Anthropologists in Arms

Critical Issues in Anthropology

SERIES DESCRIPTION: In this series, senior scholars look closely at the most pressing problems, controversies, or ideological differences that divide the discipline of anthropology. Each book is devoted to a single issue, or complex of issues, with the purpose of distinguishing problems and clarifying disputes.

The series is not limited to "objective" appraisals of current problems, though such evaluations will be an important part of the series. We also welcome proposals from scholars who are advocates for or critics of specific perspectives. The purpose of the Critical Issues in Anthropology series is to stimulate discussions along those fissures separating anthropologists from one another. To do so, we welcome both dispassionate, disinterested voices and passionate, committed voices.

BOOKS IN THIS SERIES:

Anthropologists in Arms: The Ethics of Military Anthropology, by George R. Lucas, Jr.

Anthropologists in Arms

The Ethics of Military Anthropology

George R. Lucas, Jr.

ALTAMIRA
PRESS

A division of

ROWMAN & LITTLEFIELD PUBLISHERS, INC.
Lanham • Boulder • New York • Toronto • Plymouth, UK

Published by AltaMira Press
A division of Rowman & Littlefield Publishers, Inc.
A wholly owned subsidary of The Rowman & Littlefield Publishing Group, Inc.
4501 Forbes Boulevard, Suite 200, Lanham, Maryland 20706
http://www.altamirapress.com

Estover Road, Plymouth PL6 7PY, United Kingdom

British Library Cataloguing in Publication Information Available

Library of Congress Cataloging-in-Publication Data

Lucas, George R.
  Anthropologists in arms : the ethics of military anthropology / G. R. Lucas, Jr.
    p. cm.
  Includes bibliographical references and index.
  ISBN 978-0-7591-1212-4 (cloth : alk. paper) — ISBN 978-0-7591-1213-1 (pbk. : alk.
paper) — ISBN 978-0-7591-1919-2 (electronic)
  1. War and society. 2. Anthropological ethics. 3. Applied anthropology. 4. Military
ethics. I. Title.
  GN497.L835 2009
  303.6'6—dc22   2009017748

♾™ The paper used in this publication meets the minimum requirements of American
National Standard for Information Sciences—Permanence of Paper for Printed Library
Materials, ANSI/NISO Z39.48-1992. Printed in the United States of America

Contents

Preface

On Tuesday, November 4, 2008, Paula Loyd, assigned to U.S. Army team AF-4 Blue, was conducting interviews among the local population in the small village of Chehel Gazi in southern Afghanistan. According to witnesses, she approached a man carrying a fuel jug and they began discussing the price of gasoline. Suddenly the man, Abdul Salam, doused her with the fuel in his jug and set her on fire. She suffered second- and third-degree burns over 60 percent of her body.[1] Tragically, Paula Loyd died of her injuries a few weeks later, in early January 2009.

Her teammate, Don Ayala, initially apprehended the assailant and forcibly took him into custody. When news of the severity of Loyd's injuries reached Ayala approximately 10 minutes later, he allegedly flew into a rage and executed Salam on the spot with a bullet to the brain. He, in turn, was arrested and placed in detention at Bagram Air Base pending extradition to the U.S., where (in February 2009) he eventually pleaded guilty to manslaughter in the unlawful killing of a civilian noncombatant in custody.[2]

Neither Loyd nor Ayala were American soldiers. She was a civilian social scientist, and he her private security guard. Both were employed by a private military contractor, BAE Systems, Inc., as part of a relatively new project that the Army calls its "Human Terrain Systems" (HTS). She and her teammates had been embedded with Army brigade combat teams in Afghanistan to gather cultural intelligence, provide regional knowledge and orientation, and interpret the customs of indigenous peoples to military commanders in order to mitigate conflict and minimize the kinds of misunderstandings that can lead to ill will, unwarranted violence, or inadvertent casualties. Loyd's presence as a civilian alongside combat personnel in contested areas of armed conflict—driven in turn by their need for reliable cultural understanding and accurate regional knowledge as well as linguistic skills to complement their technical prowess in war-fighting—is all part of a revolution that has transformed, and will continue to transform, the nature of warfare in the twenty-first century. The use of these HTS teams by the Army and Marine Corps are, in turn, only the most dramatic, publicly visible, and controversial facets of a much broader, evolving collaboration between scholars and soldiers, between social scientists and military, security, and intelligence forces (MIS). This emerging collaboration has come to be known as "military anthropology."

The rise of military anthropology, and the increasing recruitment and use of anthropologists in its various activities, has prompted a furious debate concerning the morality and academic or professional propriety of scholars working alongside, or otherwise providing assistance to, governments and their militaries in this fashion. The controversy in the U.S., in particular, has drawn an enormous amount of attention, set against the backdrop of grave public discord over the moral legitimacy of the U.S.-led war of intervention in Iraq, coupled with widespread uncertainty over the progress of the U.S.-led international effort to aid in reconstructing a viable government and civil society in war-torn Afghanistan. To be sure, the controversy is technically "about" anthropologists and the limits of professional probity within this discipline whenever its members are found working side by side with government and military officials. But the debate that these specific developments has generated holds wider ramifications for scholars, and for the general public, regarding moral justifications for the use of military force.

That larger debate, in turn, presents a more general moral dilemma concerning the civic and social responsibilities of scholars and citizens, which is finally what makes the debate over "military anthropology" interesting for a wider audience. Should scholars and citizens simply refrain from supporting war efforts that they find unjustifiable, or are they sometimes obliged to use their particular expertise (as doctors, psychologists, and nongovernmental organization [NGO] humanitarian assistance personnel often do) to try to ameliorate the worst consequences of war and violence, notwithstanding their individual misgivings about their own nation's participation in those conflicts?

In this book, I propose to outline and address the main features of this controversy, drawing on accounts from a variety of perspectives provided by anthropologists themselves, both individually and through their professional organizations. I then turn to the question of whether insights and methods drawn from philosophical ethics and so-called applied philosophy can assist in shedding light on some of the disputes identified. I attempt to do this for a broad scholarly and public audience, not limited to anthropologists or to moral philosophers. To meet that challenge, I will occasionally be compelled to introduce and explain background considerations that likely are already well known to anthropologists, or describe complex conceptual issues or disputes in moral philosophy in a manner intended not to mystify or alienate a wider audience. This will occasionally displease subject matter experts in both disciplines. To address their more specialized concerns insofar as possible, I have relegated detailed explanations of technical issues and scholarly controversies to the endnotes.

Notes

1. See Schachtman 2008a, Constable 2009, and Stockman 2009.

2. See Schachtman 2009, Stockman 2009. A criminal complaint of second-degree murder was filed against Ayala in the U.S. District Court of Eastern Virginia by the U.S. Army Criminal Investigation Division under the Military Extraterritorial Jurisdiction Act (MEJA) on November 18, 2008.

Acknowledgments

This work is deeply indebted to two colleagues who did much to inspire it. The first, Professor Clementine Fujimura, teaches anthropology, language, and regional studies at the U.S. Naval Academy. Her term as a resident faculty fellow in the Stockdale Center introduced our organization to this topic during the academic year 2007–2008, and it was she who encouraged the undertaking of this project. It would not have happened without her.

The second is Professor Margaret Urban Walker of Arizona State University, a longtime colleague in philosophy, dating back to her distinguished career at Fordham University. She is an accomplished social philosopher and feminist author with whom I shared my initial findings on these topics during a visit to Phoenix in late February 2008. She not only encouraged the project but also suggested the procedure described in the concluding chapter of this work as a possible way out of a very difficult conflict of interest.

Versions of several chapters were presented as colloquia or conference papers at the Stockdale Center; at Arizona State University; the University of Melbourne's Center for Applied Philosophy and Ethics; the Inamori International Center for Ethics at Case Western Reserve University; and, most recently, as the keynote address for NATO's 60th-anniversary celebration in Monterey, California. A condensed version of the overall argument of the book (essentially the preface and portions of chapters 2 and 3) was published initially as an essay in the *Journal of Military Ethics* (vol. 7, no. 3; September 2008). I have benefited from the discussions on "Mil_Ant_Net," an online association of military anthropologists and others interested in this field, especially from the list's founder and coordinator, Professor Brian Selmeski. As a registered member of the list, however, let me emphasize that no materials from that source have been quoted or otherwise used in writing this book without the express permission and acknowledgement of individual contributors.

Since I completed and submitted the original manuscript for peer review on November 30, 2008, a number of factual details have changed. The most tragic development is reported in the preface. The Human Terrain Systems (HTS) project, an important focus of controversy and hence of my analysis, had been administered through a defense contract awarded to BAE Systems, Inc., which reportedly oversaw the recruiting, training, and deployment of some 22 HTS teams to Iraq, and five to Afghanistan, beginning in February 2007. I described and raised concerns about this arrangement, which was abruptly discontinued without warning on February 18, 2009 (Stanton 2009, Schachtman 2009a). HTS personnel are now all Department of Defense civilian employees in the regular federal civil service. I have updated the coverage of these issues in chapters 5 and 6 as appropriate, but the other underlying concerns remain largely as I originally described them.

I am grateful to Professor Dena Plemmons (Research Ethics Program, University of California, San Diego), chair of the Committee on Ethics of the American Anthropological Association (AAA), for helpful clarifications of the recent history and current provisions of that code. Professor Anna J. Simons (Naval Postgraduate School) and a second, anonymous reviewer offered a number of criticisms and comments on earlier drafts of this work, most of which I have tried to include in the present version. Professors Robert Albro (of the AAA's CEAUSSIC committee) and Robert Rubinstein (Syracuse University), offered numerous helpful comments, leads, and suggestions along the way, as did philosophers Tony Coady, Rob Sparrow, and Jessica Wolfendale at the University of Melbourne. I am likewise grateful to Jack Meinhardt, acquisitions editor for AltaMira Press, for encouraging and assisting me in undertaking this project. As always, none of the above bear any blame for the shortcomings inevitably present in the final draft.

The understanding, support, and encouragement of the staff, and especially the director of the Stockdale Center, Col. Arthur Athens, USMCR (retired), were invaluable as I reached the final stages of this project. Without his confidence and tolerance, and the unfailing support of my wife and beloved philosophical companion, Professor Patricia Cook, this work could not have been completed.

Introduction

Assessing the Moral Challenge of Military Anthropology

Something is seriously awry when an official government publication, especially a military manual, can make compelling reading. But "compelling reading" is often used, appropriately, to describe the 2007 edition of the U.S. Army Field Manual FM 3-24, governing counterinsurgency operations (COIN). The first eye-catcher is that the manual was coauthored by General David H. Petraeus, just prior to his deployment to assume command of U.S.-led coalition forces in Iraq. The second is the wealth of complex, theoretical analyses of insurgency, together with intriguing examples of cultural contact and conflict portrayed in the numerous case studies—case studies that (in contrast to earlier versions, and to other Army field manuals) enrich the discussion of standard operating procedures, official policy, and enliven the usual mind-numbing rehearsal of detailed regulations.

For example, one encounters the following case study instructing military forces in Iraq and Afghanistan how to understand the historical importance of local police forces during the Malayan insurgency in the 1950s:

Police with little training and little competent leadership were ineffective in conducting operations. They also abused the civilian population and fell into corrupt practices. The population largely regarded the police as hostile; they were reluctant to give them information on the insurgents. By 1952, the insurgency had reached a stalemate. The British then established a new strategy. The strategy included reforming and retraining the entire Malaya Police Force. First, 10,000 corrupt or incompetent police officers were removed from the force.

Then, police officers who had proven the most competent in operations were made instructors in new police schools. During 1952 and 1953, every police officer attended a four-month basic training course. Police commissioned and noncommissioned officers were sent to three- to four-month advanced courses. All senior Malayan police officers were required to attend the police intelligence school. There they learned the latest criminal investigation techniques. Teams of Britain's top police officers taught them intelligence collection and analysis methods as well. Dozens of the most promising Malayan officers attended the full yearlong course in advanced police operations in Britain.

To win the ethnic Chinese away from the insurgents, the British worked closely with ethnic Chinese organizations to recruit Chinese for the Malaya Police Force. In 1952, the number of ethnic Chinese in the force more than doubled. Although the percentage of ethnic Chinese in the police force did not equal their percentage in the population, the ethnic Chinese saw this reaching out as a sign that the government was addressing their interests. At the same time, some Chinese and Malay political groups were building a coalition to establish an independent Malaya in which all the major ethnic groups would participate. The two efforts complemented each other. Better trained police officers and soldiers led by fully trained commissioned and noncommissioned officers dramatically improved the Malayan security forces' discipline. Better relations between the population and security forces resulted, . . . [such that, by] . . . 1953, the government gained the initiative. After that, the insurgent forces and support structure declined rapidly. In late 1953, the British began withdrawing forces. They progressively turned the war over to the Malayans, who were fully prepared to conduct counterinsurgency operations without a drop in efficiency. (Petraeus 2007: 6-21, 22)[1]

Those tactics, practiced by the British to bring political stability to their former colony in the early 1950s, sound remarkably similar to those put into practice by General Petraeus and his staff in war-ravaged and strife-ridden Iraq in 2006, simply replacing "ethnic Chinese insurgents" with disaffected Sunni insurgents in the current conflict. While they may not yet have achieved "victory" (whatever that term might mean in this context), these counterinsurgency tactics proved successful beyond the most optimistic ex-pectations of supporters or critics of the "Surge" by the time General Petraeus relinquished his command of U.S. forces in Iraq two years later and assumed command of the entire U.S. Central Command (CENTCOM). And, as in Malaya a half-century before, that success enabled a timetable to be set in place for orderly withdrawal of U.S. and coalition forces in favor of newly-recruited and fully trained Iraqi military and police forces.

The case studies, and just as important, the *philosophy of inter-cultural understanding and cooperation* that infuses this manual, reflect Petraeus's own previous experience in Haiti and Bosnia, and his successful practices on a prior tour as commander of the 101st Airborne Division in Mosul in 2003. But the manual itself, and its coauthor's own philosophy, *also reflect an increasing reliance, within the military, on outside "subject matter experts,"* academic scholars drawn into the inner circle of advisers at General Petraeus's own behest.[2] The influence of anthropologists, in particular, is evident, as we consider the following passage from FM 3-24 on "cultural narrative":

> The central mechanism through which ideologies are expressed and absorbed is the narrative. A *narrative* is an organizational scheme expressed in story form. Narratives are central to the representation of identity, particularly the collective identity of groups such as religions, nations, and cultures. Stories about a community's history provide models of how actions and consequences are linked and are often the basis for strategies, actions, and interpretation of the intentions of other actors. Insurgent organizations such as Al Qaeda use narratives very efficiently in the development of a legitimating ideology. In the jihadist narrative, Osama Bin Laden's depiction of himself as a man purified in the mountains of Afghanistan who begins converting followers and punishing the infidels, resonates powerfully with the historic figure of Mohammed. In the collective imagination of Bin Laden and his followers, Islamic history is a story about the decline of the *umma* and the inevitable triumph against Western imperialism. Only through *jihad* can Islam be renewed both politically and theologically. (Petraeus, 2007: 1–76)[3]

This is not typical military prose, to put it mildly. The manual goes on to describe counterinsurgency warfare as extremely complex, "war at the graduate level." It is, of course, true that Petraeus himself learned about "war at the graduate level" not only through experience, but also as a graduate student, earning his doctorate in international relations at Princeton University with a dissertation analyzing the lessons learned during America's experience in Vietnam through the lens of the French military's experience during the Algerian civil war. Chief among the lessons to be learned from that earlier war, Petraeus emphasized, was the disastrous decision of the French army to resort to torture of suspected insurgents (Algerian locals), and the attempt to retaliate in kind against Algerian civilians for terrorist attacks on French authorities (police, government ministries, and the military). By succumbing to the temptation to use torture to interrogate suspected terrorists and insurgents, as we know, the French military not only abandoned their customary adherence to international law and the rules of armed conflict, but also abandoned, along with that, any pretence to the moral "high ground" in this civil conflict.[4]

Among the practices the manual encourages military forces to adopt are:

- Focus on the population, their needs, and security.
- Establish and expand secure areas.
- Provide amnesty and rehabilitation for insurgents.
- Place police in the lead with military support.
- Expand and diversify the police force.
- Embed special operations forces and advisors with indigenous forces.

Among the unsuccessful *practices to be avoided* at all costs, are:

- Place priority on killing and capturing the enemy, not on engaging the population.
- Conduct battalion-sized operations as the norm.
- Concentrate military forces in large bases for protection.
- Focus special operations forces primarily on raiding.
- Ignore peacetime government processes, including legal procedures.

It is not altogether a surprise that a soldier-scholar like General Petraeus—apprised of such lessons and of the importance not to repeat them—has met with far greater success in post-war Iraq than his less well-prepared (or well-educated) predecessors. The recent successes in Iraq, however, also reflect the degree to which General Petraeus and the manual's current coeditor, Lieutenant General James F. Amos (U.S. Marine Corps),[5] were *assisted* in composing and compiling this now widely-read and followed handbook by civilian academic anthropologists. Anthropologists are also assisting American ground forces in attaining what is termed "regional or cultural knowledge" and greater "cultural literacy and awareness" of the areas in which they are obliged to operate—not merely Iraq, Afghanistan, and the Middle East, but also in Africa, southeast Asia, and the Pacific rim (e.g., in the Philippines). The official government mantra is that our combat warriors require a thorough awareness of the "human terrain" or "cultural terrain" in which they operate, or through which they move, every bit as much as they require knowledge and awareness of the geographical terrain.[6]

There are a number of intriguing and somewhat troubling issues buried in these new developments—including what, if anything, is meant by "culture" in these contexts, let alone how we are to understand "human terrain" as the analogue of geographical terrain. The business of providing this information to our military, this "intelligence concerning human and cultural terrain" in vastly disparate corners of our globe, constitutes one important dimension of an emerging academic sub-discipline often referred to simply as "security anthropology," or more frequently, "military anthropology."

The Ethics of Military Anthropology

In its broadest sense, "military anthropology" covers a variety of distinct activities, including, perhaps most dramatically, "embedding" anthropologists with military troops in combat zones (in Afghanistan, Iraq, East Timor, and other locations), where they assist military personnel on site with advice and consultation regarding strategic features of the local and regional culture. Training and deploying these teams constitutes the most visible and controversial dimension of what the U.S. Army terms its "Human Terrain Systems" project (HTS).

Even HTS itself, however, let alone the wider framework of "military anthropology" more generally, includes a great deal more than this specific and controversial "human terrain team" deployment program.[7] The larger HTS project also encompasses somewhat less controversial efforts undertaken by anthropologists and other social scientists to provide advice, expertise, and the results of anthropological research on "culture," and on the details of specific cultures, to military organizations for more general guidance in the formulation of effective strategy and tactics in war zones. Thus anthropologists at the Marine Corps "Center for Advanced Operational and Cultural Learning" (CAOCL) at the Marine Corps University in Quantico, Virginia, have aided the Marine Corps in composing a new handbook for operational culture (Salmoni and Holmes-Eber, 2008).[8] Anthropologists have likewise been employed by the government to write guides and study materials on local cultures for military personnel deployed around the world. With the assistance of anthropologists, for example, the cultural programming unit of the Marine Corps Intelligence Activity (MCIA), also located in Quantico, Virginia, has produced a series of training and educational materials for its troops stationed overseas, including so-called smart cards that summarize the "most essential features" of cultures encountered in nations as diverse as Chad, Sudan, and the Philippines, as well as in Iraq and Afghanistan. Finally anthropologists engaged in the broader HTS project have assisted the U.S. Army in composing two new field manuals: the aforementioned FM 3-24, on "Counterinsurgency Warfare" or COIN (Petraeus, 2007), and more recently, FM3-07 "Peacekeeping and Stability Operations" (October 2008).

The aim of these learning aids is to provide a rapid and readily-available orientation to locale for young men and women of high school age and education who may never before have traveled far from home, let alone resided or worked in some of the exotic and unfamiliar locations to which such individuals now find themselves routinely deployed. General James H. Mattis, U.S. Marine Corps, originally the coeditor of the COIN manual with General David Petraeus, is credited with the observation that "our soldiers and Marines must learn to navigate the human (cultural) terrain with as much facility as they use maps to navigate the geographical terrain."

While all of the foregoing HTS activities constitute an important form of military anthropology, the latter, much broader term, also encompasses the employment, by the U.S. military services, of anthropologists who perform routine educational and scholarly tasks for military and State Department personnel. Anthropologists teach and carry out their own individual scholarly research at federal service academies, war colleges, and language institutes. Anthropologists advise their academic employers in these institutions on how to increase cultural literacy, promote and enhance foreign language acquisition and competence among their students, and increase the "cultural awareness" and cultural sensitivities of those students. Anthropologists are being asked to assist in the development of new "regional studies" programs for the Department of Defense and its constituent military organizations. More recently, under the code name "Project Minerva," Secretary of Defense Robert Gates (himself a historian and former university president) has sought to encourage, and to generously fund, broad-based scholarly contributions to national security studies from sectors of the academic and higher education community (including the discipline of anthropology) that have heretofore been under-represented and marginally utilized for such purposes.[9]

Finally, the term "military anthropology" can be applied to a series of activities seemly distinct from all those preceding; namely, making the military itself, or its distinct organizations and/or service sub-cultures, the *objects* of anthropological study and field research. In this third, distinct sense, the military anthropologist does not render some autonomous culture or society the object of investigation in behalf of purposes entertained *by* the military. Rather, the anthropologist renders the members and sub-cultures of the military *themselves* the objects of ethnographic study. The purpose here is first and foremost simply to understand those organizations and sub-cultures more completely, as objects of scientific study, much as one is curious about the members of an alien or radically unfamiliar culture one might encounter. The results of such study might simply satisfy scientific curiosity, help the military services better understand (and perhaps improve) their own organizations, or even help societies better understand the nature and role of the military organizations with whom they co-exist.

Confronting the Controversy over Military Anthropology

It is fair to say that these recent developments, emerging gradually in the wake of "9/11" and the ensuing wars in Afghanistan and Iraq, have generated a firestorm of controversy, both within the discipline of anthropology itself, and among the wider educated public (Bender 2007; Rohde, 2007). At one extreme are anthropologists involved in the most controversial aspects of this new venture, advocating greater involvement of their colleagues in efforts to save innocent lives, reduce troop casualties, and aid in the successful rebuilding of devastated civic infrastructures, especially in Afghanistan and Iraq, two nations ravaged by decades of virtually continuous warfare and civil strife. At the other extreme are critics of any involvement of behavioral scientists and scholars with the government and military, who denounce initiatives like the human terrain teams as "mercenary anthropology," or the "militarization" of anthropology. Caught in the cross-fire between proponents of HTS and anti-war activists are the bulk of those who would identify themselves as "military anthropologists" more broadly, who complain that their work is unfairly caught up in, and their own efforts and careers unfairly impugned by, this raging controversy over merely one, controversial program in a much wider and, for the most part, morally benign area of inquiry.

Critics of military anthropology, in their turn, often object that such close collaboration with military, intelligence, and security forces inherently violates basic norms and canons of "professional ethics." Involvement in HTS, in particular, they worry, taints the profession generally, and potentially implicates participating colleagues in a variety of illegal and immoral activities (such as interrogation and torture, in which anthropologists are alleged to have assisted, both at Guantanamo Bay and Abu Ghraib prisons). HTS projects, these critics charge, aid more broadly in the prosecution of what an *ad hoc* group, the "Network of Concerned Anthropologists" described as "a brutal war of occupation which has entailed massive casualties," and what a resolution of the Executive Board of the AAA itself termed "a war that is widely recognized as a denial of human rights and based on faulty intelligence and undemocratic principles."[10]

Because of these inflammatory concerns over the HTS program specifically, many anthropologists have gone so far as to denounce *any* cooperation with the government or military *whatsoever* as "unethical," including even some of the more apparently benign scholarly studies or educational activities described above. Professor Terence Turner of Cornell University, a persistent critic of both military anthropology and, more broadly, of forms of practical, applied, or "practice" anthropology in non-academic settings, for example, firmly believes that "classified work for the military is unethical . . . and the association should have the will and guts to say so" (Jaschik 2009).

By the fall of 2007, this controversy had occasioned national press coverage, in the pages of *The New York Times*, the *Chronicle of Higher Education*, and on National Public Radio. At its annual meeting in November, 2007, in Washington, D.C., the AAA's ad hoc "Commission on the Engagement of Anthropology with the U.S. Security and Intelligence Communities" (CEAUSSIC), released the results of its year-long study of the problem, in which it began the arduous process of separating out, classifying, and examining these various controversies, and addressing the question of what (if any) official stance the profession should adopt toward each.[11]

There are a host of issues surrounding this controversy, the majority of which are most properly addressed by subject matter experts and practitioners within the discipline of anthropology itself. These "issues for experts" would include debates about the very meaning of "culture" (including whether there even *is* such a thing as "culture" in any meaningful sense), as well as methodological debates about cultural hermeneutics, "practice" theory, "essentialism" versus the "historical turn" in accounts of cultures offered within the discipline, or types of valid ethnographic writing, for example. Some of these "expert issues" or questions about proper disciplinary methodology quite clearly bear upon the scientific validity, and even the feasibility (or efficacy) of some of the projects in "military anthropology," as described earlier—such as the extent to which there are essential features of a culture which could be meaningfully or helpfully "boiled down" to a series of bullets on a laminated wallet card (as in the Marine Corps' so-called smart card project, mentioned above).[12]

This controversy has been framed by anthropologists themselves, however, as well as by the wider interested public, *primarily as a matter of "ethics" and "professional ethics."* It is this widespread *moral debate* about "military anthropology" that I propose to address in this book.

Accordingly, while I will deal in passing, and for clarity's sake, with some of the anthropological subjects cited in the preceding paragraph, it is the principal aim of this book to summarize the most salient aspects of the current public controversy over "military anthropology," and to set forth clearly the opposing viewpoints regarding the presence or absence of appropriate moral justifications for these various enterprises. I will seek carefully to identify, define, and distinguish between various types or kinds of types of military anthropology, and subject each, in turn, to critical analysis using the standard methodologies of moral philosophy, and what is usually referred to among my own colleagues variously as "applied philosophy," or "applied ethics."[13] In so doing, I propose to take account of, summarize, and evaluate the positions of critics and proponents alike, as well as to provide (where possible and helpful) the results of well-reasoned, impartial, third-party analysis of some of the main moral dilemmas identified in this controversy.

The Structure of this Project

It bears mention that there is more than a little *hubris*, and more than a little irony, involved in undertaking this project. I want to address both. The *hubris*, of course, lies in presuming that someone outside a complex and highly-specialized academic discipline could presume to comment upon it at all, let alone upon its most sensitive and divisive moral conundrums. That is, indeed, a daunting task, not lightly undertaken. I hasten to add that this was decidedly not my idea, nor am I eager to assume the role of an unwelcome guest at a party I have crashed without prior invitation. I would not have dreamed of taking on this assignment, were it not for interest and encouragement to do so on the part of several friends and colleagues who are anthropologists, and who, learning of my interest in this topic, encouraged me to "forge ahead."

In doing so, I am assisted in part by having for several years served as a senior administrator in the National Endowment for the Humanities (Washington, D.C.). The programs and program officers I specifically supervised constituted the main source of funding for research in anthropology grounded in the humanities. Most of the leading figures in the discipline at one time or another either submitted substantial research projects for our evaluation, or sat on peer review panels convened at the "Old Post Office" in Washington to advise us on funding decisions. Reading those proposals and engaging in discussions with these superb scholars was a remarkable educational experience, one that gave me a somewhat better appreciation than the average "academic on the street" of what it is that anthropologists, both inside and outside the academic world, do for a living. It also brought me into personal contact with the many remarkable scholars who comprise this field. I will always cherish those memories, and this work constitutes an opportunity to perhaps repay a portion of the debt I owe them.

Apart from this personal experience, the aforementioned report of the American Anthropological Association's "Ad Hoc Commission on the Engagement of Anthropology with the U.S. Security and Intelligence Communities" (CEAUSSIC, 2007) comes to my rescue, citing, as guiding precedent for its own investigations, the earlier history of ethics controversies within other disciplines and professions (such as medicine, journalism, and law) that quickly transcended the confines of specialized knowledge. Working on those ethics controversies over the past thirty years with scholars and practitioners from other disciplines and professions has constituted the bulk of my own teaching and research career.

What the CEAUSSIC report itself does *not* cite specifically is that the individual members and governing organizational bodies of these other professions often quickly recognized that the moral perplexities that so deeply infused many of their practices themselves constituted the subject matter of moral philosophy. And so, in the end, the troubled individual practitioners and responsible governing bodies of these other professions sought the advice and assistance of *moral philosophers* ("ethicists") as they grappled with ethical dilemmas and codes of conduct unique to their professional practice. Something like this undertaking is what I propose at least to begin in this book.

Having said this, it bears mention (or perhaps, requires an honest confession) that specialists in a profession reaching out to subject-matters experts in other fields (such as moral philosophy) did not always yield satisfactory results. Many a doctor, lawyer, or more recently, military officer might relate, through clenched teeth, how some gaunt, bearded, and bespectacled academic, boney index finger pointing toward the heavens, sonorously regaled them at length about role responsibilities, utilitarian side-constraints, moral considerability, or the distinction between "perfect" and "imperfect" duties—or, worse yet, embroiled them in a seemingly endless reading group devoted to the works of Aristotle, Immanuel Kant or John Stuart Mill—while severely underweight and medically compromised newborns struggled for their very lives in the neonatal intensive care room, or prisoners languished on death row, or combat troops awaited a final decision on the appropriateness of striking a critical, time-sensitive military target. I have many times witnessed this. Even worse, I myself have done this, for "these are the ways of my people." Members of my own discipline, long consigned to irrelevance and accustomed to dwelling on the margins of academic culture itself, were often surprised, frequently confused, and initially (in the decades of the 1960s and 1970s, at least) largely unprepared to serve as consultants or advisors in the sense required, even if we were all too eager to do so. It took some time to warm to the task, to discern just exactly what was wanted and needed, and finally to achieve a functional fusion of very different academic and disciplinary horizons.

In an important sense, the experience of philosophers in this respect runs parallel to that of anthropologists at the present moment. The latter scholars and academics, long accustomed to carrying out their research on what is sometimes lampooned as "the exotic and the useless," now suddenly find themselves likewise thrust into prominence as custodians of subject-matter expertise deemed vital to the nation's security, or to its successful conclusion of culturally-sensitive military missions abroad. It takes a little time to grow accustomed to the attention, and to warm to the task. As we shall see in this book, however, a chief difference in professional or academic experience in this respect is that anthropologists, unlike moral philosophers, are all too aware that this current polite request for expert advice is not without precedent in their discipline. Anthropologists have grave reason to view such requests with the deepest suspicion, since (in their collective disciplinary memory) such requests have been inextricably linked with malevolent intentions on the part of the State, either in oppressing or manipulating its own citizens or residents, or in projecting colonial power and authority in oppressive fashion in the developing nations of the Third World.

The history of anthropology is a complicated and—for members of the discipline or profession—a highly sensitive topic. Outsiders like myself are not qualified or equipped to write it, and indeed, given the extraordinary sensibilities of those with rival interpretations of that history, it might seem best to steer clear of it altogether. And yet, this cannot entirely be done. Here again the CEAUSSIC report comes to my rescue, pleading with the wider public to understand just how concerned anthropologists themselves are with that history, and (if I may borrow a phrase from Nietzsche) how what might be termed "bad historical consciousness" afflicts their membership, and shapes attitudes in the present toward proposals and programs like HTS and "Project Minerva"—initiatives that might seem to outsiders unobjectionable, noncontroversial, or even laudatory. So we read in the report's concluding comments:

> Despite a growing interest in anthropology, most institutions remain strikingly naïve about our discipline's fraught history with institutions of power. Many people in the military and intelligence communities are largely unaware that scandals like Project Camelot still loom enormously in the collective anthropological memory, and tend to attribute anthropologists' protests to present-day politics, rather than disciplinary history or ethics. (CEAUSSIC 2007: 22)

In the past, anthropologists have been charged (probably quite unfairly) with having consorted with colonialists and aided in the oppression, victimization, and forced migration or resettlement of indigenous peoples and cultures by powerful foreign elites. Present-day anthropologists are quite rightly sensitive about such charges, and are determined not to be deceived into complicity with such atrocities again.[14]

In light of this concern, it seems impossible simply to ignore that history. In the first two chapters, accordingly, I make reference to some recent, representative historical instances, including "Project Camelot" and the so-called Thailand Affair, that helped shape the current collective consciousness of members of the discipline. Rather than re-writing anthropology's history, however, it is my aim instead to "cross-examine" the accounts of these various historical vignettes written by anthropologists themselves, in order both to determine how anthropologists see those past experiences as shaping the Code of Ethics (CoE 1998; revised 2009; see appendix) that guides their professional and scholarly conduct at present, and also to determine how scholars generally tend to reason intuitively about such matters. It is particularly interesting for an outsider to examine the fashion in which internal disciplinary histories are, in effect, mythologized, and forged into a kind of litany, a master narrative that enunciates and reinforces widely-shared core values. As with any society or culture, care must be taken to understand, and respect must be accorded to the importance of these values as represented in the group's litany. At the same time, as with any mythology, the historical foundations turn out to be far more equivocal, and certainly less robust a source of support for the inferences drawn from them than the mythologized narrative would suggest.

"Ethics," "Morality," and the Methodology of Applied Philosophy

In undertaking this task of historical cross-examination, I take care in the first two chapters especially to differentiate internal, discipline-based debates about core values, guidelines for best practice, and responsible constraints on professional practice—all of which comprise a "code of ethics" for the discipline of anthropology—from wider concerns about justice, human rights, and concerns for general welfare that inform the broader *moral* debate about America's involvement in war and security operations (including the participation or support of anthropologists in these efforts). Accordingly, it would be appropriate here to say something about distinctions like these, as well as about the use of terms like "ethics" and "morality."

As Pat Caplan notes in the introduction to *The Ethics of Anthropology* (Caplan 2003) the terms "ethics" and "morality" are often used interchangeably, as synonyms. This is in part because the two terms themselves are derived from the Greek and Latin words, respectively, denoting shared values, customs, and fundamental guiding principles of acceptable human behavior, usually understood (as in Aristotle) in reference to a set of settled practices or a specific form of common life. So, the *ethos* of the democratic *polis* in Athens is found to be distinctively different from the militarized *ethos* of Sparta, ιυ⌐ example, while both differ sharply from that of the Persians. This kind of distinction supports the interpretation that anthropologists, since the time of Herodotus, have frequently given to both terms indiscriminately, as denoting forms of customary behavior.

Caplan also notes, however, that "some" (including philosophers) often see these terms as "different," citing the late Bernard Williams' distinction that

> ethics is any way of answering the question 'How ought one to live?' while morality is a certain kind of answer to that question, namely one involving moral obligations such as rules, rights, duties, commands and blame. (Caplan 2003: 3)[15]

Just as frequently, however, moral philosophers will reserve the term "morality" or "moral principles" exclusively for what Williams terms certain of these "answers," viz., theoretical accounts of how one ought to live (in terms of rules or guiding principles), and proceed to define "ethics" instead as *the study of* "morality" (or, more precisely, an examination and comparison of these contrasting moral "theories" concerning the right and the good).

I have long harbored reservations over that customary usage, owing to the questionable use of the term "theory" to denote what are, at best, alternative (rather than "rival") conceptions of moral reasoning, none of which could be said to rise to the level of abstract precision and internal coherence associated with a "theory." There are, unfortunately, a range of rival, largely unexamined customs rife among moral philosophers with respect to these distinctions which does little to reassure scholars and professionals in other fields that they are working in well-ordered terrain. There is something to be said, however, for dignifying an implicit assumption in Anglo-American analytic "applied philosophy" that the term "ethics" should be reserved for discussions of specific group or organizational norms and principles (as in "medical ethics," or the "Code of Ethics" for Certified Public Accounts), while the term "morality" would designate broad, widely-shared, and generally applicable *principles* or guidelines for human behavior (principles of distributive justice, for example, or basic human rights).[16]

In the third chapter, I introduce some distinctions designed to sort out the debate over the morality of military anthropology. I discuss a broad distinction, recently offered by anthropologists themselves, between anthropology *of* the military and anthropology *for* the military (Winnick 2008).[17] The Human Terrain Systems (HTS) project is clearly an example of the latter, but it is not the only example. Despite its current high profile, moreover, I find reasons to doubt whether it is even a very representative example of military anthropology. This is an extremely important observation, for both members of the AAA's Ethics Committee, and practicing military anthropologists of various other kinds, have strenuously objected to debates over their diverse concerns and activities, and over complex considerations pertaining to "secrecy" and transparency in the funding, conduct, and dissemination of scientific research, all being conflated with the sensational and politically-charged debate over the HTS project. Accordingly, I discuss the controversy surrounding all these other forms of military anthropology, and employ the methodology of "applied philosophy" to determine whether, and to what degree, there are grounds for concern over the various types of military anthropology *apart* from HTS.

There are some drawbacks or obstacles in this approach. The widespread practice of moral philosophers at present (as the eminent anthropologist, Clifford Geertz, once noted with amusement)[18] is to resort to very focused, narrowly-defined, and quite frequently hypothetical or fictionalized cases, all selected or even designed by the philosopher specifically to focus on precisely the elements of a controversy that are most in dispute, while relegating other, perhaps confusing and less relevant details to the background. This methodology has the advantage of pushing larger disputes over rival moral theories (over the relative merits, for example, of appealing to utility, virtue, duties, basic human "rights," or principles like "justice") also into the background, or out of the picture altogether.

One of my colleagues, attempting to justify this widespread practice, once claimed that the use of hypothetical examples (hypothetical scenarios involving, for example, passengers on runaway trolley cars, medical patients marooned on a desert island, or swimmers and boaters in shark-infested waters) permitted students or members of other disciplines or professions to examine and test their instinctive reactions, their "*pre-theoretic intuitions*," on the humorous conundrums that such cases often propose. The very notion of "pre-theoretic intuitions," however, is such as to leave most anthropologists (and even European colleagues outside the realm of "Anglo-American" analytic philosophy) gasping in disbelief. In addition, this methodology can itself seem frivolous, irritating, and quite irrelevant to academics and practitioners in other fields, eager to discuss their *actual* practices and problems, rather than philosophers' *imaginary* ones.[19]

I discuss, and attempt to explain the advantages (and acknowledge the limitations) of this methodology, in chapters 3 through 5, where I believe it becomes essential. That is because chapters 4 and 5, in particular, take up the controversy over HTS specifically, and it becomes important to find a way to address the controversy and the rival positions "at arm's length," with a certain degree of emotional distance and impartiality. Hypothetical cases, carefully tailored to address the most vexed questions at issue, at least help in achieving that intellectual distance from a debate that is otherwise as heated and emotional as any one is likely to encounter in the academic and professional realm. This is an especially important observation about methodology, moreover, when we discover (as we will in anthropology's case) that we are engaged primarily in a disagreement over broad principles, rather than in a specific dispute over concrete or specific instances of improper behavior.

In chapter 4, for example, it is possible to prove, through the use of hypothetical cases, that even in a war whose motivation, and whose moral and legal justification, are passionately contested and gravely in doubt, it is nonetheless morally permissible for an anthropologist to consider, at least, engaging in some of the activities subsumed under HTS without automatically violating key provisions of the current revised AAA Code of Ethics (CoE 1998, revised 2009; see appendix), let alone violating any broader and more generally applicable moral norms. That is a dramatic and substantive discovery—one which, when properly understood, ought to lay to rest, once and for all, the disagreement over principle. What emerge instead as the "ethical problems" with regard to the HTS project are: how to establish appropriate oversight and institutional peer review, in order to determine which activities might be appropriate; how to provide resources for these without engaging in conflicts of interest; and how to ensure these activities are carried out appropriately.

As I note in chapter 5, titled "CEAUSSIC Park," most of the discussion of this form of military anthropology (or rather these forms, as there are many types of HTS activities) has been a discussion of general policy, and of adhering to appropriate professional principles, and not a discussion of specific cases or actual practice. This was confirmed in discussions during the fall of 2008 with the Chair of the AAA Committee on Ethics, Dena Plemmons: namely that, during the recent discussions to re-evaluate and revise key provisions the AAA Code of Ethics, no specific instances of abuse or misbehavior were lodged as complaints or otherwise reported. In the case of HTS, neither its practitioners nor its critics have yet come forward with specific case studies of moral conflicts or questionable practices whose analysis might provide sound moral and professional guidance to others.[20] Dr. Plemmons has more recently clarified that this absence of specific case discussion is not altogether surprising, inasmuch as the deliberations of the Committee on Ethics were never devoted exclusively or even primarily focused upon HTS, or even "military anthropology" more widely, but upon broad conceptual issues and principles of professional practice pertaining to many forms of applied or "practical" anthropology. At most, the present controversy over military anthropology and HTS in particular merely represent the most recent occasion for engaging in debate over those principles, and reconsidering guidelines for best practice.

Even so, the relative absence of specific instances of concern or examples of grievance over inappropriate conduct in any of these areas, particularly with regard to so otherwise-controversial a program as HTS, is extremely unusual. I therefore examine job advertisements and position descriptions for HTS team members, and discuss anecdotal reports (including personal interviews, individual web "blogs," and media interviews) from a variety of military and civilian sources on the current status of HTS teams in combat theaters. One concern that emerges in this chapter is that critics of military anthropology may well have succeeded (to use the anthropologist's own jargon) in "essentializing culture"—in effect, creating a (nonexistent) culture by writing about it, one inhabited by no actual, individual exemplars. By contrast, in considering the scant details of actual practice, the concerns that emerge are quite different than the AAA controversy over this (nonexistent) culture would suggest. These concerns include the advisability, moral probity, and even feasibility of having private military contractors (PMCs) hire, train and deploy HTS teams, together with questions about the overall effectiveness and abilities of teams recruited and trained in this fashion to function "in theater."

The debate about this form of HTS thus merges in large part with the ongoing moral debate about the increasing presence and widening role of PMCs in combat zones generally.[21] In addition, my account demonstrates that some forms of HTS may be less effective or reliable than others, not so much because of hypothetical or speculative moral conflicts, as for simply failing to demonstrate competent or useful performance in the field of combat. We will examine scattered reports of heart-warming, if inconsistent, success in fulfilling the promise of saving lives and inhibiting the spread of misery among indigenous noncombatants in zones of combat, alongside other reports of incompetence, strife, frustrated expectations, and even selfish profiteering. Thus far, it turns out that HTS projects "state-side"—focused on writing policy, doctrine, and military guidance, and providing education and orientation regarding "culture and regional knowledge" for military personnel prior to deployment—are proving to be the most effective programs, as well as the least prone to "moral error."

Finally, in chapter 6, "Anthropologists without Borders," I summarize these conclusions and take up the problem of procedure, administration, and peer review. The title of this chapter suggests the response to this challenge that I recommend: namely, using existing or specifically-created organs of the professional society itself, in lieu of PMCs and federal funds, to provide the on-site expert advice about regions and cultures required, without engaging in the implicit conflict of interest and confusion of command authority that the present HTS system entails. This effectively converts the HTS team from the moral and legal status of employees of a private military contractor (PMC) working *for* the U.S. military, to that of representatives of a non-governmental organization (NGO) working *with*, and alongside, military forces. I cite the example of "Doctors without Borders" as the humanitarian relief organization most like what I have in mind, and hence the title of this concluding chapter.

This, then, is the outline of the task at hand. I mentioned also that there was some irony in it. The irony is of a sort I encounter upon every presentation of this topic to an audience that includes non-anthropologists. One or more participants in a colloquium on this controversy is bound to observe that many of the most prominent practitioners of the discipline, such as Ruth Benedict, spent much of their careers denouncing "ethics" as a sham, and describing "morality" as little more than "mores"—the highly-variant shared practices of discrete cultures. Upon conclusion of my initial presentation of this subject in early 2008, for example, one outraged theologian, quite distinguished in his own field, went so far as to exclaim that anthropologists simply "had no right" to avail themselves of the resources of an area of scholarship and of collective human wisdom whose legitimacy and authority they had done so much to undermine.

I must admit, as a long-time teacher of ethics, I have been obliged to read the classic essays of Benedict, George W. Stocking, and others, and patiently point out the gaping conceptual inconsistencies and informal logical fallacies running rampant in the unwarranted moral inferences these social scientists often draw from their portrayal of divergent cultural practices. As a result, I've not been above aiming a barb, in jest, at my colleagues in anthropology on precisely this point. In fairness, most react in mild embarrassment, and explain that "we don't teach that anymore," or "we've moved beyond that." Some, like anthropologist Carolyn Fluehr-Lobban, even point to the recent historical controversies, to which we now turn in this book, as demonstrating to an earlier generation of anthropologists, skeptical about the claims of morality, that there simply *are* moral norms (whatever their source or ground) pertaining to concepts like "basic rights" and "justice." Human beings must, from time to time, meaningfully appeal to such transcultural concepts for guidance in precisely the sorts of situations anthropologists now find themselves facing. In this respect, anthropologist Pat Caplan aptly observes:

For philosophers, as for anthropologists, the issue of ethics raises the hoary question of universalism versus relativism, since a comparison of different historical periods and different national disciplinary traditions suggests that the field of anthropological ethics is a shifting one. Yet . . . there is frequent invocation by some anthropologists of *moral values which they hold to be universal*: the intellectual search for some form of truth, the need for professional integrity, the upholding of the human dignity of their research subjects. (Caplan 2003: 4; my emphasis)

Evidently, the requirements for principled moral debate over canons of acceptable practice and abiding norms of decent behavior have worked to overcome anthropology's longstanding addiction to the fallacy of moral relativism, much as these same requirements inevitably do for us all.

Admittedly, there may be some who are tempted, in anthropology's case, to savor inappropriately this "delicious irony." My own concern is rather different. Many of the more strident voices in this debate at present betray a great deal more self-confidence about their own abilities, and about the discipline of anthropology's internal resources for handling these new ethical challenges, than genuine, good-faith, self-conscious reflection on this historical irony would warrant. To be sure: every individual and organization experiences, and is required to cope at some level with complex moral dilemmas. That fact alone no more makes us adept either at moral reasoning, or at formulating cogent responses to these dilemmas, however, than simply having teeth, or even practicing good oral hygiene, qualifies us all as dentists. If philosophers should not dabble carelessly in anthropology's history, then perhaps it is just as true that anthropologists should not attempt to practice philosophy without a license, and perhaps both should leave history to historians.

Such a pristine division of disciplinary labor is, of course, impossible to sustain. What might suffice in its stead is a more tolerant, less judgmental stance toward one another's forays across our respective disciplinary boundaries, and of the inevitable mistakes and misunderstandings that may occasionally arise from these interventions. No discipline has been more the champion of such tolerance than anthropology. Rest assured that I will have occasion to plead for exhibitions of that disciplinary virtue many times in the pages that follow.

For their part, what ultimately rescues my esteemed colleagues in anthropology from the ungenerous charges of hypocrisy that their colleagues in other disciplines sometimes level at them (let alone charges of *hubris* in their own right for attempting to tackle these emerging moral dilemmas entirely on their own) is what I perceive to be their collective recognition, in good

[handwritten marginalia: "ce - normative covenants? ant grounded in covenants wt peo we stud."]

faith, of a normative dimension to their own discipline. The normative dimension of anthropology is grounded in covenants the anthropologists themselves forge with the inhabitants of the societies and cultures they study, and whose modes of being in the world they fervently work to understand, preserve, and protect. Frankly, that good faith, and their good work, coupled with their earnest and evident desire not to be made inadvertent accomplices in inflicting harm, misery or abuse on precious "research subjects" who invariably also become valued colleagues and friends, is more than enough to convince me that the rest of us, seated on the sidelines of this controversy, ought to stop sniping and start pitching in to help think this all through a bit more clearly. After all, we may be next.

Notes

1. *Counterinsurgency*, eds. David H. Petraeus and James F. Amos. Army Field Manual 3–24. (Washington, DC: U.S. Government Printing Office, 2007). This manual is available as a free PDF download from the Federation of American Scientists website http://www.fas.org/irp/doddir/army/fm3-24.pdf.

2. While the present rise of "military anthropology," and the use of "Human Terrain System" teams in combat zones in Iraq and Afghanistan is often attributed to General Petraeus, and cited as an outgrowth of these wars, the germination of this increasing involvement of anthropology in international relations generally stems from the work and influence of anthropologist Robert A. Rubinstein at Syracuse University. See his seminal essay in 1988, "Anthropology and International Security," reprinted in *The Social Dynamics of Peace and Conflict*, eds. Robert A. Rubinstein and Mary LeCron Foster (Dubuque, IA: Kendall/Hunt Publishing Co., 1997), 17–34. I will discuss the larger history of anthropology in national security in my opening two chapters.

3. Actually, the language of this paragraph is from the "final draft" circulated in December, 2006. The final approved version slightly alters, and to my mind diminishes, the intellectual content of the earlier version.

4. A concise and engaging account of the Algerian case is featured in chapter 7, on "Leadership and Ethics for Counterinsurgency," (Petreus 2007: 9).

5. Such efforts are always the work of committees, and would it be more apt to describe Petraeus, for example, as the chief supervisor of the project. Earlier drafts of the manual listed General James H. Mattis, rather than Lieutenant General Amos, as the "co-author," but all of this is to emphasize the authority and "joint services" character of the doctrine set forth, rather than to credit "authorship" in the conventional sense.

6. Such advice is copious in chapter 3 in describing the effects on the operational environment of society, culture, social structures, social norms, groups, networks, and

organizations, as well as the role of identify, beliefs, and values in shaping behavior among indigenous populations in the host nation. This specific quote, the "core mantra" of the program, if you will, is attributed to General James H. Mattis, USMC, who is currently commander, U.S. Joint Forces Command (Norfolk, VA). He is cited in an unclassified CAOCL brief as setting the goal for ground forces to be able to "navigate cultural and human terrain as easily as Marines can now use a map to navigate physical terrain." http://www.dtic.mil/doctrine/education/dlcc0407_lc_usmc.ppt

7. For a wide-ranging survey of the components of this field, see the essays by a number of leading military anthropologists in *Anthropology and the United States Military: Coming of Age in the Twenty-First Century* (Frese and Harrell, 2003). For a critical account from a military practitioner perspective of how the human terrain teams approach is both failing and undermining the military's own efforts to enhance cross-cultural competence, see "All our Eggs in a Broken Basket: How the Human Terrain System is Undermining Sustainable Military Cultural Competence," by Major Ben Connable, U.S. Marine Corps: *Military Review* (March–April 2009), 57–64.

8. Anthropologists Barak A. Salmoni (Ph.D., Harvard University) and Paula Holmes-Eber (Ph.D., Northwestern University) coauthored this new handbook, *Operational Culture for the Warfighter: Principles and Applications* at CAOCL.

9. Criticisms and concerns from anthropologists regarding the orientation, administration, and likely impact of the Minerva program can be found in an AAA press release dated July 7, 2008, and located on the Association's website at http://www.aaanet.org/issues/press/upload/Advisory-Anthropologists-Critique-Pentagon-s-Minerva.pdf.

10. The phrase from the original version of the NCA's "Pledge of Non-Participation in Counterinsurgency" was widely quoted in the news media in the fall of 2007 (e.g., Rohde 2007). The original and a more recent "international" version of the pledge, somewhat more subdued in tone are available at http://concerned.anthropologists.googlepages.com. The October, 2007 resolution of the Executive Board can be found on the website of the American Association of Anthropologists (AAA 2007) at http://dev.aaanet.org/issues/policy-advocacy/Statement-on-HTS.cfm.

11. The complete report is available at http://www.aaanet.org/pdf/Final_Report.pdf.

12. The machinations involved in attempting even a succinct definition of "culture" that might be distilled for widespread consumption among non-experts would be amusing were they not simultaneously of such profound importance. One definition circulated among military anthropologists comes from a widely used textbook, and defines "culture" as "the basic assumptions within a group that govern how members should perceive, think, and feel when dealing with external and internal adaptation/integration/social relationships. These assumptions have been either invented, discovered, or developed, and then validated by the group over a period of time. They can be modified, or even eliminated, to enhance group or individual status or survival" (from E. Schein, "Organizational Culture," in D. Ancona, et

al. *Organizational Behavior and Processes*, Cincinnati, OH: Southwestern College Publishers, 1999). The Marine Corps handbook on operational culture follows the British approach to social anthropology, rather than American structuralism and postmodernism, defining "culture" as "the shared world view and social structures of a group of people that influence a person's and a group's actions and choices" (Salmoni and Holmes-Eber, 2008: 36). Finally, the COIN manual suggests that "culture" is "a system of shared beliefs, values, customs, behaviors, and artifacts that members of a society use to cope with their world and with one another," and goes on to offer this intriguing commentary: "Culture might also be described as an 'operational code' that is valid for an entire group of people. Culture conditions the individual's range of action and ideas, including what to do and not do, how to do or not do it, and whom to do it with or not to do it with. Culture also includes under what circumstances the 'rules' shift and change. Culture influences how people make judgments about what is right and wrong, assess what is important and unimportant, categorize things, and deal with things that do not fit into existing categories. Cultural rules are flexible in practice. For example, the kinship system of a certain Amazonian Indian tribe requires that individuals marry a cousin. However, the definition of 'cousin' is often changed to make people eligible for marriage" (Petraeus, 2007: 3–6, 7). This editorial suggests the lengths to which it is necessary to go to convey the complexity of an illusive term to non-academics and non-specialists deeply immersed in cultural conflicts. I will cite other definitions of culture, such as that of Clifford Geertz, in later chapters.

13. Bowling Green State University in Ohio (the first graduate program to offer a Ph.D. in "applied philosophy"), and the "Centre for Applied Philosophy and Public Ethics" (headquartered at the University of Melbourne in Australia, http://www. cappe.edu.au/index.htm), for example, use the term "applied philosophy" to denote primarily ethics, political, and social philosophy. By contrast, the University of Hull's "Centre for Applied Ethics" (in the U.K.), and a new program at Arizona State University offering a Master's degree in "Applied Ethics & the Professions" (including a required course on the "Methods of Applied Ethics") use the latter terminology to denote more specifically the application of moral reasoning, particularly the use of cases and "moral casuistry" (reasoning about practical problems, or applying moral theories to problem analysis and solution), to issues arising in professional practice or civic life.

14. Anthropology professor Anna J. Simons, in a review of an earlier draft of my manuscript, challenged the accuracy of this sweeping indictment that present-day anthropologists level on their predecessors, claiming that anthropologists during the waning days of colonialism often acted as spokespersons for the interests of indigenous peoples, and not always, or even usually in blind complicity with the malevolent schemes of colonial governments. She and an anonymous reviewer went so far as to suggest I avoid all treatment of this subject. Somewhat in contrast, Robert Rubinstein, in a presentation for a seminar on "Scholars, Security, and Citi-

zenship" at the School of Advanced Research in Santa Fe in July 2008 (Rubinstein 2008a) agreed that anthropology's own understanding of its history on these matters was "incomplete and one-sided," but suggested in addition that it deserved a fresh interpretation from a new perspective. Such concerns illustrate the challenge any author from whatever background will face in coming objectively to terms with anthropology's past.

15. Williams is a significant figure in this discussion, inasmuch as he strongly influenced the recent trend in moral philosophy away from abstract and theoretical discussions about rival interpretations of the right or the good, and more toward a focus on casuistry, the discussion of cases or examples, readily intelligible to a wider audience of non-specialists. Caplan's anthology, in turn, is of interest not only because it reflects a British, rather than American perspective on the ethics, as well as the practice, of anthropology, but also because the contributors' shared understanding of professional ethics does not seem grounded in the kind of historical litany of experiences, with the shared interpretation of a mythology of bad practice, so evident in the American context, though they make frequent reference to the American litany. In sum, while every bit as concerned as their trans-Atlantic cousins with discerning core values and best practices for the discipline, British anthropologists do not seem as haunted as Americans by guilt and bad conscience stemming from colonialism. I am not certain I am correct in this observation. But if it is true, it would make for an interesting analysis in its own right.

16. This mirrors somewhat a distinction to be found in law, as well as in the work of the contemporary critical theorist, Jürgen Habermas. It is likewise a distinction to found in the work of moral philosophers like Immanuel Kant, and in the "early" (as sharply opposed to the "later") speculative and political philosophy of G. W. F. Hegel. I will have more to say about Habermas in particular, and about this way of distinguishing "morality" from "professional ethics," in the next chapter.

17. This manner of summarizing the far more nuanced classificatory scheme utilized in the CEAUSSIC report was introduced during discussions of the final report by committee members themselves.

18. I will have occasion to recur frequently to Geertz's amusing account of these practices of philosophers, found (with specific reference to Gilbert Ryle) in Geertz's essay, "Thick Description: Toward an Interpretive Theory of Culture" (Geertz 1973: 5–10). Geertz's criticism is even more appropriately applied to Bernard Williams, as well as a number of prominent American moral philosophers, such as Judith Jarvis Thompson, all of whom (one might say) have made a career out of inventing "clever and amusing little stories." While the implied criticisms and caricatures are apt, and the practice itself is often puzzling to cultural outsiders, I do offer an explanation and defense of the practice in the following chapters. Our peculiar modern practice of moral casuistry offers a methodology that can prove useful in emotionally or politically-charged situations characterized by a high degree of ambiguity over principles, or uncertainty regarding the implications of specific practices.

19. A brief history of the emergence of this methodology and its present practice are offered in "Natural Law and the Principle of Double Effect: Six Hypothetical Cases" (Lucas and Rubel 2007: 231–37).

20. The CEAUSSIC commission has issued a call for "illustrative" case studies, both actual and hypothetical, for review and publication in a proposed volume, *Anthropology in a National Security Context: An Ethics Casebook*, to be edited by Professor Robert Albro at American University, with a target completion date of December, 2009. See http://www.aaanet.org/cmtes/commissions/CEAUSSIC/Ethics-Casebook.cfm.

21. For an account of the dramatic increase in reliance on such private contractors to perform functions hitherto within the purview of the military, especially since the 1998–1999 war in Kosovo, see, P. W. Singer, *Corporate Warriors: the Rise of the Privatized Military Industry*, updated edition (Ithaca, NY: Cornell University Press, 2003/2008). Singer is a senior fellow at the Brookings Institution and served as a member of President Barack Obama's transition team advising on this very topic. He offers a comprehensive and well-researched account, with a decided moral penchant against such reliance on the private sector in the future. For a somewhat different, and more positive account of the activities, quality of performance, and moral and legal questions involved in using such contractors in combat zones, see the work of a Heritage Foundation senior fellow, James Jay Carafano, *Private Sectors, Public Wars: Contractors in Combat* (Westport, CT: Praeger Publishers, 2008). I will return to this problem in the concluding arguments of this book.

CHAPTER ONE

⸻✦⸻

Scholars and Soldiers

"The Litany of Shame"

In March 2008, Professor Setha M. Low of the Graduate Center of the City University of New York and president of the American Anthropological Association (AAA), reported to the membership that the Executive Board had "passed a series of motions to begin the important work of revising the ethics code."[1] The "code" to which she referred is the "Code of Ethics of the American Anthropological Association" (CoE), adopted by the AAA in 1998 after years of lengthy deliberations. The 1998 CoE aimed to encompass, as well as supersede, earlier summaries of core values and statements of principles guiding responsible practice in research and teaching developed both within the AAA itself, and in its affiliate societies.

Its success in doing so, however, and the manner by which those earlier codes were either subsumed or superseded remains a matter of substantial controversy. The most recent call for review and reconsideration, for example, stemmed from a motion (introduced in November 2007 by Professor Terence Turner of Cornell University) to reintroduce specific language prohibiting "clandestine or secret research"—language that had been present in earlier versions of these guiding principles, but was omitted in the 1998 version.[2] The rationale for this motion offered by its author was that "the heightened involvement of anthropologists with U.S. military and intelligence institutions increases the danger that anthropological knowledge will be used to harm those we study and to impede the free circulation of anthropological knowledge."[3]

The so-called Turner motion reflects the broader concerns among anthropologists about the rapid growth of "military anthropology," and more specifically, the controversial Human Terrain Systems (HTS) project. While the language of the motion specifically cites the "growing involvement" of anthropologists with military, intelligence, and security forces as the rationale for its proposed changes, however, the motion itself revives concerns among anthropologists about "clandestine and secret research" and the overriding "importance of transparency and openness in anthropological research" that have a long history in the discipline, and considerably antedate the present controversy.

Moral debates about the appropriate limits of professional practice generally are forged in the crucible of specific historical crisis and controversy such as this. Professor Carolyn Fluehr-Lobban of Rhode Island College observes, "Discussions of ethics have reflected the issues and events of the day and have typically occurred during times of crisis in the discipline." This, of course, is an observation that would apply equally well to the history of a great many other disciplines, professions, and collective practices (witness the periodic crisis-driven reflections on "business ethics" as example). In anthropology's case, she notes, the ethical principles that have emerged over the past century have constituted principally "a series of crises over clandestine research," alongside other, occasionally questionable, practices by anthropologists (Fluehr-Lobban 2003: xi–xiii).

I propose that the present study of ethics and military anthropology commence, accordingly, by reflecting on significant vignettes drawn from that history of conflict within the discipline, as specialists in the field have composed it. Representative cases, drawn from the recent history of conflict and controversy, might serve to explain the extraordinary degree of concern that subject matter experts and practicing professionals in this field have displayed toward any suggestion that they collaborate with powerful governments, let alone with their military forces. Such fears appear to be well grounded in past historical precedent, and, as mentioned, have helped shape the provisions of the current Code of Ethics by which anthropologists guide their conduct as scholars and professionals today.

Anthropologists have their own lists of these controversies, a kind of "litany of shame" that informs disciplinary consciousness: the public censure of one of anthropology's most revered figures, Franz Boas, for daring to expose and denounce colleagues engaged in espionage during World War I, for example. That litany continues on to include collaboration of anthropologists in clandestine research and secret work with the Office of Strategic Studies during World War II, and later with the Central Intelligence Agency during the Cold War. Project Camelot, in the 1960s, is cited specifically in the CEAUSSIC report as a historical event of great trauma for the discipline, while other scholars single out the Thailand affair in 1970 (Price 2003).

If the debate about ethics is born in the history of controversy, however, anthropologists themselves are extraordinarily given to controversy about their history, specifically, about which events should figure in this "litany," and how each should be interpreted.[4] As Professor Fluehr-Lobban notes wryly, "The ghost of Franz Boas returns periodically both to haunt and to inspire anthropologists about engaging in secret research" (Fluehr-Lobban 2003: 19). Anthropology's history is so sensitive a topic that an outsider would be well advised to steer clear of it.

Fortunately, Professor Fluehr-Lobban herself has done a masterful a job in narrating the controversies and the provisions of various ethical codes that followed in the wake of each (Fluehr-Lobban 2003a: 1–28). The other contributors to her volume *Ethics and the Profession of Anthropology* (in both editions) have likewise commented passionately and in painstaking detail about individual events and their proper interpretation in that litany. There is no need for yet another history of these matters, let alone for a stranger to tread heavily on such sensitive, sacred, and highly contested ground.

Her volume's subtitle, "Dialogue for Ethically Conscious Practice," however, constitutes an invitation to discuss even further the meaning and interpretation of some of those events. Fluehr-Lobban describes in her introduction how it is sometimes both useful and necessary to step outside of one's disciplinary boundaries so as to view these matters (as she herself puts it) "more objectively." For her, that objectifying experience came during a residency at Dartmouth College's Institute for Applied and Professional Ethics, where she experienced an epiphany concerning her own discipline's longstanding, dismissive attitudes toward the pivotal issue of "informed consent" in human subjects research:

> I recalled many conversations with fellow anthropologists who regarded informed consent as a signed form with little cross-cultural validity or utility, as well as a paternalistic (maternalistic) attitude that an anthropologist knows what is best for his or her own people, making informed consent irrelevant.[5] (Fluehr-Lobban, 2003a: 19)

I can only imagine the astonishment with which eminent colleagues in ethics at Dartmouth at that time, such as philosopher Bernard Gert or the center's executive director at the time, Deni Elliot, must have greeted that attitude. It is an attitude, of course, that was also once prevalent among physicians, medical researchers, and the mental health professions, even after revelations of the most egregious abuses of medical research emerged at the Nuremburg "Doctors' Trials" in 1947.[6] Eventual confrontation and dialogue with outraged patients, colleagues in other fields, and the general public helped convince them finally that such unreflective and thoroughly unjustifiable attitudes lay behind many of their own professional case-litanies of abusive practice and grave moral error, even if we grant that there are undoubtedly instances where truly "informed" consent is itself difficult to achieve.

In anthropology's own "litany of shame," for example, the case that leaps out immediately at an uninitiated outsider is not that of Boas's censure (about which rival interpretations are possible), or even the oft-cited Project Camelot, but the so-called Sanchez affair.[7] What that, in turn, reveals is *not* that "informed consent" is unimportant (presumably anthropologist Oscar Lewis had some sort of informal, if not fully "informed" consent from the Sanchez family itself to live among them and write about them). It is, rather, *how difficult that long-familiar moral conception becomes to understand and ensure* when the objects of one's research are not, finally, individual human subjects themselves, but an entire group, society, or a cultural way of life that those individual subjects are taken to represent, and which is to be laid bare for public scrutiny. How does one "obtain" knowledgeable consent from "a cultural way of life," or from its members, collectively, to become the objects of scientific research, even if the researcher fervently believes such research to be in their own interests, and somehow to their benefit? And yet how, absent that understanding and consent from the subjects studied, can one presume to have a right to study them without threatening, even inadvertently, to embarrass or humiliate them, violate their privacy, or otherwise end up doing grave harm?

To an outsider, this fundamental moral tension between the claims of science on one hand, and the most basic rights of human beings and the "cultures" to which they are sometimes said to "belong" on the other, seems especially acute, and stubbornly intractable in the practice of anthropology. It constitutes an inherent and seemingly inexpugnable structural form of "bad faith" written necessarily into disciplinary practice from the outset. Even absent a research plan that is explicitly "secret" or "clandestine," the very nature of "research" in this field involves a particular kind of narrative public disclosure that cannot but pose a threat to the privacy and dignity of the individuals studied. This risk, accordingly, is seldom fully or accurately disclosed, no matter what the intentions of the researcher. Inasmuch as a scientist studying any phenomenon must try insofar as possible to minimize disturbing it from its natural state, the nature of what "living among and writing about" might really mean, for this reason also, cannot be fully disclosed, lest the individuals observed stop "behaving" and start "performing," unnaturally, instead. "Informed consent" is quite obviously compromised on both accounts. There is a danger, not only of deceiving one's research subjects, but even more of self-deception by the researcher as well, about the motivations for, and the possible consequences or public impact of, ethnographical research (Fluehr-Lobban 2003c). It is this tension, and the inability ever to entirely remove it, that constitutes what I am calling "structural bad faith."[8]

This inherent structural tension perhaps allows us to deconstruct how it comes to be that controversy over informed consent's subsidiary, entirely subordinate institutional guarantees (such as transparency, the absence of secrecy, and a concomitant obsession with "clandestine" research) are so visibly rife within the discipline. After all, the latter are not basic moral conceptions in any sense, and most certainly not conventions that are inherently either morally permissible or prohibited solely in themselves. There are many things we justifiably do in secret, while transparency, in many conceivable situations, is far from always constituting a virtue. Rather, in the instances where these are cited in rampant confusion as professional core values that "must always" be upheld, they instead turn out, in a kind of rabbinical fashion, to be simply institutional arrangements designed to ensure the upholding of even more fundamental moral values, such as security, dignity, and respect. Thus, the demand for transparency is meant to ensure, while prohibitions on secrecy and clandestine activities are intended to prevent, deliberate or even inadvertent violations of genuinely fundamental moral norms of the sort discerned in the Nuremburg Code. These include the presumed rights of biological individuals to privacy, self-determination, freedom from harm, and to fully informed and voluntary participation only in research from whose outcomes they might reasonably hope to obtain some benefit.[9]

These are, of course, complex questions in their own right. They deserve more careful and thoughtful consideration than they have customarily been given in the discipline to date. There are, for example, a number of issues that might be more precisely clarified, such as the difference between withholding research *results* from its subjects or from public knowledge, in contrast to keeping one's *research project itself* "secret." In point of fact, however, anthropologists, like most people, are seldom very clear or systematic about such distinctions, so it is probably best for the moment to rely on ordinary language conceptions and implicit understandings, unless these are found to introduce error.

For my part, I find that it is helpful to think of "secrecy" when discussing *research projects* in terms of whether or not there is full disclosure (i.e., of one's specific undertaking, its purposes, and of its sources of funding support), as well as of the presence or absence of good-faith efforts to obtain the fully informed consent of research subjects in response, prior to engaging in that undertaking. Both a failure to disclose the undertaking and its purposes (or sources of support), together with the resultant inability or unwillingness to obtain good-faith, fully informed consent of research subjects, would be sufficient to term a *research project* "secret" in the pejorative sense of "clandestine" (i.e., sneaky, underhanded, duplicitous, or otherwise deceptive).

By contrast, "secrecy" in reference to *research results* (as opposed to the undertaking itself) would pertain to withholding those results from the general public. A policy of secrecy regarding research results could be invoked to protect the anonymity and/or respect the confidentiality of research subjects themselves, in which case this policy would constitute "secret" (but importantly, not "clandestine") research. Withholding one's results from the subjects studied, or from full public dissemination for proprietary reasons, by contrast, both would constitute policies of "secrecy" that might appear "clandestine," and so would be harder to justify.

These are the sorts of finely grained nuances that a disciplinary committee on ethics, for example, would be required to parse carefully, and that rank-and-file members opposed to "secret" or "clandestine" research are likely to regard as an elaborate conceptual smoke screen. Inasmuch as anthropology has no track record of having attempted to hew to such subtly drawn distinctions in formulating its past principles of best practice, or in offering resolutions like the current "Turner amendment," I see no reason to impose so burdensome a constraint on its discourse at present. I will, however, be compelled to return to this fundamental discussion in the concluding chapter of this study.

In any case, Fluehr-Lobban's own, and subsequently the discipline's, transformation of attitudes toward the issue of informed consent suggest the value of a wider, interdisciplinary dialogue, particularly on matters pertaining to professional ethics. It would seem particularly apt for a community of scholars whose work lies in observing and accounting for "the Other" to seek out and value (rather than resist or denigrate) just such "outside" perspectives on their own (dare we call them) "cultural practices." This can be accomplished, as Fluehr-Lobban experienced, by a residency among colleagues in other fields, but it may just as easily be accomplished by widening the boundaries of the dialogue proposed, to permit those with little knowledge of, and therefore no particular "stake" in, one's professional affairs to view them at a distance, and perhaps with a different focus.

In that spirit, I would request permission to "cross-examine" a different vignette in anthropology's litany, one that runs slightly counter to Fluehr-Lobban's own description of a lack of debate at the time concerning the involvement of students of Boas with military, intelligence, and security forces in what she terms "the good war." In my somewhat contrasting interpretation, we encounter a prominent anthropologist, invited to cooperate with her government during a period of the gravest crisis, and ponder both the reasons, and even more important, the *process of reasoning*, by which she reaches and justifies her response.

Mead's Dilemma

In 1942, the prominent, provocative, and often controversial American anthropologist Margaret Mead described how, a "score of years ago" (to the reader of this book, about a century ago) the British empire had "*invented a special use for anthropologists* as advisers to the government." This is how the arrangement worked (according to Mead):

> In colonial countries, where a small colonial staff [had] to administer large areas filled with native people speaking diverse languages and practicing a large number of strange and diverse customs, there [were] always *administrative problems*: why is there a sudden outburst of headhunting in the gold-fields? Why have all the men in a certain area suddenly all gone away to work, or all refused to work? What will be the response of a tribe of two hundred fishing people if the government moves them to other land? How is it possible to stop a sudden messianic cult, which is sweeping from tribe to tribe, making everyone kill his pigs and neglect his garden? These are recurrent situations, *and some governments retained anthropologists* to find immediate answers to these vexatious questions. Trained to get the outlines of a situation quickly in cultural terms, the anthropologist was asked to find the source of the trouble, and to suggest satisfactory answers.

This description of the "use" of academic scholars and social scientists by the British imperial government might be such as to give us pause, especially when we come to realize that Mead was citing this practice with something approaching professional approval. She was herself preparing to participate in a similar attempt to "use" anthropology, fostered this time by the American government during World War II. She observed:

> So, in our own society at present, the anthropologist can comment on particular problems, based on a special type of experience. The war [that is, World War II] is putting new strains on men, women, and children; on teachers; on young people; on old people; on social workers; on factory owners; on farmers. The war is posing new problems for which there is desperate need of solutions.

In explanation and justification of her own willingness to participate in this venture, Mead famously writes:

> Six times in the last seventeen years I have entered another culture, left behind me the speech, the food, the familiar postures of my own way of life, and sought to understand the pattern of life of another people. In 1939, I came home to a world on the brink of war, convinced that the *next task was to apply what we knew*, as best we could, to the problems of our own society. . . . For my own culture [she concludes] . . . [t]he obligation of the scientist to examine his material dispassionately is combined with the obligation of the citizen to participate responsibly in his society. To the investigation of social materials to the end that we may know more, has to be added the organization of social materials that we may *do* more—here—now—in America toward fighting the war in a way that will leave us with the moral and physical resources to attack *the problem of reorganizing the world*.[10]

The core dilemma—the tension between the obligations imposed on a scientist or scholar to investigate his or her subject responsibly, and the obligations of that scientist or scholar also to function responsibly as a citizen—is here stated eloquently and passionately by an individual who, throughout her long career in the twentieth century, represented the face of anthropology to the wider public.[11] As we reflect on this particular formulation of the dilemma, we might pause to wonder, at least for a moment, just what Mead might have envisioned, at the time, as "*the problem of reorganizing the world*." We might justifiably experience even further some uneasy reservations or feelings of ambivalence about her straightforward, self-confident, and programmatic proposal to instrumentalize an autonomous discipline (and its practitioners) for nonscholarly, nonscientific—indeed explicitly political—purposes.

Some might cast an eye, either toward Mead's reference to colonial administration under the British empire, or perhaps toward the American government's numerous and varied attempts to "administer" indigenous peoples in this hemisphere during roughly the same period, and argue that, in principle, such collaboration of scholars with government and military officials ought never to be sanctioned. Others, with more caution than Mead herself evinces, might nonetheless be open in principle to the idea of responsible collaboration, but might, at minimum, demand a working knowledge of what the ultimate purposes were in the case of either British colonial administrators or the U.S. government (then and since). We might reasonably demand to know, in particular, whether those purposes were sufficiently "other-regarding"—that is, either beneficent, or at least non-malevolent, in their intent. Still others might recognize that, notwithstanding even the best of intentions, most prior attempts to "engineer" culture, or to put cultural knowledge at the service of government or empire, have ended badly.[12] There would, in all these instances, be ample grounds for caution concerning even the most ideal of ends, if not suspicion about means.

Of course Mead was, at the time, proposing that the United States should "use" anthropologists—indeed, describing how she herself willingly proposed to be used—to help America "win the war" against Nazi Germany and Imperial Japan. To her credit, she acknowledged at the time that wars might better be won by nations that deserved to win them, and that "deserving to win" ought to translate into both *having a morally worthy or justifiable cause*, and also into *being* a particular sort of nation and people. Indeed, the problem with which Mead seemed to be wrestling throughout *And Keep Your Powder Dry* (Mead 1942) was discerning just what sort of nation America itself was at that time, and the extent to which anthropology as a discipline could usefully shed light on that question.

But why even pose such a question at this time and in this way? Implicit in her inquiry seemed to be another, perhaps deeper and more general question, one quite familiar in philosophy, if not in anthropology. That question concerns whether being a nation whose own government and people collectively give every appearance of wanting to live together peacefully, with liberty and a reasonable degree of equality, accompanied by what we might reasonably describe as a commitment in principle to other basic human rights for the majority of its citizens, would also *morally entitle* that nation (at least, in the extreme circumstances in which America found itself at that time) to *wage war in its own defense*. It is that deeper, embedded, implicit question that renders Mead's anthropological ruminations in this work of general interest for our inquiry, for that is a question that all citizens, reflecting on their role and responsibilities in society, must at some point or other ask themselves.[13] It is a question that is just as well addressed to scientists or scholars, as to any individual in any other walk of life. No one, despite their beliefs or occupations, is entirely immune from asking it, certainly not in a time of grave crisis, such as the threat of world war.

What Mead clearly, at the time, did assert explicitly (and perhaps with unwarranted confidence) is that anthropology and its core methodology of field ethnography provided a scientific approach to the study and understanding of culture that might examine and conclusively demonstrate whether the U.S. itself constituted a nation and a people that would, in fact, be morally entitled to defend itself and protect its interests with force, if necessary. If anthropological knowledge and expertise, she thought, could provide a positive answer to this broad and basic question, it might also be able to inventory and understand just what unique cultural strengths such a nation and people might bring to the fray to help them prevail against ruthless, determined, and utterly unprincipled enemies.

Nations make use of their scientists and scholars for many purposes, in formulating and enforcing policies during peacetime, and in prosecuting campaigns during wartime. Galileo used his newly invented telescope and his mastery of ballistics to help Venice defeat the invading Ottoman navy (Sobel 1999: 30ff). America marshaled its physicists in the Manhattan Project to try to defeat Germany in the race to develop an atomic weapon. But these are not activities in which we would want citizens, let alone scientists, to blindly or unreflectively engage. Instead, we would want to counsel any citizen, and surely any citizen armed with the power and the responsibility that scientific knowledge may capably impart, to wonder about the purposes to which their efforts might be put, and the moral worthiness of the governments and institutions that importune their cooperation in this fashion.

To be certain, what is (or was) being studied and manipulated in these well-known instances are materials, armaments, or technology in an arms race, and decidedly not human beings and their cultural proclivities. Is there not something even more sinister and potentially insidious about using behavioral sciences, such as psychology and anthropology, in an effort to manipulate and control human behavior in such situations? And is this not an especially troubling question when we consider the transparent abuses to which these behavioral and human sciences have been put by tyrannical and totalitarian governments in Germany and the Soviet Union during the all-too-recent past?

And finally: even if Galileo apparently felt no qualms whatever about assisting his Venetian political masters in their military projects, we know that many physicists since have, for their part, expressed profound ambivalence about these practices and their participation in them, as well as about the *subordination of science itself to political ends*.[14] It is as if, somehow, the scientists, as distinct from ordinary citizens, might by their collaboration be found to betray the most fundamental values inherent in scientific inquiry itself. Bohr refused to be drawn into the conflict on either side. Einstein, and more especially Robert Oppenheimer (Mason 2006),[15] worried deeply about their involvement on the American side, while Werner Heisenberg, by his own account at least, passively resisted participation in the military aims of his own nation, whose moral stance he claims to have questioned. This betrayal of the most fundamental core values of scientific inquiry itself seemed, as well, to be the unpardonable sin for which Franz Boas denounced his colleagues after World War I. Shouldn't Margaret Mead, we wonder, have felt a similar reluctance to subordinate anthropology to politics? Shouldn't she have proven, in the end, more hesitant than she apparently did to employ her expertise in the study of human cultures for military ends—especially if the overriding purpose was, in some sense, external social control, what Mead herself described with chilling self-confidence as "social engineering?"

Her diffidence is particularly unsettling when we consider examples of other anthropologists from this same period, including Mead's husband at the time, Gregory Bateson, who likewise engaged his anthropological expertise to assist the Office of Strategic Services (forerunner of the CIA), but later came to regret his decision (Price 1998a). In a telling prelude to the contemporary debate about "mercenary" anthropology, some scholars complained publicly by 1944 that anthropologists had become little more than "technicians for hire to the highest bidder."[16]

The determination with which Mead, at the time, appears to have brushed such uncertainties aside, and the confidence with which she enumerated and celebrated her own nation's position of innate moral superiority during World War II, is cited here precisely because of the obvious parallels between her confident evaluation of American moral superiority then, and the present determination and moral confidence with which many contemporary American political and intellectual leaders have decried the immorality of terrorism, and justified the defense and even cultural promulgation of democracy and a commitment to basic human rights in the "war on terror." There is, to be sure, an eerie resonance between the spirited discussions and debates at present over neoconservative politics and America's wars in Iraq and Afghanistan, and Mead's acknowledgment during the Second World War of "the moral . . . superiority of democracy as a way of life over totalitarianism as a way of life" (Mead 1942: 108). Likewise we perceive some instructive overlap in her frank acknowledgment of the tactical disadvantages and handicaps a democratic state experiences when engaged in what Mead herself describes as the "democratic cultural style" of waging war—a style she contrasts with the morally unprincipled ruthlessness with which totalitarian states (or, we might add, fanatical nonstate actors) can be shown to prosecute such wars.

Anthropologists in the present acknowledge and bemoan their discipline's troubled history of having sometimes come out on the wrong side of such questions. And by citing with approval, rather than condemning, earlier uses of anthropology in similar contexts by the stewards of the British empire in the nineteenth and twentieth centuries, Mead herself perfectly exemplifies the uncritical and incautious mindset and the attendant practices that many contemporary anthropologists are determined not to see replicated. Mead herself was, of course, roundly criticized at the time, and since, for her stance on this matter during World War II. Her credentials as a scientist were questioned, and even more the scientific validity of her approach to this questionable anthropological project. She herself equivocated mightily between assuming the mantle of respectability and impartiality of science, and advocating the stance of a concerned, committed, loyal, and patriotic citizen. Her accounts of American cultural life and practices in this project are themselves often condemned as naïve and one-sided. (She blithely ignored the pernicious and invidious racism of the time, for example.) She is criticized for having, in works like this, fallen far short of the most basic ethnographic standards, and for engaging in little more than opinionated editorializing, rather than accurate, comprehensive, and impartial ethnographic field observations. In sum, Mead was criticized then, and since, for having, through this venture into war and politics, undermined the core values of her fragile discipline and brought her profession itself into possible disrepute.[17]

The criticisms leveled at Mead for subordinating anthropology to political ends in the past century are identical to the criticisms leveled at military anthropologists by their colleagues at present. And the questions we would want anthropologists engaged in such collaboration to propose now are identical to those we would have like to have seen her propose more carefully then. They are precisely the questions of principle with which we are concerned in this book. To what extent, if ever, is it possible for anthropologists in particular, and for scientists and scholars in general, to collaborate with governments and with military and security forces in conducting their operations without betraying the most fundamental, core values of their disciplines?

We perceive Mead grappling, at the time, with fundamental moral values concerning her nation and its practices (even if she did not do this as fully and comprehensively as we might wish). We see her grappling also with the core strengths and insights that her discipline might offer in behalf of morally worthy ends (whatever those might be). But we do not see her asking, at least in this instance, whether in so doing the *core values of the discipline itself* might thereby be compromised. Such an examination on her part would have been aided, and perhaps more specifically evoked, by a clear and unequivocal statement or summary of precisely what those core values were. Such a summary was, at the time, nonexistent. Whatever the core values of anthropological scholarship were, they remained implicit, a set of presuppositions, perhaps thought to be obvious in the light of history and practice or subject to contextual debate within the discipline, but nowhere codified or clarified.[18]

Many anthropologists, even those critical of Mead, acknowledge the valuable insights provided to the American provisional governing authorities in Japan after World War II by the work of Mead's close friend, the venerable anthropologist Ruth Benedict, in her classic study *The Chrysanthemum and the Sword* (1946). Even had it not been the case that General Douglas MacArthur and the American occupation forces in postwar Japan urgently needed all the understanding they could glean at that time to assist them in making and keeping the peace, still such a study would have been scientifically and intellectually valuable for its own sake.[19] Indeed, Sidney W. Mintz's memoir argues that students of this work are "unanimous in the opinion that this is Benedict's crowning achievement in the study of national cultures," and that "few scholars would gainsay the penetrating originality of her analysis."[20]

It might be (as Fluehr-Lobban also implies) that the self-confidence of Ruth Benedict, Margaret Mead, Mead's husband Gregory Bateson, and many other anthropologists at that time about the collaboration of scholars with military and intelligence forces during what they regarded as a justifiable war of self-defense against tyranny rendered them less cognizant of the increasing dangers of moral turpitude that their students and successors would face during the far more morally ambiguous wars of counterinsurgency, as in Vietnam, Cambodia, and Thailand, that would soon follow during America's "Cold War."[21] Before turning to these, and to Mead's own role in professional oversight and peer review of them in the next chapter, it is worth making note of the implicit procedure she invoked to explain her stance to her colleagues and to the public.

Morality and "Professional Ethics"

The account of Mead's reasoning that I presented above entails two very distinct sets of considerations. The first are quite general in nature, and do not pertain specifically to anthropologists. These include her recognition, for example, "that wars might better be won by nations that deserved to win them," and that "deserving to win" ought to translate into both "having a just cause," and also into "being a particular sort of nation and people"—one (I took her to be implying) whose own commitment to peace with justice, and to liberty, accompanied with basic human rights for all its citizens, entitled it to wage war in its own defense. What we find Mead doing is offering a justification for her own actions (including using anthropological knowledge and expertise) by aligning them within a much larger justificatory scheme—in this instance, involving a nation's (i.e., *her* nation's) decision to go to war. The background demand is that this larger decision, which she now proposes to support and enable through her own professional and scholarly activities, be perceived as having been *morally justified.*

Such a discussion transcends anthropology, or any other specific discipline or professional practice. It is a *moral* discussion, and in this case, leads to a *moral evaluation* of a decision to go to war. Without being able to understand, represent, and finally assent to this larger moral evaluation, the professional or scholar is unable to offer support for collaboration in some larger effort. But reaching that perspective requires resources and expertise that no one professional or scholarly field monopolizes. In fact, what we see Mead doing here first is engaging intuitively in what moral philosophers would identify as "just war" reasoning. She is asking hard questions about the "causes" of the war—by which she (and we) mean "the good (or bad) reasons for it" rather than descriptions of the political or economic factors that may have "caused" it in the sense of "brought it about."

This kind of reasoning has a long history in Western culture, but it is as far from being merely a Western cultural artifact as the practice of war itself. If warfare constitutes a highly variable form of "cultural performance" worthy of anthropological study,[22] one might also observe that such performances are routinely accompanied by equally unique forms of cultural discourse concerning the circumstances under which the performance is to be staged, and to what extent, and by whom, against whom, and most important, for what ends. Arjuna and Krisna debate precisely these questions in the *Bhaga-vad Gita*, while laws in ancient India clearly defined those who were to be exempt from attack in the midst of war. Sun Tzu famously offers delicately nuanced and understated views on precisely these questions in *The Art of War*. Chairman Mao denounced his own culture's earlier forms of discourse and limitations on the practice of combat as "asinine," but then proceeded to proclaim his own "Eight Points for Attention" outlining constraints on his own insurgency forces in their conduct of guerrilla war in 1938. The Qur'an and its accompanying Hadith declaim frequently and at length upon when, how, and to what extent to make war upon unbelievers, along with when, if ever, Muslims should raise the sword against fellow Muslims.

The renowned political philosopher Michael Walzer writes, "For as long as men and women have talked about war, they have talked about it in terms of right and wrong. . . . Reiterated over time," he observes, "[these] arguments and judgments shape what I want to call *the moral reality of war*—that is, all those experiences of which moral language is descriptive or within which it is necessarily employed" (Walzer 1977).[23] The "necessity" of this moral discourse, moreover, is one born not of compulsion but precisely of our collective agency—our freedom—our ability to decide, to choose, to act or refrain from acting, and to offer better or worse accounts of what we have done and why. This is precisely the sort of discourse that Margaret Mead invoked to account for her actions in 1942; it is precisely the form of discourse that opponents of military anthropology have invoked to explain the background of their concerns and their principled opposition to collaborating with military forces in Iraq and Afghanistan at present.

My own account of this extensive and multicultural history of "just war" reasoning is that it simply represents a form of what critical theorists (led by the Kantian philosopher Jürgen Habermas) term variously "communicative action" or "ideal public discourse" (Habermas 1984–1987).[24] When an individual decides to defy authority, break an important moral rule, or otherwise step outside the normal realm of justifiable behavior (as in an act of civil disobedience, for example), an account is usually given, and in fact demanded, to explain and justify the decision, often as much to the individual undertaking the action, as to skeptical others observing and criticizing it. Such reasoning is subject to public review and criticism—what any scholar or academic would immediately recognize as review by a de facto jury of peers. Just war reasoning is exactly such a form of discourse concerning one of the gravest and most important moral decisions any society can make: deciding to commit its soldiers and citizens to the risks of harm in war.[25] An account is demanded, and usually (even if only for political reasons) given, and, in any just society, at least, such an account is subject to criticism and review. This is true, no matter what political system or philosophical orientation toward morality reigns. The account may be framed in terms of self-interest or national interests, for example. But as such, even so thin a justification is subject to review and challenge (Thucycides 431 BCE).[26] Certainly in a society, in a democracy for example, in which the political order is organized around respect for the basic rights and freedoms of each citizen, such a conversation is of paramount importance.

Just war reasoning is a tradition of moral philosophy, however, that recognizes (as does the practice of moral philosophy generally) that some forms of reasons are "better" than others. Reasoning that leads to war on account of some compelling act of injustice, after a "harm has been inflicted,"[27] for example, and only after all recourse short of war has been exhausted, seems to represent a stronger case than one in which war is resorted to haphazardly, impatiently, on the basis of faulty intelligence or misleading information, rather than after a long period of deliberation and exploration of alternatives. This is as much true for tyrants and totalitarian states as it is for states committed to minimal justice. Where the differences come to light is that inherently unjust regimes, or regimes that are largely uninterested in the guarantee of basic rights for their citizens, frequently offer less compelling reasons for going to war than do just regimes, and the causes for which they urge recourse to violence are often especially weak. A claim of a right of national self-defense as a reason for taking the nation to war is decidedly less convincing when offered by a dictator like Idi Amin in Uganda, for example, or by the military junta in Argentina during the Falklands War (following more than a decade of egregious domestic human rights abuses) than when put forward by a widely popular and historically fair-minded hereditary monarch, let alone the legitimately elected leader of a democratic state.

Quite remarkably, it is precisely this entire conception of justification that Mead has intuitively "lasered in on." We see echoes of this profound and enduring form of reasoning in Mead's own assessment of the moral worthiness of her own nation (despite its flaws), and in her judgment that it is important for all citizens of her nation to join in defending it from forms of political order and military violence that (she also expects her readers intuitively to recognize and agree) would be decidedly worse.

I claimed, however, that there were two sorts of considerations embedded in her defense of her own decisions and in her appeal to her colleagues at the time. That second set of considerations pertains specifically to anthropology, defining what the field itself represents, what it stands for, or what it offers to the public, and also what its practitioners are permitted, or even obligated, to do. So we find Mead turning almost instinctively to anthropology's core methodology of field ethnography, which, she believed, provided a scientific approach to the study and understanding of culture that might examine and demonstrate both whether the U.S. at the time constituted the sort of nation and people worthy of defending, and if so, as she put it, help further to inventory and understand just what unique cultural strengths such a nation and people might bring to the fray that might help them prevail against "ruthless, determined, and utterly unprincipled enemies."

These latter concerns, in sharp contrast to the widespread (I would say general or universal) *moral* debate about war, are quite specific and limited. Critical theorists, following Habermas (see endnotes 24 and 25), would describe these as "*ethical*" concerns, very focused and particular in their content and limited in their jurisdiction, as distinct from the universal rhetorical appeal of moral discourse. In somewhat plainer language Mead is inquiring, What are the "core values" of the discipline of anthropology? What is it to be an anthropologist, that is, to study the members of distinctive organizations and societies, to conduct ethnographic research in their midst, and to share and disseminate these results? What are we about, and indeed who are "we," when we engage in such activities? These, in contrast to human rights practices, or the justification of a decision to go to war, are precisely not the sorts of questions that every citizen should ask, but that only some few should ask, namely, those who identify themselves as members of a discipline, or perhaps a profession.

In sum, that second set of questions that Mead addressed falls within the domain of what philosophers sometimes label "ethics and the professions," the specific investigation of the core values attached to recognized professional practices (such as medicine), together with discussion and evaluation of the kinds of practice-specific cases and problems that arise in the course of professional activities. One might justifiably wonder to what extent discussions of ethics and "professional practice" can be brought to bear upon academic disciplines.[28] Frankly, there are no well-formulated answers to those questions, in part because there have been few prior occasions to extrapolate in precisely this fashion. What is required is a formal move from the relatively recent development of this area of "applied ethics" or "applied philosophy," undertaken (as I outlined in the introduction) wholly in response to needs and requests from specific professions (such as medicine or psychology), to the kinds of problems and debates that an academic discipline such as anthropology faces in present circumstances. That should not be hard to do in principle, and indeed one sees a kind of intuitive analogy already at work among scholars in the discipline reflecting on professional ethics, moving between the identification of core values of the practice to guidelines for best practice and the formulation of prohibitions and constraints defining the limits of acceptable and unacceptable practices.[29]

Thus, as related to anthropology specifically, we would simply observe that the answers anthropologists might collectively give to questions concerning their shared core values, examples of best or exemplary practice, and any constraints they would feel compelled to impose collectively upon questionable or unacceptable practices by other members of their discipline and academic society, might be said to constitute the intellectual grounding, the foundation, of anthropology's "Code of Ethics." Moreover, such collective ruminations by anthropologists would constitute their code just as reliably and authoritatively as the answers physicians and health care professionals give to their own questions serve similarly to forge the Code of Ethics of the American Medical Association.

It is important to note, however, that where uncertainties lurk over which specific values are indeed "shared," or over which sorts of practices ought to be constrained or outlawed, there also lie the origins of genuine and principled disagreements over what provisions such a professional or disciplinary code should contain. In the realm of core values, for one obvious example, how important is the value of enhancing and disseminating scientific knowledge for the benefit of humankind (ensured by institutional arrangements like transparency), in relation to the respect for the most basic rights of the subjects studied to security, privacy, or freedom from other injury that might be incurred in the pursuit of that knowledge (ensured by confidentiality and informed consent)? That particular, quite familiar conflict is hardly unique to anthropology, but it has constituted a festering sore in the history of this discipline as much as it has in any other where human subjects are the objects of research.

Such conflicts, and the principled disagreements of practitioners over them, finally, demonstrate the tacit reliance of the limited and focused professional discourse about "ethics" upon the wider public discourse about morality generally. It is the interdependence of these two otherwise distinct forms of moral discourse that is quite often poorly understood.

Disputes about secrecy, for example, or collaborating with military and intelligence forces in the performance of their operations, can only be resolved and enshrined in (or removed from) a profession's code of ethics on the basis of appeal to general considerations that transcend the intellectual boundaries of that code. Supporters of the "Turner amendment" as the basis for revising the AAA's earlier (1998) Code of Ethics, for example, were presumably not engaged simply in harking back nostalgically to a time when that code contained more explicit guidance about clandestine research than it does now. Instead, they appear to argue that the absence of such specific guidance at present permits actions that they believe to be *morally unjustifiable*. Quite obviously, the unjustifiability of such actions cannot rest upon provisions of the CoE that no longer explicitly prohibit them. Instead, the argument must appeal beyond either the 1971 "Principles of Professional Responsibility" (Fluehr-Lobban 2003) or the 1998 CoE to a stance outside of both, from which vantage point the alleged superiority of the language of the former to that of the latter can be argued and defended.

That such arguments frequently degenerate into hopeless circularity is hardly to be wondered at, when the broader foundation of general moral presuppositions upon which any such argument rests are themselves poorly understood or hidden from view. In the present instance, those tacit moral generalizations have to do with the morality or immorality of war, preparations for and conduct of war, and the moral legitimacy of specific activities of military and intelligence organizations during war.

Anthropologists in particular, long portrayed as uncomfortable with the notion of generalizable, cross-cultural norms of behavior, might dispute such a contention. They might prefer to attempt to forge an entirely self-contained, self-referential solution to this dilemma—simply trying to argue, for example, that the professional activities and core values of anthropology as a behavioral science are somehow incompatible with the latter kinds of wartime activities and organizations. Such an attempt is doomed to hopeless incoherence, however, unless it appeals to some general considerations that lie beyond the domains of both anthropology and the military and intelligence forces (in this instance), sufficient to account for *why and how* the very nature of the former is incompatible with the latter. These more general moral reasons invoked in the justification of personal action or professional values are precisely what we find Margaret Mead, in the historical vignette above, struggling to discern.

As I pointed out earlier, Mead does not herself appeal to any specific "code of ethics" for anthropology. She evinces instead what was, at the time, a widespread faith in the virtues of impartiality and truth as the hallmarks, the core values, of scientific investigation generally. She then sets forth the kind of truth or valuable insights regarding culture, cultural differences, and her own culture's unique strengths, that her particular brand of science might offer the nation in its pursuit of a just war against fascism and totalitarianism. The linking of these two sorts of considerations, "just war" reasoning and any sort of discipline-specific code of ethics, are particularly difficult to negotiate when the code itself lies nascent, unformulated, and imprecise, let alone when the war in question is of dubious justification. The former, and decidedly not the latter, was Mead's challenge in the midst of the Second World War.

In our present circumstances, by contrast, in the midst of morally contested wars in Iraq and Afghanistan, the situation is reversed. Indeed, the self-confidence concerning justifiable wars and the scientist's role in them that Mead exuded in 1942 was a great deal harder to come by a scant two decades later, as the U.S. once again asked its anthropologists for assistance as it struggled to contend with incipient communist insurgencies in Latin America, and was subsequently drawn into wars of counterinsurgency fought against communist partisans in Vietnam, Cambodia, and Thailand.

Notes

1. *Anthropology News* (March 2008).

2. Gerald D. Berreman offers his own background history of the earlier codes and principles of professional responsibility, and of the arguments leading up to their replacement with the current Code of Ethics in "Ethics versus Realism in Anthropology: Redux," (Fluehr-Lobban 2003: 51–83). A summary of the relevant deletions

pertinent to our inquiry is at p. 64, and analysis of loss or weakening of restrictions on secrecy and clandestine research at pp. 66–69.

3. The precise wording of the motion and summary of the historical background was included in a more recent letter from President Low to AAA members, reporting on the progress of efforts to respond to this motion and to revise the CoE, circulated via e-mail on Wednesday, September 24, 2008, and posted on the association's website at http://dev.aaanet.org/issues/policy-advocacy/Proposed-Changes-to-the-Ethics-Code.cfm. These proposed changes were adopted by a majority vote of the association early in 2009: http://dev.aaanet.org/issues/policy-advocacy/2009-Ethics-Code.cfm. The revised CoE (CoE 1998; rev. 2009) is printed in appendix A.

4. Some readers, most likely specialists, may have immediate concerns about whether, in this account, I have selected the right vignettes or figures to feature, or whether I have included enough of these to be representative. I emphasize that the cases and illustrations I have featured are derived directly from historical accounts written by prominent anthropologists themselves. Even so, the specific details and the interpretive significance of each are subject to great controversy: "Why discuss Smith, when Jones is an even more egregious example," and so forth. Any partial selection also involves omission, which can itself be grounds for suspicion or offense. I intend neither. What I trust cannot be denied (even if other scholars would have chosen different cases) is that the particular vignettes I have chosen suggest all too readily the mindset that otherwise reputable and morally responsible scholars can develop, absent a certain self-critical caution and humility.

5. Fluehr-Lobban offers a detailed account of her own, and the discipline's, struggle to understand and incorporate a workable conception of "informed consent" into the current (1998) CoE. See Fluehr-Lobban 1994.

6. Informed consent was the very first of six, and ultimately 10, principles of proper medical practice (including human research) imposed in the verdicts issuing from those trials. It states: "The voluntary consent of the human subject is absolutely essential. This means that the person involved should have legal capacity to give consent; should be so situated as to be able to exercise free power of choice, without the intervention of any element of force, fraud, deceit, duress, over-reaching, or other ulterior form of constraint or coercion; and should have sufficient knowledge and comprehension of the elements of the subject matter involved as to enable him to make an understanding and enlightened decision. This latter element requires that before the acceptance of an affirmative decision by the experimental subject there should be made known to him the nature, duration, and purpose of the experiment; the method and means by which it is to be conducted; all inconveniences and hazards reasonable to be expected; and the effects upon his health or person which may possibly come from his participation in the experiment." See *Trials of War Criminals before the Nuremberg Military Tribunals under Control Council Law, Vol. 2, No. 10* (Washington, DC: U.S. Government Printing Office, 1949), 181–82. In fairness to anthropologists, it requires some extended analogical reasoning to see how this

principle would bear upon ethnographic field studies, and it was the work of several decades to translate this specifically medical insight into a wider principle limiting the practice of research of any sort on human subjects generally.

7. Fluehr-Lobban (2003a: 9) reports on the outrage that broke out in the Mexican press following the translation into Spanish of anthropologist Oscar Lewis's study of one impoverished Mexican family in *Children of Sanchez* (1961).

8. Dena Plemmons comments that Dutch anthropologist Peter Pels is even more blunt than I in his assessment of anthropologists' moral failings as "tricksters" (Pels 1999; Pels and Salemink 2000). I think that perhaps overly harsh. Self-deception (Sartre's "bad faith") and paternalism are serious enough failings, if also less odious in their intentions. My point, moreover, is not to sit in judgment or join anthropologists in this self-flagellation, but to suggest the underlying moral problem is embedded in the discipline's fundamental methodology. That is a different and an altogether (and, I think, far more serious) point.

9. My own initial, entirely intuitive reaction to the HTS program, prior to knowing anything specifically about specific provisions in AAA's CoE, let alone the association's interesting history with the concept of informed consent, was: "How on earth would an HTS team member obtain any kind of meaningful informed consent from the local populace for the work he or she proposed to engage in under combat conditions?"

10. Margaret Mead, *And Keep Your Powder Dry: An Anthropologist Looks at America* (1942), hereafter cited in the text as Mead 1942. New York: Berghahn Books, 2000, pp. 1–5; rearranged to summarize her larger argument; my emphases. The Oliver Cromwell quotation (see p. 103) from which the book title is taken reflects Mead's own Cromwellian sensibilities regarding "taking matters in hand" and the goals of what Mead herself describes approvingly as "social engineering." Given the ruthlessness with which Cromwell himself then proceeded to invade Ireland and attack the foundational institutions of Roman Catholicism, it is not clear that Mead would have so wholeheartedly approved the original project.

11. This simple fact about Mead's extraordinary public persona in the 20th century largely accounts for my choice to begin with her statement of her dilemma at the time. An additional justification for this choice emerges in the account of her role in mediating disputes among anthropologists over the Thailand affair, toward the end of the Vietnam War, that led to the second formulation of the AAA Code of Ethics in 1971 (Fluehr-Lobban 2003a). Others might choose to develop a different narrative and ignore her altogether. I am fully aware, of course, of the debates within the discipline over her public role and her leadership in the AAA, as well as her own credentials as a scientist. Again I must beg indulgence: not only do I not wish to join that controversy, but there is in fact nothing in or about it, or about one's personal view of Mead herself, that would prove at all relevant to, or in any way alter the argument of, this chapter. It would merely result in an alternative narrative, featuring different figures but making essentially identical points.

12. Examples of such disasters in the wake of good or at least honest intentions to provide cultural solutions to intractable cultural problems abound in the history of anthropology. One of the most disturbing in America's history was the U.S. government's "Indian removal" effort at Bosque Redondo, a reservation established for Mescalero Apache and Navajo peoples, championed by U.S. Army Brigadier General James H. Carleton in the 1860s. Carleton was a well-educated and well-read man who fancied himself a kind of amateur ethnologist or cultural anthropologist. The forced exodus of nearly 9,000 Navajo to this site at Fort Sumner in eastern New Mexico, resulting in the death of hundreds, is known in Navajo history as "the Long Walk." One recent and vivid account of this episode is that of writer and popular historian Hampton Sides in *Blood and Thunder* (New York: Random House, 2006), 445–50. (This title is taken from the popular ethnocentric and anti-indigenous accounts published at the time, concerning the exploits of "Indian fighter" Kit Carson.)

13. Indeed, I find it remarkably prescient that Mead is posing the question in this way, since an affirmative answer concerning any nation's "right" of self-defense has customarily been presupposed in moral theory and international law without much critical reflection. Whether nations routinely possess this right, let alone when (if ever) it is moral for them to exercise it, is a topic of great current interest in my own discipline, prompted in part by the brilliant and provocative challenge to the prevailing assumptions about this recently issued by Oxford philosopher David Rodin (Rodin 2002).

14. Einstein remarked, "If I had known that the Germans would not succeed in constructing the atom bomb, I would never have lifted a finger." Robert C. Batchelder, *The Irreversible Decision: 1939–1950* (New York: Houghton, 1962), 38. Quoted in Walzer 1977: 263.

15. Alone among the otherwise copious literature on Oppenheimer, Bohr, and others, this work focuses on the scientist's choice as an occasion for moral reflection on the nature of scientific curiosity and the purity of "research" as appropriate motives for inquiry, as well as on the nature of professional and academic responsibility for one's scientific pursuits and findings.

16. Anthropologist Laura Thompson, quoted in Price and Gonzalez 2007: 3, also in Price 2008. Price (2004, 2008) is certainly the most exhaustive historical treatment of the topic of collaboration with the military. His selection of topics, evidence, and the resultant narrative accounts, however, are heavily theory-laden, driven largely by the a priori conviction that such collaborations are wrong in principle. I diverge from his pattern of emphasis simply because my goal in this chapter and the next is to cross-examine existing historical accounts by anthropologists like Price, precisely in order to determine whether there are grounds for holding this conviction. My own argument is that this conviction requires a pattern of wrongdoing by individuals engaged in such collaboration, which pattern cannot itself be established simply by showing, as Price surely does, that anthropologists engaged in them, or even that doing so in turn involved them in "secret research." The ongoing pattern

of such research must, in turn, be shown to be persistently malevolent in order to justify a professional principle forbidding it; less stringently, such "clandestine" collaborations may be shown to be prone to malevolence, establishing a prima facie burden of proof against engaging in them. (The latter, in Price's account, appears to be the tacit misgiving shared by many anthropologists engaged in government work during World War II, which they overrode for reasons I offer in my account of "Mead's Dilemma" in this chapter.)

Price's earlier work uncovers a pattern of prejudicial intent by the FBI against anthropologists engaged in civil rights and antiwar movements in the twentieth century (Price 2004). That is an altogether different matter, shameful in its own right but largely irrelevant to the problem of either "secret research" or the professional probity of collaboration with military and security forces. What is required is clear evidence of wrongdoing by anthropologists while they occupy these roles. There is little of this, largely because the evidence Price uncovers clearly shows that anthropologists did not, in fact, accomplish much of consequence one way or the other in such roles. There are some instances of genuine abusive or unprofessional behavior, as we shall see, while anthropologists engaged in contract work sometimes made exaggerated claims for the military or security advantages their expertise might offer that are disturbing, and certainly unprofessional in their content. But these claims were spurious and self-serving, and Price provides no evidence that anyone else believed them, let alone acted upon them.

17. The above account of scholarly reaction to Mead's war efforts is drawn from the introductory essay by Hervé Varenne to the 2000 edition of Mead's *And Keep Your Powder Dry*. David Price, in a review of my earlier work on this topic, objected to this summary not only because he felt there were better examples, but because "Margaret Mead's work remains suspect among many anthropologists because of her faulty ethnography on adolescence in Samoa, not because of her support of the war effort." But that view is countered by the several reliable anthropological sources I cite here. It is simply false that her wartime collaborations were not the object of intense criticism. There may be, of course, other examples of such collaboration besides hers, but, as I've indicated earlier, that is beside the point. Hers is an excellent illustration of the dilemma faced for anthropologists at present. As I stated, it is not my task to write history, only to cite it, and to subject its authors' conclusions to evidentiary cross-examination on their own terms (that is, using the accounts they have written, and the evidence they themselves have cited). In addition to Hervé Varenne's account, a similar mixed assessment of Mead is offered by Sydel Silverman in her concluding reflections on Mead's career (Silverman 2004: 213–18). Silverman includes a thorough, balanced, and often positive assessment of Mead's wartime and postwar experiments with "public" anthropology and her role in investigating the involvement of anthropologists in counterinsurgency efforts in Thailand in 1970.

18. Carolyn Fluehr-Lobban, discussing the role of anthropologists during a "just war," confirms the absence of any formal statements or guidelines governing anthro-

pological research prior to the 1948 formal declaration of "Ethical and Professional Responsibilities" of the newly formed Society for Applied Anthropology (SfAA). Indeed, she reports that as late as 1963, an entire volume on the teaching of anthropology published by the AAA contained little in the way of references to ethics and professional practice (Fluehr-Lobban 2003: 5–7).

19. Like many issues in anthropology, this work is clouded in controversy. For one thing, Benedict was unable to carry out field studies, and had to rely on literary sources and discussions with Americans of Japanese birth and ancestry. The extent, moreover, to which her work played a role in decisions about ending the war and influencing the subsequent policies of the provisional occupational authority are subjects of scholarly controversy. The claim that Benedict's work on national character was instrumental in influencing the American government's decision to retain the Japanese emperor as a figurehead at the end of the war was offered supportively by Mead herself, and is likely exaggerated (Silverman 2004: 214). Those disputed historical details, mercifully, are beside the point in this assessment.

20. Sidney W. Mintz, "Ruth Benedict," in Silverman 2004: 112.

21. David Price alleges as much, suggesting that "the various actions undertaken by American anthropologists . . . during World War II . . . no doubt presupposed them to accept" a number of subsequent appointments in or collaborative projects with the State Department and the CIA during the early years of the Cold War (Price 2003: 33).

22. This characterization is one of several offered by the editors of a varied and brilliant collection of anthropological studies of differing war practices (Ferguson and Whitehead, 1992: xxiii).

23. Walzer is, of course, the author of what I and my colleagues collectively celebrate as the preeminent contribution to "just war discourse" in the 20th century, now in its fourth edition. The quotations are from the opening chapter, "Against Realism," pp. 1, 15; the citation of ancient Indian law concerning classes of noncombatants can be found in chapter 3, "Rules of War," p. 43; and the description of Mao Tse-tung's doctrine of just war in chapter 14, "Winning and Fighting Well," pp. 225–27.

24. As the size of this two-volume work suggests, this is an immensely complicated topic, and is itself the subject of nearly as much criticism and counter-argument as anthropologists heap upon conceptions of "culture." To make matters worse, my account qualifies as falling under the third of three distinctions that Habermas makes regarding such discourse: logic, dialectic, and rhetoric. Moral discourse, in the third realm, aims at persuasion through appeal to criteria that are deemed by listeners as universal. That summary is going to strike a cultural anthropologist as mystifying, to say the least. And to make matters worse again, Habermas differentiates moral discourse from "ethics" discourse, which is limited and culturally specific. As I mentioned in my introduction, moral philosophers do not always or consistently follow Habermas in this respect, though the distinction emerges quite clearly in discussions

of professional practice and discipline-specific "codes" of ethics. I have endeavored in my simplified account of just war discourse to avoid entangling my claims in the fine points of the critiques of Habermas's discourse theory, and instead couch it in terms that readers who had never heard of any of this could nonetheless find intelligible and, I hope, not unreasonable.

25. Habermas has attempted to apply his theory of "communicative rationality" and the procedural emphasis of what he terms "discourse ethics" to problems of just war, such as the NATO Balkan intervention (Habermas 2000) and, more recently, to the significance of the global "war on terror" for his larger cosmopolitan project of international law (Habermas 2004). I have not found his own approach to these topics very enlightening, and endeavor to give a more coherent and, I hope, intelligible interpretation of what I take to be the thrust of these concerns in the account offered here.

26. The ancient Greek historian Thucydides, for example, provides a dramatic example of how this self-limiting and self-correcting community of discourse functions, in his account of the debate in the Athenian Assembly, specifically between Cleon and Diodotus, over the proposed military response to the rebellion by one of Athens's colonies at Mytilene. See Thucydides 431 BCE: Book III, chapters 36–49, pp. 176–83.

27. For example, according to the Spanish Dominican philosopher Francisco de Vitoria, "The sole and only just cause for waging war is when harm has been inflicted" (Vitoria 1539/1557: 303). Vitoria goes to some length to specify what sorts of "harm" he has in mind: he includes the harms inflicted on their hapless subjects by ruthless tyrants, necessitating humanitarian military intervention and regime change. See his "fifth just title, in defence of the innocent against tyranny" (Vitoria 1539/1557: 287–88).

28. There are certainly further important distinctions to be made here between "disciplines" and "professions." The former usually denote areas of subject expertise alone, while the latter encompass such expertise in recognized forms of public service, usually including a code of conduct or a set of ethical principles governing membership in the profession and constraining the behavior of its members. "Anthropology" is arguably a hard case, inasmuch as there are distinct subdisciplines, such as cultural or physical anthropology and linguistics, together with practices that may be, but need not be, oriented principally toward public service. For simplicity's sake, it might be well to allow the "discipline" to continue to identify itself also as (or as involving) a "profession" of some sort, as seems to be implied in the 1971 "Principles of Professional Responsibility" (PPR; reprinted in Fluehr-Lobban, 2003), the immediate ancestor of the current AAA Code of Ethics (CoE 1998; appendix), to key provisions of which Professor Turner's motion would now recur.

29. This is explicitly the case in Fluehr-Lobban 2003, and also, somewhat more diffusely, in the contributed essays reflecting on ethics from a variety of practitioner settings in the U.K., in *The Ethics of Anthropology: Debates and Dilemmas* (Caplan

2003). Although the conceptual landscape is far from clear, psychology would provide a useful example, in that it, like anthropology, appears as a discipline in the academy, in which the primary activities are teaching, research (involving human subjects) and dissemination of knowledge, and also as a clinical profession outside educational settings, providing counseling and health care services to patients and clients. It is likewise far from clear how, apart from "informed consent," the code of conduct governing the latter's professional decorum, public service, and treatment of patients carries over and applies to those strictly engaged in the academic study of psychology.

CHAPTER TWO

"Rain in Camelot"

Scientists and Spies

Both kinds of moral discourse discussed in the previous chapter, that of professional ethics and that of moral philosophy (specifically, of justifiable and unjustifiable wars), are transparent in one of the key "defining moments" of anthropology's moral history, what I termed its "litany of shame." That defining moment was the censure by the American Anthropological Association[1] (AAA) of one of its founding members, Franz Boas, for his open letter denouncing the role of anthropologists engaged in espionage and clandestine activities immediately following World War I.

Alexander Lesser, in his account of this regrettable incident, makes the role of both elements clear in defining Boas's stance as a "citizen-scientist" during anthropology's most formative years. Boas was, Lesser writes, "a pacifist, opposed to the war from the beginning." He was actively engaged in promoting U.S. neutrality in what he regarded as "an imperialist war," and also in attempting to counteract wartime hysteria against German culture following America's entry into the war in 1917 (Lesser 1981: 11). His disagreement with his colleagues, however, was framed as an instance of straightforward unprofessional behavior—in effect, a violation of the core values of scientific inquiry itself. In Boas's 1919 letter in the *Nation*, titled "Scientists As Spies," he wrote, "The point against which I wish to enter a vigorous protest is that a number of men who follow science as their profession, . . . *have prostituted science by using it as a cover for their activities as spies.*" It is difficult, however, as the letter subsequently makes clear, to determine just how closely Boas's views of the conduct appropriate to the

(see also p 108)

scientist are bound up in his wider moral stance in opposition to war. He goes on to write:

> A soldier whose business is murder as a fine art, a diplomat whose calling is based on deception and secretiveness, a politician whose very life consists in compromises with his conscience, a business man whose aim is personal profit within the limits allowed by a lenient law—such may be excused if they set patriotic devotion above common everyday decency and perform services as spies. They merely accept the code of morality to which modern society still conforms. Not so the scientist. The very essence of his life is the service of truth. We all know scientists who in private life do not come up to the standard of truthfulness, but who nevertheless would not consciously falsify the results of their researches. It is bad enough if we have to put up with these, because they reveal a lack of strength of character that is liable to distort the results of their work. A person, however, who uses science as a cover for political spying, who demeans himself to pose before a foreign government as an investigator and asks for assistance in his alleged researches in order to carry on, under this cloak, his political machinations, prostitutes science in an unpardonable way and forfeits the right to be classed as a scientist. (Lesser 1981: 12–13)

Think what we will of him for having written such a letter, let alone of the AAA voting by a margin of 2 to 1 to censure Boas for it, it is abundantly clear from his argument that Boas's evident devotion to science as a morally worthy activity springs from his conviction that the pursuit of "truth" in science is (or ought to be) free from the moral taint of these other activities (specifically, of engagement in clandestine activities in support of a morally dubious war).[2] His powerful rhetoric in this letter appears, moreover, to constitute an attempt at a self-contained, self-referential account of his opposition to espionage, of the sort whose validity I challenged in the previous chapter. That is: one way of characterizing his underlying argument is that the two kinds of activities are simply incompatible. Science, as the pursuit of truth, should be free of the "moral taint" of secrecy and clandestine activity, both of which appear to be inimical to the pursuit of truth, very much in the same fashion that the scientific pursuit of truth is thought to be free from any ties to the scientist's own race, religion, or ethnicity (a principle that Boas likewise defended courageously throughout his career).

As the earlier vignette on "Mead's Dilemma" makes clear, however, the issue cannot be disposed of this simply. The conflict between the two practices presents us, not with a settled resolution of the conflict based upon straightforward, self-contained (or self-referential) professional principle, but rather with a moral dilemma—the moral dilemma faced by Mead herself, and also by Oppenheimer and his colleagues in the Manhattan Project. That moral dilemma was more intense for them than it appears to be for Boas, precisely because the wider moral perspective to be taken on their war, and on their nation at that time, presented them with a stronger case for the moral justifiability of engaging in that war (and for scientists collaborating in it) than the circumstances of America's participation in World War I presented to Boas.

Indeed, I take his stance in this letter, and the passion of his rhetoric of denunciation, as demonstrating how strongly Boas's views on "professional ethics" and the professional responsibilities of scientists depended upon his underlying moral assessment of the appropriateness of America's involvement in Europe's "imperialist" war.[3] Many others might likewise assent to Boas's view of the proper conduct of the scientist, at least as a general rule. But they might disagree sharply with his sweeping moral indictment of both soldiers and diplomats (if not, perhaps, of business "men"), and might rightly complain about the accuracy or fairness of his passionate juxtaposition of so unflattering a moral portrait of these activities with what he derisively describes as "patriotic devotion" and public service.

Boas, in this instance, painted self-assuredly, even self-righteously, with a rather broad brush. One wonders how plausible, for example, his portrait of the soldier "whose business is murder as a fine art" would seem to the families of G.I.s who would lose their lives a little over two decades later in the invasion of Normandy or in the Battle of Okinawa. Since our reasons invariably transcend any particular conclusions or historical circumstances in which we offer them, we ought, as a rule, to be perhaps more cautious and even-handed in offering them than was Boas in this instance. He was, to be sure, angry—nay, outraged. And as often happens in such circumstances, his moral eloquence at the time was eclipsed by the entirely unintended clumsiness of his uncharitable rhetorical excesses. To engage in this sort of careless and unreflective moral condemnation of so many disparate and complex activities is equally (on his own terms) a "grave disservice to science." Not only is his account of the moral deficiencies of these other human activities one-sided, stereotypical, and generally unworthy of so eminent and accomplished a social scientist, but also his laudatory moral assessment of science itself is highly idealized, and (we now know from numerous sociological and historical studies of it) deeply flawed.[4]

His righteous outrage over war has rather clearly clouded his scientific judgment—clouded it, surely, but did not wholly obscure it. To his credit, Boas does not name names nor engage in slander, and hence the vote of censure leveled against him by his disciplinary colleagues at the time seems entirely unwarranted, perhaps even (as anthropology's litany chants it) "shameful." But neither does he cite evidence or give accounts of exactly what these alleged turncoat anthropologists were supposedly doing. Simply denouncing them as "spies," or even claiming they were engaged in intelligence-gathering activities is not sufficient, absent a far more compelling argument than he develops here. The profession would have been better served by simply allowing Boas this personal, impassioned statement of dissenting opinion. That it did not, enraptured as public opinion was at the time in equally exaggerated and misplaced expressions of nationalism and patriotism, had the decidedly unintended and unfortunate consequence of establishing a poorly reasoned and thinly substantiated argument as settled professional principle, and enshrining its proponent ever after in the discipline's history as a martyr for that principle.[5]

Unless we were likewise principled pacifists, or else committed (if somewhat unreflective) anarchists, we would require much more than Boas provides in order to convince ourselves to join him in his protest. And we would, one hopes, have been less given to hysteria and self-righteousness about the "moral failings" of our fellow citizens from other walks of life in deigning to stoop so low as to engage in secretive or deceptive practices, and perhaps more humble about the role of science and scientists in resisting these putative failures of character. Oskar Schindler, for example, was a "business man" decidedly engaged in deception (if not, finally, in outright "espionage"). Would our favorable moral assessment of his activities, less than two decades after Boas published this rhetorical denunciation of all his kind, change one iota if Schindler had instead been a scientist, somehow using *that* role to shield the prospective victims of genocide by employing them in his laboratory, and eventually sending them abroad (and thereby into asylum) allegedly to attend scientific conferences or gather data for his research? If we would hesitate to denounce these activities under such circumstances, then, quite clearly, it cannot be the secrecy or even deception per se that is morally objectionable but the intentions behind them. We would need at least to know something about the moral justifiability of the overall strategy behind such activities, as well as the end toward which they are employed.

Moral philosophers, loath to countenance discretionary violations of important principles, sometimes distinguish between absolute and prima facie duties.[6] The duties of the scientist to maintain transparency and to avoid secrecy and deception are clearly of the latter sort. Boas is quite correct to intuit that they denote a professional stance, one that we weaken or relinquish at great peril. What the recognition of such duties does, however, is impose a strong burden of proof that can only be overridden in exceptional circumstances. It is difficult to function as what the nineteenth-century

American philosopher C. S. Peirce described as a "self-correcting community of like-minded inquirers," if the results of scientific research are clandestinely withheld or one's activities as a scientist are shrouded in secrecy. How, under such conditions, can there be a "community," and how on earth can it be "self-correcting?" And so there is, rightly, a strong prima facie presumption in favor of transparency and against "secret research."

It would require exceptional circumstances to override these presumed duties of the scientist to integrity, truthfulness, disclosure, and transparency. Such circumstances might arise rarely, for example, in a decision to with-hold results of experiments in nuclear physics, or to deceive fellow scientists about those results, if one had extremely good reason to fear those results might otherwise be used for horrific, destructive purposes by a malevolent government (or nonstate actor) that otherwise somehow might get hold of them. Even such considerations would not justify or legitimize either secrecy or clandestine research on the part of the scientist. Instead, the exceptional circumstances would constitute grounds for overriding those normal duties of transparency and full disclosure in that instance. We would describe that scientist, in those circumstances, as caught in a conflict of rival duties. His or her resulting moral dilemma is then sometimes described as a choice of "the lesser evil" since, strictly speaking, it is always morally wrong to fail to uphold the duties we have.

Thus, when Professor Fluehr-Lobban invokes this "ghost" of Franz Boas who "returns periodically both to haunt and to inspire anthropologists about engaging in secret research," it is this presumption against secrecy, attached to any attempts at collaboration with one's government, that in fact does the haunting. This symbolic role of the Boas case in anthropology's litany of shame, however, is as puzzling as it is ironic. It is not, after all, "secret research" or "clandestine research" that Boas himself denounced (though no doubt he would have objected to these activities as well). His own objection was to the *deception*, to the putative deceitfulness of the other scientists in question, and not at all to their "research activities" (of which none were alleged). His complaint focused on their "prostituting" their role as scien-tists in order to carry out "their political machinations," as he so colorfully phrased it. The irony is thus that, in anthropology's litany, the name of Franz Boas is chanted in invocation of a principle condemning activities, like clandestine research, that he himself never once mentions, let alone ac-cuses anyone at the time of having undertaken. What is hopelessly obscured thereby, moreover, is the principle he very clearly *did* mean to articulate: that the scientist ought never to use, or to subordinate, his or her *role as scientist* in order, deceptively or deceitfully, to carry out other activities of any sort—and certainly not activities (like spying in wartime) that the scientist *as moral agent* might determine to be morally objectionable. It is a significant mistake simply to conflate those two very different concerns, each of which must be made to stand or fall on its own, specific moral deficiencies.

The Rise and Fall of Project Camelot

This equivocation over the proper objects of moral condemnation (as well as over what, exactly, it is that the Boas case properly symbolizes) came once again to the fore with Project Camelot. The AAA CEAUSSIC report (2007) cites this incident, the only event specifically mentioned by name, in its plea for greater public understanding of its current crisis of conscience over military anthropology. Over and over in anthropology's "litany of shame," Project Camelot looms large in the collective consciousness of the discipline as a watershed event. As in the Boas case, however, its outsized mythological significance in that litany does not perfectly accord with the actual historical details.

"Project Camelot" itself was not quite the social sciences' "equivalent of the Manhattan Project," as it was sometimes portrayed at the time,[7] but it did constitute an extremely large, complex, and potentially lucrative and prestigious grant for social scientists. Conceived as a "three to four-year effort to be funded at around one and one-half million dollars annually," the project was designed "to determine the feasibility of developing a general social systems model which would make it possible to predict and influence politically significant aspects of social change in the developing nations of the world."[8] Specifically, researchers were first to "devise procedures for assessing the potential for internal war within national societies," and second to identify actions that a government might take to "relieve" those conditions, which are implicated as "giving rise to a potential for internal war." Initially, the project was envisioned to focus primarily on countries in Latin America, but the methodology quickly grew to encompass other geographical regions as well.

In effect, what was being proposed at the time was development of what we would now term a "state-failure model" for predicting and responding to civil society or governmental collapse and the concomitant rise of insurgencies or, worse, humanitarian disasters. Many eminent political scientists have been working collaboratively at a number of academic institutions in the U.S. and Europe since the early 1990s to develop just such a model to plan for and cope with the collapse of effective governments and the onset of humanitarian crises and genocide (as in Bosnia and Rwanda).[9] Some ideas seem destined never to die. Embedded in the methodology of Camelot, however, were proposals for eventual "field studies" during the final stages of the project to be carried out within a smaller subset of the selected countries, from Iran and Thailand to Venezuela, Bolivia, and Peru. These were presumably intended to test and ratify the project's preliminary findings, based more on literature and archival research. The moral dilemma posed by the project's overall focus on the rise of insurgencies, however, was whether those final field studies would constitute genuine ethnography, or espionage.[10]

What is interesting, in light of this more recent work on state failure and genocide, as well as in the midst of the present controversy over military anthropology, is Project Camelot's description of the U.S. Army's willingness even to consider sponsoring such research. After all, the Latin American governments in question considered themselves quite adept at counterinsurgency: simply round up the dissidents and protesters and shoot them. This project revealed the emergence of a somewhat more nuanced theory of counterinsurgency. "Within the Army there is especially ready acceptance of the need to improve the general understanding of the processes of social change if the Army is to discharge its responsibilities in the over-all counterinsurgency program of the U.S. Government," states the initial memorandum of invitation, extended to a broad range of scholars in the United States and Latin America in December 1964. Subsequently, an initial government White Paper prepared as a brief for the Army chief of staff concerning the project offered this account of its overall rationale:

> If the U.S. Army is to perform effectively its part in the U.S. mission of counterinsurgency it must recognize that insurgency represents a breakdown of social order, and that the social processes involved must be understood. . . . A country, viewed as a social system, is made up of many different and interdependent groups of people in pursuit of various goals. When groups fail to function so as to provide for the needs of the people that make up these groups, there is a tendency for them to break down and for their symbols to change meaning or lose value.

Whoever coined those passages must have survived long enough to return to work for General David Petraeus.

Even if Project Camelot cannot meaningfully be compared with the Manhattan Project, an anthology, *The Rise and Fall of Project Camelot*, compiled in its immediate aftermath by Irving Louis Horowitz (Horowitz 1967), might be somewhat more accurately described as Project Camelot's equivalent of the Warren Commission report. Horowitz himself takes pains to describe the roles and assumptions behind the initial funding of the project by the U.S.

Army's Special Operations Research Office in 1964, and, on the basis of official project files and data gathered from interviews from its initial participants, to describe their attitudes toward their work and what they perceived as the shortcomings of the project.

Like the Warren Commission report, these accounts provide excruciating details and extensive, sometimes withering, criticism: in this instance, of deeply flawed scientific assumptions that led to formulating the project, and of vague, inappropriate, and occasionally absurdly inflated expectations of the value that social scientists' presumed regional knowledge or expertise in "local cultures" might add to political, military, and intelligence forces' understanding of incipient insurgencies in Latin America. Horowitz himself reserves his sharpest criticisms for the lax, incompetent, and perhaps even negligent oversight of the project by the grant's recipient institution, American University, in Washington, D.C. That institution, he charges, seemed motivated entirely by what, at the time, were lucrative rates of administrative "overhead" to be garnered from the grant, and thus appeared to have been willing to serve as little more than academic camouflage for a government project that was not simply "externally funded," but was truly external to the institution's own system of financial and managerial accountability and scholarly peer review.

But, in marked contrast to subsequent portrayals, this early account pointedly denies any intention to engage, and finds no evidence that any participant did knowingly or purposively engage, in "cloak-and dagger" spying or secrecy, let alone in any "clandestine research." Horowitz reports, on the basis of interviews with the involved social scientists:

> None of them viewed their role on the project as spying for the United States government or for anyone else. The only person who even touched on this discordant note was an assistant professor of anthropology whose connection with the project was from the outset remote and tenuous. (Horowitz 1967: 8)

Indeed, Fluehr-Lobban, who otherwise assimilates this project as the keystone in the AAA's subsequent efforts aimed at the "abjuring of secret research" (Fluehr-Lobban 2003a: 10) correctly notes that "the project itself was neither classified nor designed to conceal those who were the sponsors" (Fluehr-Lobban 2003a: 8). Horowitz's account supports this view, and extends it to cover project personnel and the formulation of the plan of work, all of which were carried out in full view of the scientific public. Indeed, it was the invitation, cited above, extended in December 1964 to an open working conference on the project scheduled in the U.S. that coming June

1965,[11] to an eminent Norwegian sociologist, teaching at that time in Chile as a member of UNESCO's Latin American Faculty of Social Sciences, that helped foment the ensuing uproar over Camelot. The scientist, Johan Galtung, refused in principle to participate, and cited several objections in a letter to the project's director (dated April 22, 1965), including sponsorship of the project by the U.S. Army, what he termed the "imperialist features" of the research design, and its "asymmetry" in focusing solely on U.S. interests in Latin America without inquiring about Latin America's similar concerns with the United States.

Horowitz offers a detailed, blow-by-blow account of the sequence of events. He places the blame for the radical misconstruing of the true nature of the project as a "vast continental spy plan," and for the widespread public furor and embarrassment of anthropologists, in particular, at the time, squarely at the feet of an assistant professor of anthropology at the University of Pittsburgh, one Hugo G. Nuttini.

A former citizen of the Republic of Chile, Nuttini apparently hounded the project's director with his ardent desire to "participate in Project Camelot in whatever capacity was deemed most useful." He was finally retained in a limited and decidedly informal capacity as an outside consultant, charged to explore the feasibility of "cooperating" with social scientists in Chile on the project, "and in general to do the kind of ethnographic survey that has mild results and a modest honorarium of $750." Notwithstanding, the ambitious young scientist "somehow managed to convey the impression of being a direct official of Project Camelot and of having the authority to make proposals to prospective Chilean participants" (Horowitz 1967: 12).[12] A perfect storm of controversy thus ensued when this opportunistic young scholar scheduled a meeting with the vice chancellor of the University of Chile to discuss prospects for local collaboration on Project Camelot. In that meeting, Nuttini was confronted by a member of the faculty with a Spanish text of the original conference memorandum, as well as with Galtung's response. The vice chancellor then indignantly demanded an explanation of the aims of the project, its sponsors, and its possible political implications.

The affair was taken up in the Chilean Senate, and subsequently in the national press, where it was characterized as "intervention," "imperialism," and a "vast continental spy plan known as 'Operation Camelot.'" The U.S. ambassador to Chile, Ralph A. Dugan, sent strongly worded communiqués to the State Department, denouncing the project and demanding its termination. This scandal erupted in the midst of steadily deteriorating relationships in the United States among the project's various stakeholders (most especially the State Department), and amid deepening skepticism over the worthiness of the project's "scientific" value, and the feasibility of its wider aims and goals. Senator J. William Fulbright led the call for a congressional investigation of the project, and it was ultimately terminated after only a year, as Horowitz notes, "before it ever really got under way" (Horowitz 1967: 14).

For all that, Chile was not even on the list of countries in Latin America cited for study in the original project design, either in a larger group of countries selected for "comparative historical studies" in Latin America, the Middle East, the Far East, and elsewhere (including France and Greece!), let alone the smaller subset proposed for "Survey Research and Other Field Studies" (to include Bolivia, Colombia, Ecuador, Paraguay, Peru, Venezuela, Iran, and, finally, Thailand: see Official Document #3; Horowitz 1967: 57–59). Notwithstanding, it has passed into mythical lore as "the infamous and ill-fated Project Camelot, a U.S. counterinsurgency research plan for Chile in 1965" (Berreman 2003: 52).[13]

In historical perspective, according to the accounts of those who knew it best, "Project Camelot" was an ill-conceived, inappropriately sponsored, poorly coordinated, badly administered, bone-headed, ham-handed attempt to develop regional and cultural knowledge to guide government policy in response to socialist revolution and counterinsurgency in Latin America and other regions of the globe. It might be fair to denounce it and to remember it as a nitwit, hairbrained waste of taxpayers' dollars. It might be good also to note its resemblance in this respect to a great many other ill-conceived and badly run government projects, especially those, as Horowitz warns in conclusion, "in which the mystique of social science seemed to have been taken for granted by friends and foes . . . alike" (Horowitz 1967: 17). But it is also important to recognize that the actual project, as contrasted with the mythical or symbolic "Project Camelot," entailed absolutely no "spying," no "secret" or "clandestine research," and indeed, hardly involved anthropologists at all. As Fluehr-Lobban perceptively notes, "It was not the high crimes of anthropologists involved in Project Camelot . . . but the effects that a bollixed operation had on future research in Latin America" that constituted the real problem posed by this disaster (Fluehr-Lobban 2003a: 8).

There were, however, good and sufficient reasons for the symbolic significance of Project Camelot to be exaggerated in collective imagination, and its meaning thoroughly misunderstood as somehow involving anthropologists in "secret activities" and "clandestine research." The project was, after all, conceived under government sponsorship only a few years after the disastrous Bay of Pigs invasion in Cuba. The United States initiated a military intervention in the Dominican Republic in 1965, at the height of the Camelot controversy. The entire affair unfolded against America's deepening involvement in the war of counterinsurgency in South Vietnam. The CIA, for its part, was heavily involved in the internal affairs of Chile, and did ultimately intervene, several years later, to engineer the overthrow and assassination of the democratically elected Marxist president, Salvador Allende, in 1973, although there is no hint or suggestion of any CIA involvement in Project Camelot itself.

Nonetheless one can easily understand how, at the time, this project could come, in the collective consciousness of anthropologists, to be linked symbolically, as Fluehr-Lobban describes, with Boas's "Scientists As Spies" letter of some fifty years earlier. In response to this scandal, she reports that the AAA's 1967 "Statement on Problems of Anthropological Research and Ethics" included the provision that "except in cases of declaration of war by Congress, anthropologists should not undertake research for exclusive government contracts nor lend themselves to clandestine activities." Moreover, the AAA statement of 1967 observed:

> The international reputation of anthropology has been damaged by the activities of individuals . . . *who have pretended to be engaged in anthropological research while pursuing other ends.* There is good reason to believe that *some anthropologists have used their professional standing and the names of academic institutions as cloaks for the collection of intelligence information* and for intelligence operations. (Fluehr-Lobban 2003a: 9; my emphasis)

Thus, Fluehr-Lobban comments, "Boas's sentiments of a half-century before are repeated and officially sanctioned and he is vindicated."

This conclusion, however, seems the wrong one to draw from this episode, in several important respects. First, as we have seen, in direct contradiction of the AAA's 1967 statement, there are no good reasons whatever to believe that "some" anthropologists behaved in this ethically questionable manner. In fact, only one otherwise insignificant self-promoter has ever been identified. More important, neither he nor any one else attached to the project apparently had it as their purpose or mission to engage in "the collection of intelligence information" or otherwise engage in intelligence operations, nor is there any evidence, as Horowitz notes, that they were authorized or expected to do so. If Boas's position on such matters even requires "vindication," it would not be forthcoming from the details of this incident. Instead, as we have duly noted, his original condemnation (as well as this final paragraph from the AAA's 1967 statement) aims at condemning the use of one's identity as a scientist and scholar for purposes of deception and misrepresentation. This, in turn, is quite distinct from the concern Boas never specifically mentioned: namely, engaging in secret or "clandestine research."

It is, of course, quite possible to imagine how these two issues might conceivably be linked in some sort of malevolent project to obtain significant cultural data clandestinely, and then use such data to gain military or intelligence advantage over the individuals studied by manipulating them to their disadvantage, perhaps enslaving or even killing some of them. We consider several hypothetical examples of this kind of "abusive anthropology" in subsequent chapters, alongside allegations that such abusive anthropology has in fact been practiced at Abu Ghraib or Guantánamo Bay. Fears of such abusive anthropology form the cornerstone of objections to the Human Terrain System in particular: that it will involve the collection and use of proprietary anthropological data and clandestine, secret research to assist military and intelligence forces in determining "who to kill." We will reserve these considerations for later.

For the present, merely observe that, whatever it might have become, or however it might have evolved if allowed to do so, Project Camelot was never envisioned as such an operation, and the public documentation of the project and anthropologists' own most authoritative historical accounts of it demonstrate this. Ill-conceived, naïve, or incompetently administered as it may have been, there is no evidence of its having harbored malevolent intentions, or (as Horowitz again notes) of its personnel or participants having engaged in "unethical practice" as defined by codes of conduct in force in the discipline at the time, or since. This remains the case, whatever the Chileans may have made of the unauthorized overtures and shameless influence-peddling of their expatriate colleague, the sole anthropologist associated with this project, Assistant Professor Hugo Nuttini.

Nevertheless, this episode gets taken up, absorbed, "sublated" (*aufgehoben*, a Hegelian might say) within anthropology's self-indictment for what it fervently believes to be its own members' ongoing involvement in "CIA-sponsored espionage," and (what is quite distinct) secret, clandestine research.[14] Not only is this mythology historically inaccurate, it misses the more salient lessons to be properly drawn from this affair—lessons that are more directly applicable to the current controversy over military anthropology.

Those lessons to be learned are far less about dark conspiracy theories than about government impatience and scientific ineptitude. Margaret Mead self-confidently described her own project during World War II as one of "social engineering." One might classify Project Camelot more accurately, however, as an attempt at "*over*engineering," *over*reaching, falling prey to precisely that "mystique of social science" against which Professor Horowitz wisely cautioned. That caution cuts in both directions. Governments, for their part, are too prone to seeking out quick solutions to complex problems, and prone to move abruptly from dismissive indifference of academics to overappreciation of their subject-matter expertise and potential usefulness. It is easier for governments, militaries, and indeed, any organization to throw a great deal of money at a problem, and expect neglected outsiders to step in and address it instantaneously for them, than it is for them to painstakingly support the gradual development through education, mentorship, and nurture, of appropriate expertise within their own ranks (Selmeski 2007b).[15] Meanwhile scholars, resentful of their marginalization, are all too vulnerable to responding positively to those sudden, sporadic expressions of interest and (perhaps even more seductively) the lure of lucrative funding for themselves and their research. It is highly seductive to become, all at once, the repository of expertise vital to the national interest or to national defense, and, in the mix, to be able, finally, to pay the bills.

Anthropology on the War Path in Thailand

Untangling factual historical accounts from subsequent theory-laden interpretations, and ultimately from the settled mythology of the "litany of shame," is every bit as complicated as unwinding so-called derivatives, the bundled securities and credit-swap transactions at the heart of the global financial crisis of 2008–2009. Just as in those examples, however, the eventual historical unwinding does finally unmask a core of cases and historical instances involving morally questionable or ethically unprofessional behavior that are rightly considered "toxic." Again, as in the financial analogue, lingering uncertainty about the size and significance of that "toxic core" of bad behavior erodes disciplinary confidence and destroys professional trust in a disproportionate manner.

Thus, even if Project Camelot wasn't, in the end, "about" Chile at all, let alone about secret or clandestine research per se, there are many other instances anthropologists could legitimately cite in which research was carried out covertly, and for which the cloak of secrecy was meant to conceal ends that seemed radically at odds with the normal expectations and responsibilities laid upon scientists and scholars to seek the truth, behave with integrity, and above all, to inflict no harm, nor even increase the risk of harm, to their human research subjects.

David Price, for example, has published a number of studies documenting the involvement of anthropologists (and even "secret agreements" with the AAA itself as an organization) in carrying out or cooperating in research for the CIA, the State Department, and other branches of government involved in clandestine activities during the Cold War (Price 1998b, 2003,

2008).[16] Price frequently takes pains to contextualize the decisions of many of the principals, whom he identifies by name, and to excuse many of them for acting (even if wrongly, in his judgment) on strongly held beliefs, in the aftermath of their collective experiences during World War II, about what they believed was likely in the nation's best interests. He identifies other instances, however, in which anthropologists behaved deceitfully as researchers, and even made their colleagues the unknowing subjects of data collection for intelligence and national security purposes of which those subjects were entirely unaware.

Though he discriminates thoughtfully in this fashion, Price does not seem to acknowledge the wider implication of his own studies. If one can, in the end, meaningfully discriminate in this manner between individuals, or even projects that are more or less blameworthy, then it cannot be the case that *all* such work, or *all* the individuals who engaged in it, were morally wrong to do so. Likewise it cannot simply be the case that such work per se constitutes a violation of professional standards simply because it is secret, or simply because it involves working with the government, or even with "clandestine or covert organizations" like the CIA. Instead, the ultimate moral judgment of professional misconduct depends critically upon what, specifically, was undertaken with these organizations and in this clandestine fashion, and most especially, what ends were served by this work.

This is powerfully illustrated in the various accounts, by Price himself and a number of other anthropologists, of our final vignette, the so-called Thailand affair or Thailand controversy. The affair itself seems to involve precisely the kinds of activities feared—namely, the pairing of covert or deceptive misrepresentation of "spies" masquerading as scientists, and the involvement of those spy-scientists, by turn, in clandestine, "mission oriented" research with malevolent intentions. It also subsequently came to involve anthropology's public maternal figure, Margaret Mead, toward the end of her life, in a massive cover-up of the incident, and so symbolically (if somewhat tragically) completes the circle of her own involvement with ethics and military anthropology.

There are a number of graphic accounts of this episode and its tumultuous and divisive aftermath. Gerald Berreman, whose own career and professional reputation were impugned in the controversies leading up to, and following the so-called Mead Report, commends Eric Wakin's monograph *Anthropology Goes to War* (1992). To that account, written when Wakin was a doctoral candidate in history at Columbia University, and recently reprinted in the light of our own current controversy over military anthropology, Berreman (2003) adds his own recollections as a central participant in the turmoil surrounding the debate over the Mead Report.[17] Like the Watergate conspiracy, which followed closely in time, the Thailand affair appears to exhibit two components: the covert operations undertaken in Thailand with the support of at least one prominent American anthropologist; and the subsequent investigation of the incident by a special committee of the AAA, the Ad Hoc Committee to Evaluate the Controversy Concerning Anthropological Activities in Relation to Thailand, chaired by Margaret Mead (at this time appointed to positions at both Columbia University and the American Museum of Natural History). And, as with the Watergate conspiracy, the subsequent investigation ended up doing the greatest actual damage and generating the most enduring professional controversy.

After reviewing the Camelot controversy as background, Wakin tracks the funding of anthropological research and the use of proprietary data in classified accounts primarily by three distinct government agencies: the Advanced Research Projects Agency (now known as DARPA, the Defense Advanced Research Projects Agency, usually focused entirely on technology development); the Institute for Defense Analysis (IDA) at the Department of Defense (not, importantly, the CIA); as well as the U.S. Agency for International Development (USAID, reporting to the Secretary of State). All three agencies apparently sponsored various forms of analysis of communist insurgencies in critical regions of Southeast Asia in several "regional study groups" formed for this purpose, including the Thailand Study Group at the IDA, and SEADAG, the Southeast Asia Development Advisory Group at USAID. The normal division of labor among such agencies and study groups would have the former, in this case, focusing on military threats and appropriate military and political responses to these, while leaving the questions concerning the underlying economic causes of insurgency and prospects for economic development as a form of counterinsurgency to USAID/SEADAG. It is likewise routine practice for such groups either to include or to seek as consultants academic subject matter experts from their own ranks or from the wider civilian academic community: economists, political scientists, sociologists, and (in this instance, at least) anthropologists.

During the waning days of an unpopular and politically divisive war in neighboring Vietnam, it was this last practice that ignited the controversy. A student employee of a UCLA anthropology professor, Michael Moerman, submitted photocopies of letters, reports, grant proposals and abstracts, and other contents from his research files to members of the Student Mobilization Committee to Stop the War in Vietnam (SMC). These documents appeared to implicate a number of scholars from several disciplines, including anthropology, in collaborating on several different projects sponsored by the aforementioned agencies to study and combat communist-inspired regional insurgencies. The organization published some of the most damning documents in its newspaper, *The Student Mobilizer*, in April 1970. SMC also sent advance copies of these materials to several scholars (including Berreman), who subsequently joined SMC in denouncing this "counterinsurgency research" by their colleagues.

This research for the most part appears to have continued along the vector originally established by Project Camelot: that is, undertaking (or, more correctly, proposing to undertake) fieldwork designed to better understand the causes of political discontent and alienation, and the resulting willingness among local partisans to abandon existing civil society and governing structures in favor of incipient insurgent movements. Unlike Camelot, however, at least some of the proposed projects in Thailand had gotten underway, and project personnel were conducting research and gathering data on the habits and attitudes of local villagers and peasant farmers in Thailand. In the wrong hands, especially if misinterpreted, such information (indeed, the very act itself of conducting such inquiries) could have subjected the research subjects to retaliation, either by the Thai army or local police or (as also happened in Vietnam) the insurgents themselves. There is no good or safe way for members of a local population living in a politically contested and unstable area to participate in such "fact-finding," even if it is ostensibly designed to collect information that might somehow redound to their benefit. And it is hard to argue, in any case, that a project abstract, allegedly written by an anthropologist employed at the "Military Research and Development Center" in Bangkok and titled "Low Altitude Visual Search for Individual Human Targets," was designed to benefit its ostensible research subjects.

Perhaps most damning was a grant project for which Moerman himself had apparently served as an outside consultant, "Counterinsurgency in Thailand: The Impact of Economic, Social and Political Action Programs." The proposal, which included two anthropologists (only one of whom was a member of the AAA) as coauthors, was submitted to DARPA in 1967 by the American Institutes for Research at the University of Pittsburgh (the institution that had earlier employed Project Camelot's infamous Hugo G. Nuttini). It proposed to develop "preventive counterinsurgency measures" for Thailand, and to generalize the resulting methodology to "other countries" (including, presumably, the United States itself). It was funded, Berreman reports (2003: 60), in the amount of $500,000, whereupon its subsequent semiannual progress reports were classified. Rather chillingly, the proposal describes "three different types of operations": securing allegiance and political stability by dint of ever-increasing tangible benefits (as was likewise proposed in Project

Camelot), alongside far more ominous measures, such as military confrontation "to counteract or neutralize successes already achieved" by insurgents, and preventive measures designed to inhibit or preempt the achievement of such successes, including "assassinating key spokesmen and strengthening retaliatory mechanisms. The social scientist," the proposal concludes, "can make significant contributions to the design of all three types of operations" (quoted in Berreman 2003: 60).

It is difficult to understand, in the light of such documents, how the Ad Hoc, or "Mead Committee," could have simply exonerated those few of the AAA's own members involved in this project from charges of wrongdoing or unprofessional conduct. Certainly anthropologists or other social scientists ostensibly involved in projects with aims such as these had crossed a very bright line. Berreman, still understandably angry about his own shameful treatment, and the generally dark tenor of the political intrigue surrounding the investigation of the controversy, alleges that the committee chair was absent in the South Pacific for much of year during which, on its account, more than 6,000 pages of documentary material were "carefully studied" by the committee in reaching its conclusions. Both Berreman and Fluehr-Lobban describe the role played by members of the fledgling AAA Committee on Ethics in joining and even leading the public condemnation of the clandestine work that had been exposed. Fluehr-Lobban remarks, however, that "as in 1919, the AAA publicly sanctioned the messengers more severely than those whose professional behavior had been called into question."[18]

The rejection of the Mead Committee's report, however, was equally harsh, even if, at the time, it seemed deservedly so. By overwhelming majorities, the membership appeared to reject both Mead's status as a public icon of anthropology, and to renounce its own Executive Committee's handling of the crisis. As anthropologist Sydel Silverman notes, the AAA's rejection of the Mead Committee's conclusions and recommendations regarding principles of responsible practice constituted, for her, a humiliating personal repudiation from which she never fully recovered (Silverman and Metraux 1981: 216).

Forging a Professional Code of Conduct

It should by now be possible to appreciate the extraordinary efforts, and often profound and painful personal investments, that have gone into forging an acceptable code of conduct for the discipline of anthropology. Even more, it should be possible more completely to understand and appreciate why a great many anthropologists at present are opposed so vehemently to "secret or clandestine research," and deeply suspicious of invitations to collaborate with military, intelligence, and security forces. And from this, in turn, one can appreciate more fully just what is at stake in proposals like the Turner Amendment to amend the AAA's current Code of Ethics in order to strengthen its commitment to transparency, and its principled opposition specifically to "clandestine and secret research."

My purpose in these opening two chapters was never directed toward providing a comprehensive account of the AAA's current and past codes of ethics or statements of professional principles and responsibilities. Neither did I intend to write, let alone rewrite, the history of the discipline that offers a background for understanding these codes. Both of these tasks have been undertaken thoroughly, several times, by specialists in the field. The point of the preceding discussion was rather to "cross-examine" those histories to determine the basis for the current controversy within the discipline over the rise of "military anthropology." If this metaphor of a historical cross-examination is allowed to stand, then it seems appropriate to conclude it with a final summation for the jury.

The importance of Project Camelot and the Thailand controversy, no matter what the underlying facts or interpretation of the facts one attaches to them, is that both incidents occasioned profound reflection and deliberation, resulting in key formulations of important ethical standards for the profession. I commented in passing in the preceding chapter upon the effect that the absence of such an explicit code had on the moral deliberations of anthropologists upon their own professional versus civic duties, even during a war that was at the time deemed necessary and morally justifiable. The current chapter suggests, by way of contrast, how much more explicitly painful and divisive are such professional deliberations when carried out against the backdrop of wars whose justification is deeply contested. This is true even when individuals like Franz Boas stand on their progressive or pacifist principles against the prevailing tide of public opinion, let alone when (as with the Vietnam War, or now Iraq) public opinion itself on the justification of the war in question is deeply divided.

War and its justification are not the only backdrop for discussions of ethics and anthropology.[19] Fluehr-Lobban's historical reconstruction includes the impact of a variety of other completely independent concerns that helped forge specific provisions of anthropology's moral self-understanding, such as the custody of Native American patrimony (ancestral burial grounds, or cultural artifacts and skeletal remains housed in museums) or the wider impact of anthropological research upon indigenous cultures. I singled out the Sanchez affair in the preceding chapter. Given the nature and focus of the discipline, one might have expected these sorts of issues to dominate discussions of professional ethics, and largely determine the content of any resulting formal codes or statements of professional principle. Yet surprisingly, in the accounts written by anthropologists themselves, as well as in their shared historical litany, it is war and "clandestine" activities that dominate. As Fluehr-Lobban herself remarks, "It is fair to conclude that without the Camelot affair, no statement regarding ethics and professional behavior would have been forthcoming from the AAA" (Fluehr-Lobban 2003a: 10).

In light of the several different historical accounts of anthropology and ethics that we have examined, I certainly find no reason to doubt the accuracy of that claim. Yet it also constitutes a rather extraordinary (if entirely unintended) judgment of the discipline concerning its professional stance and moral responsibilities, one that I find both puzzling and more than a bit troubling.

I maintained that there might be some value in having an outsider—specifically, a nonspecialist with no stake in the outcome—examine the reasoning, the experiences, and the interpretations attached to the experiences that helped forge the collective self-consciousness of the discipline. Perhaps this is the proper moment to ascertain whether that surmise is correct. For I take Fluehr-Lobban's summary statement, reinforced in the singular and specific citation of Project Camelot in the CEAUSSIC commission report's conclusion as well, to constitute a rather explicit description of that collective self-consciousness.

What is abundantly clear is that there is a great deal of emotional investment by individual members of the discipline in these matters, with strong feelings on all sides, born of more than a century of acrimonious debate over broad social issues like war, espionage, clandestine activities, and allegations of secret (and presumably nefarious, invidious, and unscrupulous) research projects carried out by anthropologists for branches of government and the military. And though anthropologists tend to cite the Boas censure and Project Camelot in order to invoke and to symbolically recollect all this, I have found (and explained) grounds for doubting the prevailing interpretation of the former event, and for doubting the very significance of the latter.

Boas, as we have seen, was opposed to war, and to scientists deceptively posing "merely as" scientists in order to engage in espionage in the furtherance of war. He did not mention "clandestine research." And Project Camelot, in the end, as an understated British comedian might remark, "involved no actual *project*." Even more to the point, it involved no actual anthropologists (other than the star-crossed Nuttini).[20] Finally, as Horowitz painstakingly documented at the time, nothing about it was secret, clandestine, or even classified. I think it less a sign of careless scholarship and more a sign of some sort of mesmerizing pathology that, over and over again, his work is listed as a key reference by numerous authors in this field, ostensibly to provide their documentary confirmation for characterizations of that project and its significance that he himself, in contrast, had taken the greatest possible care to *refute*.

On the basis of accounts provided by experts within the discipline, the Thailand affair seems by far the single most grave and sinister incident. It entailed far more tangible damage being done, or at least threatened, by anthropologists engaged in it, and even greater damage being done by anthropologists to one another in arguing about it. One cannot read the abstract on "human targeting" from that "military research center" in Bangkok, let alone the excerpts on "assassination and retaliation" drawn from the American Institutes for Research grant proposal for DARPA in 1967, as examples of "operations toward which social science can make a contribution," without wondering what on earth its project directors could have been thinking. Likewise, an outsider cannot ponder Gerald Berreman's dramatic account of the reading out of those passages in open challenge to both the veracity and fidelity of the Mead Committee report in November of 1971—let alone the wider, deeply pained, and excruciatingly detailed accounts of the invidious, undemocratic backroom machinations, unscrupulous academic politicking, and vicious personal betrayal that accompanied it—without hanging one's head in pity, and perhaps also in shame. After all, it is the latter sort of secrecy and clandestine activity with which we in the academy generally, and not just anthropologists, are all too familiar: the solicitous colleague, with the kindly hand on the shoulder, withdrawn to reveal a slender dagger inserted delicately, and ultimately fatally. Our concerns about clandestine activity are indeed well-grounded.

Perhaps this series of events, more than the others that are ritually "forefronted" in the disciplinary litany, truly accounts for the deep professional ambivalence and soul-searching that led to the robust reformulation of the AAA's "Principles of Professional Responsibility" in 1971.[21] The Thailand affair, more readily than the other symbolic events in the "litany of shame," offers genuine grounds for appreciating the unease with which anthropologists have greeted invitations from our present government and military forces to contribute their scholarly expertise once again to grand projects aimed at promoting greater "cultural understanding" on the part of American and allied combat troops deployed in distant regions of the globe, engaged in wars whose moral and legal justification are profoundly in question.

And for those like Berreman himself, and Terence Turner, who suffered through those earlier struggles, it is all too clear why the subsequent elimination, in the 1998 version of the AAA's Code of Ethics, of specific language opposing "secret or clandestine research" and cautioning against collaboration with military and security forces would be greeted with bitterness, biting sarcasm, and deep suspicion.[22] Those revisions and omissions responded at the time to the needs and desires of so-called practice anthropologists, engaged in proprietary research for the government or the private sector, for whom prohibitions on secrecy seemed an unfair and inappropriate restriction. The Turner Amendment, by contrast, sought to reintroduce precisely the formulations of ethical principles originally forged in opposition to the Thailand affair, in part to oppose the recent widening involvement of anthropologists with the conduct of morally contested wars in Iraq and Afghanistan.

It is one thing, however, to come to an appreciative understanding of historical phenomena. Without doing this, others of us cannot possibly understand why anthropologists are as sensitive to these topics as they are. It is quite another thing, however, to assent to the authenticity of this self-understanding. Ludwig Wittgenstein once opined that philosophy must itself be understood as a kind of therapy. And it is sometimes the task of therapy (if not the therapist) to force a confrontation, a crisis of confidence, in the authenticity of the narratives that patients stubbornly (and sometimes self-destructively) weave for themselves. If we have unwound the underlying history, perhaps it would be well to consider reweaving more authentic narratives.

Let us then ponder, for a moment, what exactly would follow, even if every feature of the current narrative, the litany of shame, from Boas to Thailand, were historically valid in every respect. Let us "reckon up" all the activities of questionable professional probity proposed or engaged in by anthropologists, and even the sum total of all the harm done to one another in disputing them. (The last appears by far to be the single largest entry on this particular reckoning.) That hypothetical reckoning would, I submit, pale in significance to a second, well-known one, consisting of the actual deeds, involving allegations by actual victims of actual harm done to them, all stemming from the activities of actual (as opposed to imagined) anthropologists conducting what were until quite recently considered routine anthropological research projects involving perfectly "conventional" methodologies.

To be sure, these events, too, figure in the historical litany: the Sanchez affair, the Yạnomamö, the Pehuenche, "Kennewick Man," and the entire controversy over control of the cultural patrimony of indigenous peoples. But unlike those involving military collaboration, somehow these other incidents do not, shall we say, enjoy the pride of place that would, and perhaps should, be accorded them. This seems to be the case whether we choose to accord "space and place" purely on the basis of a stark utilitarian calculation of actual harm inflicted, or do so instead based upon a deontological assessment of the priority of fundamental moral duties or core professional obligations that may have been violated.

Let me be clear: I am not engaged in finding fault, I am merely, as it were, "toting up" and comparing damage claims. Moreover, I am well aware that anthropologists themselves have long taken these issues with the utmost seriousness, and indeed, may be said to have knotted themselves an entirely separate cord for self-flagellation on these accounts. It is the *judgment of relative importance*, of comparative significance, that I am questioning. More than that, *it is the manner in which the discipline has chosen to tell its story* that piques my curiosity and concern.

I say "the discipline" because the narrative exhibits a structural unity and uniformity over many authors (including even collective authorship, as in the CEAUSSIC report). There is some kind of tacit agreement on what the story is, on what it contains, on how it should be told, on which events to highlight in the foreground, and which to include only in the margins. There is surprising consensus in the sequence of events, in the way in which minor errors of fact get transmitted from author to author, and even how other factual discrepancies, when noted, do not seem to matter.[23]

This is somewhat surprising, especially among scholars. I can report that no such uniformity would be forthcoming or even remotely achievable in my own discipline. Instead, to put the matter politely, such narratives would be (are, in fact) highly idiosyncratic—both in the literal sense of depending upon the perspective of the individual narrator, or metaphorically, depending upon the sect or community perspective whose significance was celebrated. We handle discord simply by leaving "the Other" out. And there is, I'm embarrassed to admit, no tradition of shared reflection, let alone agreement, on the "morality" of what we do.[24]

From my limited experience, that is common practice in scholarly disciplines in the humanities and social sciences, characterized as they are by methodological strife and partisanship. This is what makes the case of anthropology's moral narrative so surprising: first, simply the fact that there is one at all; and second, that anthropologists seem to agree so profoundly on its contents and their meaning, even while disagreeing violently about practically everything else.

Those characteristics are more to be found in the moral narratives of professions, enshrined in the preambles of their own codes of conduct. I've spent the better part of my own career reflecting on these, examining and applying (or criticizing) their provisions, sometimes even helping to write them or revise them, but certainly never (at least until now) reflecting more generally (if I may say this) on their anthropological significance. Medicine's self-narrative, for one example, is profoundly moral in its account of its mythic figures (like Hippocrates, Galen, Harvey, and Pasteur), and in its emphasis of key provisions, such as *primum non nocere*, and otherwise to act always in behalf of the welfare and best interests of its patients. In particular, medicine's moral narrative confronts centrally the most egregious failings of certain of its practitioners (Jonson 2000). It lifts up, often by name, certain of its members who have gone morally astray, and enshrines those acknowledged failings in guiding principles, like the Nuremburg Code, designed to prevent their recurrence.

Anthropology's moral narrative, its litany of shame, more resembles a professional than a disciplinary narrative. It, too, lifts up mythic figures (like Boas), articulates core values and principles—the quest for knowledge, the welfare of its research subjects—and ostensibly confronts its moral failings, and seeks to enshrine these in principles, like transparency and the prohibition of secrecy, that are designed to prevent their recurrence.

So far, so good. But, in comparison to the medical example, anthropology's moral narrative seems distorted, out of proportion, focused somehow on the wrong events. And if I am right in this observation, this distortion has serious and decidedly negative consequences for the moral self-consciousness of the discipline.

How are we, for example, to compare Camelot, or even Thailand, to Nuremburg? They are incommensurate. Camelot was a political and public relations disaster for the nation and its social scientists, to be sure, an embarrassment, a mortification, but in every other respect more pathetic and misguided, even (in a sense) comic, than malevolent. How is such an event to be compared to vivisection of untold numbers of helpless victims for the purpose of illustrating medical textbooks? Even Thailand, with the chilling descriptions of the manner in which "social science" (whatever that pretentious term means) could be "useful" in operations like assassination and retribution does not measure up, because "social science," and certainly not anthropology, are not, finally, all that useful for such matters. Margaret Mead's much-maligned committee was right about that, at least: it was all self-aggrandizing, self-promoting, hyperinflated rhetoric designed to impress grant agencies, which, like DARPA, were, for their part, at least temporarily working far outside their own domain of expertise. Outrageous, unprofessional, and inexcusable, and properly punishable (unlike Boas) by censure, perhaps; but in the end, no one, and certainly no anthropologist, actually did anything of consequence, nor did any victims or their relatives come forward to demonstrate harm or complain otherwise. The Thai villagers, whose interview transcripts Wakin so meticulously documents, recognized at once the grave danger these bumbling and incompetent field researchers posed for their safety and angrily sent them away.

These incidents ought not, in any sense, to be compared to years and years of the most monstrous and cruel human experimentation ever imagined, for the putative benefit of wounded German soldiers, or for no good purpose at all, by Mengele and Wirths at Auschwitz and Birkenau. Instead, they should be relegated to the margins of anthropology's moral narrative. Project Camelot as a cautionary tale of hubris in particular should be consigned, once and for all, to the footnote immortality that Irving Horowitz intended for it, and perhaps the Thailand affair along with it. To think otherwise of these affairs is to succumb to the very temptation of which he warned, and that brought them about: the (wholly inappropriate and undeserved) mystique of social science (Horowitz 1967: 17).

What, then, should take the place of these relatively inconsequential incidents in anthropology's litany? Canonize Boas, if one must, for having the courage to speak out for intellectual freedom, against war, in the teeth of public insanity, but please do not, in the process, dignify his elitist, smug, and condescending moral judgments of classes of people, including soldiers, who would very shortly prove themselves his moral equals, if not superiors. Instead, canonize Theodore Downing, one of those despised and maligned "practice anthropologists" who, at considerable risk and personal sacrifice, did exactly what anthropology's Code of Ethics required, coming to the defense of his research subjects, the Pehuenche, in opposition to the aims of his employers (Fluehr-Lobban 2003a: 21–22). Forefront the complaints of the Sanchezes, and the Yąnomamö (even if their specific claims to harm or abuse were exaggerated or spurious; see Fluehr-Lobban 2003b). The lesson those cases teach, regardless, is about using the lives and experiences of others for personal gain, with little regard for the consequences. Chant, instead, the cautionary litany of our own Native peoples from both American continents, describing "how your ancestors displayed the bones of our ancestors, and defiled the sacred soil of their graves, for the amusement of children."

Whatsoever things are morally good and true through such reflection, dwell ever after on *those* things, and on the lesson of Nuremburg: "Never again!" And simply let it be forgot that once there was a lot of pointless, foolish nonsense that was known as "Camelot."

Notes

1. Reflecting the significance of this event, two accounts of it, both highly sympathetic toward Boas's stance, nonetheless differ in their presentation of the historical particulars. Carolyn Fluehr-Lobban (2003a: 3) reports that the 20:10 vote of censure was taken by the Executive Board of the Anthropology Society of Washington, and that neither their original resolution "nor any variation of it" was passed by the AAA. She cites Alexander Lesser's account (Lesser 1981) as her documentation for these assertions. His own account in that work, however, is that the longer resolution of the Washington Anthropological Society [sic] was set aside in favor of a much briefer statement of censure, passed by a "vote of about two to one" at the December 1919 meeting of the AAA itself (Lesser 1981: 13–14). I am thus following Lesser's account.

2. David Price spends a good deal of time discussing the Boas case as a lead-up to the involvement of anthropologists with the military during World War II. On Price's account, which, not surprisingly, offers a radically different and more favorable interpretation of Boas, "Boas's anthropology and *progressive political beliefs* informed this critique, and while his critical interpretation of the cultural inculcation of patriotism can now be seen as a theoretical analysis of social superstructure, during the war such views were simply seen as subversive" (Price 2008: 3). This account seems accurate in all respects. I do not fault Boas's progressivism, and certainly not his "subversiveness." I find the case for censure inadequate, and the action itself (which was finally and fittingly "undone" by the AAA in 2005) invidious. I do not entirely share, however, in the heroic mythologizing of Boas himself, as will become clear.

3. In this respect, it is useful to compare his rhetoric and his positions on these matters with the rhetoric and the underlying positions on the unjustifiability of America's war in Iraq, in particular, evident in the statement of the "Network of Concerned Anthropologists" against the "militarization" of anthropology (NCA 2007).

4. Ironically (again) the chief rebuttals of this self-confident portrayal of science would come later, both in the form of a well-known history of the sociological features of scientific inquiry generally by Thomas Kuhn (Kuhn 1962) and, even more authoritatively, a study of its day-to-day practices by two eminent sociologists, Bruno Latour and Steve Woolgar, that question its very objectivity (Latour and Woolgar 1979). The manner in which scientists compete egotistically is captured vividly in James D. Watson, *The Double Helix* (Watson 1968). Moreover, these serious reservations concerning scientific impartiality and objectivity were already being widely discussed in Boas's time, and in his circle of influence (Whitehead 1919, 1920, 1925). In short, there is not, nor was there ever, anyone answering to the description that Boas invokes, and thus any implied principles of proper professional conduct based upon so superficial an understanding of science must perforce themselves be suspect. For an authoritative account of this issue from the standpoint of the history of anthropology itself, see the introduction to Rubinstein 2001.

5. Note that in 2005, the AAA passed a resolution officially lifting the censure of Franz Boas after nearly ninety years.

6. This useful distinction is first made in *The Right and the Good* (1930) by the early 20th-century Scottish moral philosopher and Aristotelian scholar Sir William David Ross. In contrast to an "absolute" duty that could never properly be overridden by other considerations, a prima facie duty is a duty (e.g., to fulfill a promise I made to a friend) which, on "first glance" or intuitively, "on the face of it," I would be expected to honor. Ross's argument was that most specific moral duties fall into categories (such as refraining from harming others, doing good things for others, being honest and truthful) that, in turn, can be ranked intuitively according to degree of priority or seriousness. Accordingly, this particular deontological moral theory is sometimes called "ranked-rule formalism," to distinguish it from Immanuel Kant's account of moral duties, which (implausibly) can never come into conflict, because (as Kant says) "Reason cannot contradict itself."

In Ross's account, by contrast, moral dilemmas arise precisely whenever prima facie duties are found to conflict with one another. Those of lower priority may then be overridden by those of higher priority. I have prima facie duties, for example, not to lie or deceive others or, as a scientist, to avoid secrecy in my research. But these duties may be overridden on some occasions by more pressing obligations: I may conceal my research if making it public would endanger the lives of the research subjects or, in subsequent, and now widely used example, if Nazi Gestapo agents knock on my door and inquire if any residents in my building are Jewish, I may justifiably lie to or otherwise mislead them (on Ross's account) in order to fulfill the more compelling duty to save others from harm.

7. Horowitz (1967: 27) is the source of this characterization, though it is clear from his comments on the magnitude and scale of funding that he is reporting and discounting what was a widespread view of the project among his contemporaries. This characterization gets taken up, and wrongly attributed to Horowitz himself, however, in subsequent accounts.

8. "Project Camelot, Official Document #1" (Horowitz 1967: 47–49).

9. The State Failure Task Force (now known as the Political Insecurity Task Force) was originally formed at the behest of President William Clinton and senior U.S. policymakers in the aftermath of the Rwandan genocide. Its purpose was "to design and carry out a data-driven study of the preconditions of state failure, defined to include ethnic and revolutionary wars, adverse or disruptive regime transitions, and genocide and politicides." See Barbara Harff, "Assessing Risks of Genocide and Politicide," in *Peace and Conflict* (2005), eds. Monty G. Marshall and Ted Robert Gurr. Available from the "Genocide Watch" website at http://www.genocidewatch. org/aboutgenocide/harffrisksofgenocide.htm.

10. Project Camelot Official Document #3 (Horowitz 1967: 56).

11. This is the time frame cited by Horowitz for the proposed four-week planning conference, although the original memorandum of December 4, 1964, specifies that

the gathering would take place at Arlie House in Virginia in August of that year. See "Project Camelot Official Document #1" (Horowitz 1967: 47).

12. While the eminent anthropologist Marshall Sahlins weighed in mightily on this controversy at the 1965 meeting of the AAA (Sahlins 1965), it was his colleague, political scientist Kalman H. Silvert of Dartmouth College, who was actually conducting field research in Chile during this period, and interviewed all the principals mentioned in an effort to get to the bottom of the controversy that threatened his own investment of 25 years in that country. Silvert offers the most detailed account yet of Nuttini's machinations, particularly his clumsy attempts at name-dropping and influence-peddling as Nuttini attempted to portray himself as an important and well-connected member of the project staff. It was his denial, initially, of knowledge of the U.S. Army connection, when confronted with Galtung's evidence and open letter of invitation, that precipitated the ensuing crisis and gave it the appearance of a clandestine operation. Silvert makes it quite clear, however, that he and others knew this was not the case, and that Nuttini was a fraud (Silvert, 1965: 82–88). Interestingly, Silvert confirms that Nuttini was the only anthropologist directly involved with the project in any way at that time. Its staff, he notes, were primarily sociologists and political scientists.

13. Berreman cites "Horowitz 1967" as his source, despite the fact that Horowitz specifically and decisively shows that this was not the case, as does political scientist Kalman Silvert (Silvert 1965), included in Horowitz's anthology. Litanies offer vivid symbols, but often selective or inaccurate history.

14. Thus Price (2003: 30), Berreman (2003: 52), and Sahlins (2000: 261–68) all cite Horowitz (1967) as their source for these persistently inaccurate characterizations, even though Horowitz's conclusions are precisely the opposite of what they imagine.

15. See Selmeski's illustrative account of the fate of anthropologist Edward T. Hall at the U.S. State Department's Foreign Services Institute (FSI) in the early 1950s, at pp. 9–10.

16. Price's *Anthropological Intelligence: The Development and Neglect of American Anthropology in the Second World War* (2008) subsumes these earlier accounts, and is the most detailed and authoritative study of the interaction of anthropology with military and security forces to date. I have earlier stated my reluctance to rely exclusively on its findings, though his accounts must be read and critically pondered. I have tried to do that fairly, as he himself has tried to remain open-minded about the degree of culpability to attach to the various intrigues his research has uncovered.

Colleagues in history, however, cite an additional dilemma: that since much of the contents of the archives necessary to undertake this research remain classified, Price's work, as he acknowledges, is obliged to rely heavily on Freedom of Information Act (FOIA) inquiries. Somewhat contrary to his own enthusiasm for these sources (Price 1997: 12–15), such sources by themselves are not, in fact, fully representative or even especially reliable, owing to the selective and often highly interpretive manner in which these requests may (or may not) be fully complied with, and even more to the fact that such requests are routinely "fobbed off" onto untrained and largely uncooperative support staff, for whom all this constitutes a lot of extra nuisance work piled on top of their normal duties simply to "satisfy some crackpot or trouble-maker with a political agenda." As Price himself laments, "Covert research (when it is properly conducted) often remains unknown and thus generally unrecorded in the annals of history"—at least in those annals readily accessible to scholars (Price 2003: 30). We simply cannot know how much we don't know, and the temptation, in that instance, is quite often to imagine more than is really there. This last observation constitutes perhaps the strongest moral argument against secrecy, even in behalf of morally worthy ends: it breeds suspicion and mistrust, undermines any good that might otherwise come from one's activities, and so should be avoided at all costs.

17. Berreman (2003) accidentally mis-cites Wakin's subtitle as "Professional Ethics and Counterinsurgency in *Vietnam*." The focus of the book, however, is almost exclusively on Thailand, in which the author had traveled extensively.

18. Fluehr-Lobban 2003a: 12; see also Berreman 2003: 57 for a slightly altered account.

19. As I noted earlier, Pat Caplan's anthology (Caplan 2003) stands in marked contrast to Fluehr-Lobban's on this account. Involvement of anthropological expertise in wartime is certainly a theme of concern in some of those essays, but does not come close to dominating the discussion in the manner we see in this country. Fluehr-Lobban herself suggests that the British concern is reflected in discussions in its leading journal, *Anthropology Today*. Examination of selected issues of that journal, however, reveal that what is of interest to British anthropologists is primarily the American controversy over military anthropology and Pentagon support for anthropological research (such as Project Minerva). The articles on such topics are commissioned from American rather than British anthropologists (e.g., Catherine Lutz of the Watson Institute at Brown University), and frame issues in terms of a debate between contributing authors about issues like the Human Terrain System and the formation of AFRICOM, the unified command of coalition forces stationed in Africa (e.g., see volume 24, number 5 in 2008). What is absent is any evidence of a corresponding outcry in Britain itself, among British scholars, about its own scholars' past or present engagement with military, intelligence, and security forces. For a review of contents of recent issues, see the website of the Royal Anthropology Institute at http://www.therai.org.uk/pubs/at/anthrotoday.html.

20. These conclusions are suggested by Horowitz (1967) and confirmed by Silvert (1965). This appropriation by anthropologists of narratives drawn from the history of related disciplines such as sociology is another prevalent but puzzling feature of their mythologization of their moral history. Anthropology shares a family resemblance with sociology by traditional association, but shares just as close a conceptual resemblance to history and political science. And in fact, the family resemblance is not very strong. We might label this eclectic tendency by anthropologists the "juris-

dictional fallacy," and it has several manifestations that I will take up once again in my concluding chapter. One is this selective assimilation of the history of distinct disciplines. It is sociology, and perhaps political science, and surely *not* anthropology, that ought to apologize for Camelot, unless one also wishes to broaden boundaries to include physics and the Manhattan Project, or the endlessly similar machinations of economists and political scientists within the proper moral purview. And this no one seems to propose doing.

The second manifestation is to label persons "anthropologists," and to accept responsibility for their deeds, regardless of their actual professional background or qualifications. Human Terrain System (HTS) teams, as we shall observe, are composed of "social scientists" only in the loosest possible sense: they advertise for anthropologists if they can get them, but are willing to accept nonterminal degrees in everything from history to theology in their place! This hardly constitutes the "militarization" of anthropology, though the practice raises (as I will note) other disturbing questions about the nature of professional qualifications and expertise in HTS. Perhaps it would be simpler if we agreed that the term "anthropologist" for purposes of moral argument designates one who holds an advanced and preferably a terminal degree (i.e., Ph.D.) in one of the recognized subfields of anthropology, and who is a member of the AAA or an equivalent professional society. Further, we agree to permit the weaving of narratives of moral responsibility only if they involve the participation of "anthropologists" so defined—in which case Project Camelot must perforce be omitted entirely.

21. Members of the discipline, and specific authors like Berreman and Price, use this date, but Fluehr-Lobban notes the finished draft was not actually completed and ratified until the following year. More important, it bears repeating that the reformulation was based on an original draft, written in 1967, in the aftermath of Project Camelot, from which I quoted in my account of Boas, above. Again, my point is not to quibble with the chronology, which is beyond dispute, or even with prevailing notions of historical causality (the Camelot scandal *was* without question the "cause" of the original PPRs, as Fluehr-Lobban attests). Rather, I am inviting deeper and more thoughtful reflection on the meaning and interpretation of that chronology.

22. That is how I characterize and account for Berreman's own denunciation of the specific revisions of the current (1998) CoE as having, in sum, replaced "ethics with greed" (2003: 68). His individual arguments over specific provisions or objectionable revisions are always impassioned but frequently ungrounded, and occasionally just plain mistaken. While his treatment of "secrecy" and "clandestinity" are brilliant, vituperative diatribes that make great reading, that alone does not render them true. His denial of any meaningful difference between the adjectives "secret" and "clandestine" is, for example, quite false: we take "secret ballots" on the shop floor so that neither management goons nor union thugs can intimidate workers in reaching decisions about whether, and by whom, to be represented for bargaining purposes. There is nothing "clandestine" (i.e., sinister, sneaky, underhanded) about

that. Quite the opposite, in fact! I think, however, that to engage in such "logic-chopping" with the author is to miss the larger moral force of his principled position on these matters.

23. I've flagged a number of examples of both in the endnotes of this chapter and the last, not initially to prove this point but to prove instead that I've been trying to pay close attention. My judgment of the pattern here could certainly be quite wrong. It is, finally, for thoughtful members of the discipline in response to determine whether there is anything to these observations.

24. Plato's early portrayals of Socrates have him offering a moral defense of philosophical inquiry, alongside an indictment of the moral bankruptcy of his rival Sophists' pursuits. Nietzsche's general indictment of the "cruelty" inherent in logic and reason might be taken as a general moral denunciation of the profession, of course. Bruce Wilshire's *The Moral Collapse of the University: Professionalism, Purity, and Alienation* (New York: State University of New York Press, 1990) includes a scathing review of analytic philosophy's alleged moral shortcomings, taken up in greater detail in the author's *Fashionable Nihilism: A Critique of Analytic Philosophy* (Albany: State University of New York Press, 2002), but those are criticisms of the alleged failings of one school or approach, not the discipline as a whole. There are, in addition, numerous critiques of the moral failings of individual philosophical figures, such as Martin Heidegger. The point is, however, that there is nothing remotely similar to anthropology's collective reflection on and agreement concerning its own moral failings as a profession.

CHAPTER THREE

Anthropology of,
and for, the Military

A long-simmering debate among American anthropologists over the rise of the newest form of "military anthropology" erupted into a wider public controversy in the weeks leading up to a key annual meeting of the American Anthropological Association (AAA) in Washington, D.C., toward the end of November 2007. Descriptions of the new Human Terrain System (HTS) were featured in programs and publications ranging from the *New York Times*, the *Boston Globe*, the *New Yorker*, and the *Chronicle of Higher Education*, to WAMU Radio's nationally syndicated *Diane Rehm Show*, where reporters and commentators joined with anthropologists and Army officers in discussing proposals to use anthropologists as cultural advisers in ongoing wars of counterinsurgency in Iraq and Afghanistan. AAA members were invited to opine in published interviews and on radio talk shows, as well as in Internet journals and blogs, on the morality and professional probity of HTS in particular, as well as on the wider controversy over the increasing engagement of colleagues with military, intelligence, and security forces in a variety of other fashions during the past several years.[1]

Anthropologists Roberto Gonzalez (San Jose State University) and David Price (St. Martin's University) appeared to lead the charge of critics against what they termed "the militarization" of anthropology, complaining that:

> The Pentagon is increasingly relying on the deployment of "Human Terrain system" (HTS) teams in Afghanistan and Iraq to gather and disseminate information on cultures living in the theater of war. Some of these teams are

assigned to US brigades or regimental combat units, which include "cultural analysts" and "regional studies analysts." . . . Although proponents of this form of applied anthropology claim that culturally informed counter-insurgency work will save lives and win "hearts and minds," they have thus far not attempted to provide any evidence of this. . . . If anthropologists on HTS teams interview Afghans or Iraqis about the intimate details of their lives, what is to prevent combat teams from using the same data to one day "neutralize" (read "assassinate") suspected insurgents? What would impede the transfer of data collected by social scientists to commanders planning offensive military campaigns? Where is the line that separates the professional anthropologist from the counter-insurgency technician? (Price and Gonzalez, 2007)

Price and Gonzalez do not claim that such professional abuses are actually occurring, although Gonzalez himself does describe and specifically denounce the role of "biscuit" teams (Behavioral Science Consultation Teams) in discovering and exploiting areas of cultural sensitivity for the purposes of interrogation and torture in Guantánamo Bay and at Abu Ghraib (Gonzalez 2007). Price, Gonzalez, and their fellow critics do acknowledge that there are positive examples of cooperation from the past. But, as the reference to the Pittsburg AIR project indicates, they think they remember Camelot, but appear to remember Thailand. They draw the line, accordingly, at anthropologists, serving under contract at the State Department's counterterrorism office, or assisting the Department of Defense (DOD) in forging doctrine or writing policy (such as providing substantive advice and input in authoring the Army counterinsurgency manual).

One of the academics who assisted the DOD, and more recently the U.S. Department of State in understanding the intricacies of counterinsurgency, is Dr. David Kilcullen, an Australian national with a Ph.D. in political anthropology. He now lectures widely on the details of counterinsurgency, sharing lessons he learned firsthand as an officer in the Australian National Defense Force. His experience includes tours of duty in Iraq (2006, 2007), Afghanistan (2006), and "pre-9/11" tours, serving in the Australian-led U.N. intervention force in East Timor. From these experiences, he observes, he learned that insurgencies, including supposed Islamic "extremism," are local, not global. His presentations on the day-to-day operations of counterinsurgency—how to patrol neighborhoods and provide enhanced security, for example, without incurring increased animosity—aim to convince military audiences that a working knowledge of cultural specifics by commanders in the field goes far toward defusing hostilities and preventing needless casualties, all elements vital to winning over an insurgency (Packer 2006).[2] Whatever its merits (or lack thereof), this is a far cry from the rhetoric of

AIR in 1967, in which social scientists would "contribute" to "neutralizing competing (cultural or insurgency) inputs" through assassination and "other forms of retaliation."

Another anthropologist working on this project, Montgomery McFate, is strong-willed and confrontational, and celebrates this important new vocation for anthropologists, believing that promoting more nuanced cultural awareness and sensitivity for the average soldier, sailor, or Marine through HTS will actually help save lives and avoid needless casualties, even while assisting in the war on terror (Schachtman 2008). McFate has been especially critical of her discipline's unwillingness to consider the merits of such collaboration, an attitude, she claims, that stems from the discipline's radical, postmodernist turn toward "self-flagellation." Interestingly, she does not seem to acknowledge anthropology's troubled past associations with such efforts, nor does she address the "bad conscience" of the discipline on these matters. Rather, she either ignores, dismisses, or ridicules this history.

So, for example, when describing some of the current needs for cultural understanding in the so-called war on terror, and anthropology's past history of providing such insights during pivotal conflicts, she observes that, at present, "Although anthropology is the only academic discipline that explicitly seeks to understand foreign cultures and societies, it is a marginal contributor to U.S. national security policy at best." She contrasts its present status as a purely academic discipline, intent on studying the "exotic and useless," with other social sciences, such as political science and economics, that are deeply involved in evaluating and formulating public policy. She attributes this attitude rather offhandedly to the "deep isolationist tendencies within the discipline" following the Vietnam War, and the rejection of its historical ties to colonialism. She does not mention Camelot or the Thailand affair by name. Instead, she offers the following provocative critique of the discipline, hinting at this history:

> Thus [in the post-Vietnam era] began a systematic interrogation of the contemporary state of the discipline as well as of the colonial circumstances from which it emerged. Armed with critical hermeneutics, frequently backed up by self-reflexive neo-Marxism, anthropology began a brutal process of self-flagellation to a degree almost unimaginable to anyone outside the discipline. (McFate, 2005a,b)

Other participants in this debate, such as the AAA's director of external, international, and governmental relations, Paul J. Nuti, find themselves simply perplexed at the genuine efficacy of some of these efforts. Nuti, for example, is skeptical about attempts by the Marine Corps Intelligence Activity program in Quantico to employ anthropologists in the task of "boiling down" the essentials of complex cultural mores onto laminated, wallet-sized "smart cards" for use by what they characterize as a typical "19-year old Marine lance corporal from Iowa, who may never have traveled overseas, let alone fought in a middle-eastern war zone" (Nuti 2006: 15–17; Nuti and Fosher 2007: 3–4).[3]

On October 31, 2007, the Executive Board of the AAA issued a statement strongly opposing the U.S. military's "human terrain system," and strenuously objecting to the participation of members of the society in this program:

> In the context of a war that is widely recognized as a denial of human rights and based on faulty intelligence and undemocratic principles, the Executive Board sees the HTS project as a problematic application of anthropological expertise, most specifically on ethical grounds. We have grave concerns about the involvement of anthropological knowledge and skill in the HTS project. The Executive Board *views the HTS project as an unacceptable application of anthropological expertise.*[4] (AAA 2007)

The specific concerns were numerous, and potentially grave for the profession. As we have noted, such work might constitute a violation of the AAA Code of Ethics, specifically Section III-A.1 (see appendix), by having HTS participants engaged in work that could result in harm to the cultures inhabited and studied. Such work, they charge, involves an inherent conflict of interest between the supervising employer's needs and the welfare of the peoples and cultures studied. Field anthropologists engaged in HTS projects for the military would likely not be able to disclose their activities and obtain reasonably informed consent for such work from the subjects of their study.

Finally, cooperation with the U.S. military in this way might compromise the professional identity of anthropologists in the future, damaging their autonomy and integrity in the eyes of potential research subjects, and making it impossible for them not to be identified merely as "tools" of foreign government policy, rather than as impartial (and harmless) scientists engaged in legitimate research. Moreover, critics are wont to criticize the potential of this work as constituting yet another invitation to "secret or clandestine" research, of the sort that is not now explicitly identified as constituting unacceptable professional engagement in the current CoE. As we noted, it is this lacuna that the proposed Turner amendment aimed to redress. The Executive Board statement did, however acknowledge:

> that anthropology can and in fact is obliged to help improve U.S. government policies through the widest possible circulation of anthropological understanding in the public sphere, so as to contribute to a transparent and informed

development and implementation of U.S. policy by robustly democratic processes of fact-finding, debate, dialogue, and deliberation. It is in this way, the Executive Board affirms, that anthropology can legitimately and effectively help guide U.S. policy to serve the humane causes of global peace and social justice. (AAA 2007)

Classifications of Military Anthropology

At this same watershed meeting in Washington, D.C., during November 2007, an ad hoc committee, the Commission on the Engagement of Anthropology with the U.S. Security and Intelligence Communities (CEAUSSIC 2007), released the results of its yearlong study of the problem. The commission (which included some practitioners of various types of military anthropology, as well as critics of engagement with the military, intelligence, and security communities) refrained from endorsing the AAA Executive Board's earlier strong opposition to the HTS project. In contrast, the report distinguished a number of different types of engagement with (or employment by, or in the service of) military, intelligence, and security organizations (MIS), and attempted to give a balanced and fair-minded assessment of these very different types of engagement with MIS communities, counseling caution and restraint in engaging too readily or uncritically in such endeavors. [5]

In this report, the CEAUSSIC commission members took care to distinguish broadly between a number of quite distinct activities. These ranged from teaching and educating the members of MIS communities about culture, or studying these organizational cultures themselves, all the way to writing policy and doctrine for these organizations, providing cultural analysis and assessments of foreign cultures and communities for them, or assuming other analytical or operational roles, such as embedded service in deployed military units in foreign countries (the Human Terrain Systems).

Table 3.1. Types of Military Anthropology

Symbol	Type	Description
MA$_1$	Anthropology *of* the military	Anthropological study of military culture
MA$_2$	Anthropology *for* the military	Human Terrain Systems (HTS)
MA$_3$	Anthropology *for* the military	Educational programs (language, culture, regional studies) at military academies

The guiding ethical framework proposed for evaluating these different activities stressed four core principles:

> to do no harm; to provide disclosure of one's work and role [in order] not to deceive; to uphold the primary responsibility to those involved in one's research; and to maintain transparency, making research accessible to others to enhance the quality and potential effects of it as critique. (CEAUSSIC 2007: 14)

One simplifying distinction, proposed during the discussions of the commission report and its findings during the AAA 2007 annual meeting, is that between anthropology *of* the military, and anthropology *for* the military (Winnick 2008). What the report itself described as "organizational study," employing interviews, focus groups, and participant observation to make recommendations for organizational improvement and change, would be an example of an anthropological study *of* the military. So, more generally, would broader attempts to study military cultures (their precepts, habits, history, rituals, and behavioral codes), regardless of how such studies were funded. HTS, by contrast, would constitute a use of anthropology *for* the military. So also would accepting employment in order to write policy and doctrine (for example, providing anthropological advice and insight for composing the Army's Counterinsurgency Manual or the Marine Corps Handbook on Operational Culture), as well as what the CEAUSSIC report itself described as "cultural training" and "analysis," in order to provide MIS organizations' members with "greater cultural literacy and trans-cultural awareness."

This broad, dualistic distinction is useful at one level, though probably not sufficiently detailed, in part because of an equivocation regarding what might be meant by "*for* the military." As the commission report itself reveals, anthropology "for" the military embraces a wide range of activities carried out "for" the military as employer, or "customer," or beneficiary, at least some of which might be benign or morally unobjectionable. And, as the report itself also seems to indicate, it is simply not the case that *all* forms of anthropology *for* the military—in which MIS organizations serve as an employer, recipient of service, beneficiary, customer, or client in a variety of different senses—are to be brought under indictment.[6] Instead, the principal focus of moral concern is upon those activities in which harm might be done (whether intentionally or inadvertently) to members of the culture studied, or where secrecy[7] or an absence of transparency might result in either failing to obtain fully informed consent of human subjects for one's research, or withholding the publication and dissemination of results of such study for reasons independent of scholarly knowledge or the benefit of those subjects studied. In sum: the threat of possibly doing harm, coupled with the fear of inappropriate secrecy or the absence of appropriate scholarly transparency formed the nucleus of the CEAUSSIC commission's own reflections and advice regarding all forms of military anthropology it identified.

The distinction "of" versus "for" appears to have made its way into these discussions, however, simply because many participants in the wider discussion of what they themselves took to be "military anthropology" did not always make such distinctions. That is, quite a few anthropologists, as judged from their comments on and attitudes expressed toward this debate, are of the opinion that any sort of engagement whatsoever with the military ought to be proscribed. We have traced the origins of this broader, more general antipathy in the preceding two chapters. For its part, the commission, having noted this attitude, quite clearly distanced itself from such a broad condemnation of engagement with MIS, and instead took great pains to distinguish and exonerate what, I think, is the primary "ordinary language" meaning of the term "military anthropology."

For convenience, we'll label this primary meaning of military anthropology MA_1: this consists of making the military itself, or its distinct organizations and/or service subcultures, the objects of anthropological study and field research. The objective in MA_1 is not to render some autonomous culture or society objects of investigation for the purposes entertained by the intervening military. Rather, MA_1 renders the members and subcultures of the military themselves the objects of ethnographic study. The purpose here is first and foremost simply to understand those organizations and subcultures more completely, as objects of scientific study, much as one is curious about the members of any alien or radically unfamiliar culture one might encounter.

While the report did not specifically say this, it is often this sort of military anthropology that is, in fact, practiced by anthropologists employed by military services and organizations. This activity involves living among, visiting, chronicling, describing, and interpreting the rituals and traditions of military subcultures. Anthropologist Clifford Geertz, a leading proponent of "cultural hermeneutics," once aptly described culture as the webs of interpretive interconnectivity[8] that bind an organization's or society's individual members together. This is what anthropologists engaged in "military anthropology" in the first sense undertake to study.

On the one hand, such activity might seem to outsiders, unfamiliar with anthropology's recent history and "bad conscience" on these matters, to be as morally unobjectionable, prima facie, as any other kind of anthropology. We have, however, established at least the basis for such antipathy, even though I criticized the narrative from which it results as distorted or disproportional to the actual deeds undertaken, or harm done by anthropologists engaged with

MIS in this fashion. Perhaps at this juncture, we should pause to consider whether there remains any good reason, outside of the mythologized case offered in that "received" historical litany, to harbor suspicions about the scholarly and professional validity, or the moral probity, of engaging in MA_1.

It seems clear that the Executive Board of the AAA does not think so, and that the members of the CEAUSSIC commission went to some lengths not to seem so. They, in turn, were obliged to go on the record as defining and exempting this sort of activity because, according to widespread reports from a host of anthropologists, a substantial number of AAA members nonetheless harbor suspicions about even this kind of legitimate and relatively benign activity. Anthropologist Kerry Fosher, for example, reports on the reaction of colleagues in the profession, upon learning of her interest in the Marine Corps work on "cultural intelligence," who warned, "If you lie down with dogs, you'll end up with fleas," while other colleagues equated her earlier interests in police and security with "giving a sympathetic portrayal of concentration camp guards" (Fosher 2008).[9]

As we have seen, this generalized prejudice concerning "security anthropology" (as some now also call it) is the major driving force behind the current controversy. While the specific focus on HTS has been the centerpiece of the controversy, *HTS is probably in many ways not the best example or most comprehensive illustration of the sort of work that anthropologists do with and for the military,* or in the public sector generally (e.g., in the DOD, the State Department, at Homeland Security, or at federal educational institutions in support of what is often termed "professional military education," or PME). So Dan Henk, a retired Army officer and a Ph.D. anthropologist who serves as director of the Air Force Culture and Language Center at Air University in Montgomery, Alabama, writes:

> The controversies over HTS have largely obscured an arguably much more fundamental way in which anthropologists (and scholars from related disciplines) are engaged with the US Department of Defense. This is a very concerted effort to use professional military education to better equip US military members to communicate, negotiate and build relations in culturally complex environments. . . .We are endeavoring to use our educational system to build Cross-Cultural Competence (3C), which we in the Air Force define as the ability to quickly and accurately comprehend, then appropriately and effectively act, to achieve the desired effect in a culturally complex environment—without necessarily having prior exposure to a particular group, region or foreign language.
>
> . . . we teach language and regional issues, but are even more interested in the ability to go anywhere, particularly on short notice, and communicate,

negotiate and build relations. Understandably, the world's attention has focused on our ongoing wars in Iraq and Afghanistan, but our US military "steady state" is probably best characterized as coalition partnerships and complex humanitarian emergencies. So the "bottom line" to our educational efforts is the ability to work well with others, whether coalition partners, NGOs, local civil society actors, or traumatized victims of humanitarian disasters.

There is nothing covert about our educational efforts. The anthropologists engaged in US military education are in regular communication with counterparts in US academe and with civil and military counterparts in other countries—Canada, UK, Netherlands, Germany, Sweden, and others.[10]

In my estimation, the leadership of the AAA and the members of its ad hoc commission were correct in their own assessment of this matter, as against the deeply held prejudices of some of the membership stemming, as we have seen, from its historical litany and collective self-consciousness. Apart from that deeply flawed and historically unsubstantiated narrative, however, there are simply no firm grounds or reasons that can be given in support of the view that MA_1 is anything other than morally benign. To demonstrate this, consider one example of what Geertz himself once bemusedly derided as "those little stories that Oxford philosophers like to make up for themselves" (Geertz 1973: 7).

Imagine a wholly perverse, wicked martial subculture, morally abhorrent in every respect: brutal, arbitrary, authoritarian, unjust, and cruel (in sum, a society that closely resembles my own discipline's professional organization). Would an anthropologist try, if possible, to study it? I assume so, provided only that it were possible to do so safely. One's moral assessment (especially if it is little more than a personal subjective assessment, more akin to a prejudice) has no bearing whatever on the moral suitability of the study of that culture, so long as such study does not extend somehow to aiding and abetting that culture in the performance of its brutality. Provided such study caused no additional danger and was feasible, it would be perfectly appropriate to undertake it. It warrants affirming the conclusion of the AAA CEAUSSIC commission itself, that blanket opposition to "anthropology *of* the military," MA_1, has no basis in fact or in argument.

That doesn't quite finish the matter. Perhaps there is still reason to question the moral validity of MA_1 on account of some ancillary purposes for the military that it might be alleged to serve. One ancillary purpose of MA_1, if one exists at all, might be both to help the leaders and members of the individual cultures come to a greater self-awareness and self-understanding, and perhaps, thereby, come to be more effective and authentic in living out their professional roles, or discharging their professional obligations. When present, the latter purpose would not differ substantially from the broad pedagogical purposes of education more generally, and especially practical moral education and character development. These likewise aim at self-awareness, and through this, at individual and group betterment. In another sense, the purposes of this kind of activity would not differ from those of psychological counseling and therapy—likewise aimed at understanding individuals (and sometimes groups). We do not in principle (or in general) hold these latter kinds of educational development and attainment of improved self and group understanding to be morally problematic. Why, if ever, would we object to military anthropology in the MA_1 sense as morally objectionable, let alone reprehensible, apart from adhering to a groundless historical litany that, as we have discovered, profoundly needs to be rethought, and rewoven?

Unless we were either seriously confused or confounded by the failure to distinguish MA_1 from the various senses of anthropology "for" the military to which we might more legitimately object, we would hold MA_1 to be morally problematic only in the same rare and rather exceptional cases in which we hold moral education or psychological counseling to be morally problematic: that is, when the client and beneficiary of the education or therapy, who is thereby enabled more effectively to live out his or her life and carry forward his or her projects, is inherently corrupt or morally degenerate. So, for example, we do not think it quite right to extend the benefits of counseling, therapy, or presumably educational self-awareness to an underworld "hit man," and by extension, certainly not to a genocidal tyrant—not, at least, unless we hoped thereby to dissuade them (or better, have them dissuade themselves) from any further pursuit of their immoral objectives. We certainly don't wish to assist them to become better at these activities or more comfortable with themselves in performing them.

Thus, while we think psychological treatment or educational development is in principle the right of any individual (or, by extension, group), we would, at the very minimum, encounter a moral dilemma in the form of a conflict of duties and interests in extending such support to a cold-blooded murderer or a ruthless tyrant. In the example of Franz Boas, we saw that Boas himself did hold views of this sort regarding "spies" and scientists who stooped to espionage. He also apparently thought that his countrymen who were soldiers and politicians were little more than cold-blooded murderers and deceitful tyrants, and apparently he thought even less of business "men." It would follow, especially for a pacifist like Boas, that providing any sort of aid and quarter, let alone collaborating with them or joining them in pursuit of their activities, would constitute morally unacceptable behavior in the extreme. In anthropology's "litany of shame," we have also seen that his role as a kind of symbolic martyr for the cause of academic freedom and freedom of speech as a result of expressing such unpopular views, has had the effect of endorsing, not merely the *principle of free expression* of such views, but *something very much like those views themselves* in the collective consciousness of the discipline.

So it might seem reasonable to an admirer of Boas to conclude that *the very act itself* of collaborating with military or intelligence forces (such as the CIA) is morally suspect or even blameworthy. It would be enough to show merely that such collaboration occurred to have grounds to condemn it,[11] without being obliged to inquire further (as we observed Margaret Mead trying to do in 1942, at least) about the moral orientation of the nation or government whose military and intelligence forces these were—or even further, about the moral probity of the specific activities in which these forces themselves were engaged.

In like fashion, in order to suggest that there is inherently something tainted about the pursuit of MA_1, we must be prepared to argue that the American (or, for that matter, the British, or Australian, or Canadian, or French) military, their various organizations, their subcultures, and/or their individual members, despite their vast differences in background, tradition, or even purpose, are uniformly tainted, uniformly devoted to purposes that are wholly undesirable and morally unworthy, and so subject to blanket moral condemnation. Undoubtedly there are some individuals who do accept this blanket condemnation of all things military. I think them mistaken in holding such views, but such views are held. I do not think, however, that such views can withstand critical scrutiny or bear the weight of evidence. For those reasons, I do not think those views are representative or widely held (certainly not by the rank and file of educated citizens outside higher education, for example). Nor do I think it the point, finally, of responsible critics of "military anthropology" (by which they presumably have in mind one of the various senses of anthropology "for" the military, discussed below) simultaneously to advance such blanket generalizations, or to espouse such uncritical, unfounded, and ultimately unsupportable views.

Individuals and groups have negative views of police, politicians, lawyers, and the military. Franz Boas, as we saw, clearly entertained such views. Those individuals from minority communities who have been victims of police brutality, along with political prisoners or victims of rendition and torture, for example, have very good reasons to hold those negative views, together with substantial evidence to support them. In most cases, however, such broad and sweeping generalizations are unfounded. Indeed, MA_1 might offer the hope that improved self-understanding and awareness would improve function to bring high moral purpose in line with conventional practice and to lessen incidents of mistakes and moral failings due to error and misunderstanding. Indeed, as Horowitz shows with respect to Project Camelot, some very naïve version of that aspiration was what appeared to motivate many of the social scientists who did sign on with the project. It was not their commendable motivations, but their utterly spurious "scientific" assumptions and their deeply flawed work plan (along with the machinations of Professor Nuttini) that did them in.[12]

Fortunately no such naïve and grandiose assumptions form any part of the primary purpose of MA_1, which is, like all anthropology that claims to be "scientific," aimed at improved knowledge and understanding for its own sake. It would be odd in the extreme to argue against attaining greater, more reliable understanding of what has historically proved to be one of the most influential and important organizations in this nation's history.

Hence, our first definitive conclusion is that MA_1 can and must be distinguished from any and all of the various meanings of anthropology "for" the military, and that military anthropology as the study of military culture (whatever that may turn out to mean or to be) can, should, and indeed, must proceed unfettered by undue regulation, misguided resolution, or invidious personal prejudice. It is a worthy, even fascinating endeavor with potentially important outcomes that the wider anthropological and scientific community is entitled to pursue and deserves to study.

So much for "anthropology *of* the military," the primary meaning of "military anthropology," MA_1. I have spent this much time on it only because of the inordinate difficulty of bringing to the surface, scrutinizing, and dismissing visceral prejudices that subconsciously taint the better angels of our (rational) nature, and that are certainly unworthy of academics and professionals whose own expertise and research is directed in part against such blind prejudices in other cultural arenas. We labored in the preceding two chapters to develop a sympathetic understanding of the origins of these prejudices of collective conscience, and I concluded there, as I repeat here, that it is probably time for members of the discipline to confront and exorcise them.

Before turning in the next chapter to the commission's second category, the controversial "human terrain" projects (MA_2), let me conclude this chapter by considering some of the other possible meanings of the remaining broad category, "anthropology *for* the military," that the commission report identified.

Exploring the Implications of the "Boas Principle"

I worried that the broad dual distinction between "of" and "for" the military that anthropologists introduced into their initial discussions of the CEAUSSIC report in November 2007 was probably insufficient. The commission report, for example, identified a third type of military anthropology that is certainly "for" the military. Accordingly, let us label this MA_3, encompassing anthropologists who work for the government or military in a routine capacity (for example, as language educators and behavioral-science faculty members in federal educational institutions—service academies, ROTC units, war colleges, language institutes, and so forth). Although this surely qualifies as a type of "anthropology *for* the military," the commission report seems clearly to indicate that these activities should not simply be conflated with Human Terrain Systems in the current debate.

In contrast to the commission's second category, the controversial HTS projects (MA_2), those engaged in MA_3 simply do what any anthropologist does: teach and conduct research with the goal of improving our (and specifically, their students') general knowledge of societies and cultures. The commission report identified several presumably unobjectionable activities, such as serving as a conventional faculty member at a military academy or defense university.[13] It should not matter in principle, in a democracy, and in a higher-education system that places the premium on academic freedom that Boas believed it should, that the paycheck happens to come from "Uncle Sam" or the DOD, any more than it matters inherently that the paychecks of others come from the private sector, state government, or, say, a Jesuit institution.

If we believe, once again, that the mere existence of these organizations is itself a moral abomination, then, of course, it would follow that working for them in any sense, no matter how benign the work was in itself, somehow compromises our intellectual integrity or impartiality, or perhaps is morally objectionable on some other grounds we would be obligated to specify. If not, or if we cannot meet the foregoing burden of proof, then we must allow these organizations, like any others, to hire and employ anthropologists for the purposes of teaching to that organization's members general facts about languages, cultural symbols, generic rituals and relationships (such as birth, marriage, and death) in a variety of cultural settings, along with all the other elements that go into fostering enhanced cultural awareness. We would have no grounds for thinking less of, let alone condemning anthropologists for accepting such appointments, unless the specific institution for which they worked, or they themselves, were engaged in morally questionable or objectionable behavior.

The larger point to be appreciated here is this: if we were to acknowledge the validity of some sort of moral argument made against military anthropology merely on the grounds adduced above, then that argument would extend to many other disciplines and individuals as well. We would be obliged to extend our moral condemnation beyond merely anthropologists, and include moral philosophers, for example, who helped a federal academy develop a philosophy program in the hopes of promoting a better liberal arts learning experience for students at such an institution, or improving the students' understanding of the moral underpinnings, legal constraints, and moral obligations incumbent on the members of their profession. The same would apply, mutatis mutandis, for scholars teaching history and military history, religious studies, or literature. And the argument against the moral permissibility of such collaboration would hold, whether the teaching was done to cadets or midshipmen at federal service academies or to university students who happened also to be enrolled in ROTC programs of various types. Our moral condemnation would quickly exceed our reach, and very probably our jurisdiction, and would likely come to encompass we ourselves—for there is a very decent probability that at least some of the students we end up teaching or mentoring during our own careers at any institution in this land will one day end up either collaborating with, or working for, government agencies, military services, and domestic or international constabularies, intelligence, and security forces.

Surely we can't mean to condemn all of this, sight unseen and out of hand! This guilt by association, in fact, constitutes the ultimate reductio ad absurdum of what we might rightly call the "Boas principle." It is what gives condescending moral self-righteousness a bad name. When we look down our moral noses at large swaths of our fellow citizens about whom we actually know very little, the implications of what seem to us as valid moral judgments of their inferior worth end up circling back to haunt and condemn us as well. Hegel, with reference to Robespierre, offered an observation to this effect in his own ruminations on "culture" in the *Phenomenology* (1807), painting a stark portrait of the toxic effects of such judgmental, self-righteous, moralistic factionalism in which, at the end, the guillotine becomes the final leveler.[14]

The Case of the "Jurisdictional Fallacy"

For my part, let me try to demonstrate just how fatuous and intellectually unworthy the Boas principle is, by applying it in an entirely different context. Indeed, I will put it at first in a context far removed from our present debate, but one in which it seems to have the strongest possible claim of meaningful application. Surprisingly, we will return several times in subsequent chapters to the findings of this seemingly irrelevant case, for what it does is help us examine our underlying conception of *moral responsibility*, and the limits on liability that preempt the kind of "guilt by association" that seems to lie at the heart of Boas's own stance. The case helps highlight, in a helpfully altered context, a fallacious form of reasoning that I term "the jurisdictional fallacy," in which individuals or organizations might erroneously assume responsibility for events that are out of their jurisdiction and beyond their reasonable control. The findings in this hypothetical case will thus prove of vital importance in negotiating the appropriate limits on the jurisdictional authority and moral responsibilities properly belonging to the discipline of anthropology, as distinct from "the social sciences" more generally. Thus, if I may plead for a moment's patience, here is the case I have in mind.

Suppose that I am teaching accounting and finance at a nationally renowned business school. One day in class we discuss an arcane accounting topic, "Special Purpose Entities" (SPEs), also known as "Special Purpose Vehicles" (SPVs). These are legally acceptable, perfectly conventional, and widely used procedures for aggregating capital from many sources (such as banks, wealthy investors, and pension funds) for the purpose of purchasing expensive capital assets (e.g., aircraft), which are, in turn, leased by the SPE to companies that need them, but don't have (or don't wish to invest) the capital to purchase them (e.g., most airline companies throughout the world). This is pretty boring, tedious, but important material. Although I am entirely unaware of it, however, there is a bright student in my class (we'll call him "Andy") who realizes that such procedures could also be utilized, perfectly legally, to aggregate debt. The reason for doing so, he recognizes (as I do not), is that neither the assets nor, in his instance, the debt of SPEs or SPVs show up on the accounting records of the parent or contributing companies. The same accounting rule covers both, though the resulting lack of transparency regarding corporate indebtedness was never the intention of the rule (which was meant, quite the opposite, to prohibit companies from double-booking capital assets and thus appearing wealthier or more profitable than they actually were).

"Andy" subsequently goes to work for a large corporation (call it "Enron"), where he discusses his theory with his accountant (call him "Arthur") who agrees with Andy's theory and helps him set up several of these entities, to which they transfer most of the indebtedness of Andy's corporation, making it appear to investors and government oversight agencies much more profitable, and much less debt-leveraged than it really is. At the same time, Andy's school girlfriend (call her "Darleen") goes to work for the Air Force and realizes that a SPE would be a terrific way to buy surplus unsold aircraft from a private company (call it "Boeing"), retrofit them as fuel tankers, and lease them to the Air Force, which has neither time nor budget to build a desperately needed new fleet of tankers from scratch. As a condition for aggregating the deal, however, Darleen wrangles a job for her daughter and a cushy post-retirement vice presidency for herself in the SPE's parent company.

Meanwhile, a few years later, Andy's friends from business school, who always thought Andy was a genius rather than merely a criminal doing time for the collapse of Enron, recommend a complex version of his theory to their boss (call him "Lehman"), and together they proceed to aggregate debt from a variety of sources good, bad, and ugly, blending and "winding" them until even they can't really tell which is which. They run them past their usually grouchy, suspicious and "Moody" investment oversight board, which falls for the ruse and rates these securities as "investment-grade bonds," allowing them to be sold to otherwise conservative investors like banks and pension funds (say, in Iceland). Since Andy was in my class, and I taught him about SPEs, am I to blame for Enron's collapse, the Boeing aircraft scandal, or, finally, the collapse of the entire global financial and credit system?

Under the "Boas principle," I am surely responsible, since I am a business professor and these are businessmen and businesswomen. These are the sorts of immoral things that they routinely do. What else could one expect? I should never have consented to teach them, let alone collaborate or otherwise consort with them, and I am as much to blame as they for their egregiously immoral, widely destructive behavior.

Most of us would probably agree intuitively, however, that I'm not really responsible for all this, even though we'd like to find someone to blame for this mess.[15] But how can I be guiltless, since my knowledge (and Andy's being in my class and learning all this) are ultimately the cause of all the harm?

What we routinely say in moral philosophy is, that in order to hold someone responsible for something, three conditions have to be met: their actions have to be the cause of the problem (mine were, ultimately), and they had to have acted both freely (I did), and knowledgably (i.e., with foresight and intent). Each of these three conditions is a necessary condition for my being responsible, meaning that if any one of the conditions is not fulfilled, then I am not responsible for what eventually happened. Thus moral responsibility differs from, and is a more stringent concept than, legal responsibility, which requires only the first two of the three conditions above. And it is that last condition, acting knowledgeably, with foresight and intent, that seems to be absent in this case. I did not know, foresee, or intend that one or more of my students and their friends would pervert my otherwise arcane teaching in this fashion.

Once again, however, that "ghost of Boas" who is said to frequent our professional consciousness might want to argue that I could have foreseen this, simply because all the people who go to a school like mine in order to pursue a profession in business possess the deficient moral character traits he ascribed to them in his letter denouncing "scientists as spies," for which he was censured. Of course I suspect that most readers realize he could not have really meant this: it was a thoughtless, ill-advised rhetorical flourish, not a considered judgment, that detracted from what was his central moral message (which was inflammatory enough) denouncing both jingoistic war fever and deceptive, duplicitous colleagues who "prostituted" their scientific identities to further it.

At least, so I hope. And if I hope rightly, we would have to backtrack and unwind any remaining trace of moral substance from this otherwise silly and unjustifiable prejudice, which would help remind us (in the present case) that not all schools of business or students of business are remotely as unscrupulous (and probably, also, not as brilliant) as "Andy." And so I could not, finally, have foreseen or intended any of this, and I as "Andy's" teacher am not morally responsible or blameworthy for bringing about the collapse of Enron or the subsequent global crisis based upon the same gimmick, even if my teaching efforts were somehow implicated as the material cause at the heart of these disasters. That principle, in such instances as we have envisioned here, limits our own moral liability or culpability for the unintended consequences of our actions, especially when such consequences not only are not intended, but also could not even be reasonably foreseen. Of course, if the principle protects some, it protects all who fall under its domain of jurisdiction, including colleagues engaged in teaching or conducting research at West Point, Quantico, or the FBI academy.

In the preceding case, note that I have made the most damning possible case against the position I want now to defend. Even in this worst-case instance—that is to say, where the students I have influenced engage in such terrible deeds—I cannot be held liable, nor should I be ostracized for having consented to teach them, because there is absolutely no reasonable way (apart from the worst kind of elitist, ungrounded prejudice) that I could have suspected or foreseen that any of my students would behave in this way. If we now agree, however, to unwind the negative judgments that Boas made about "business men," even in an instance where a small subset of them did, in fact, do egregious harm to others, then we might likewise wish to unwind his similarly unflattering comment about soldiers. For we must recognize that their case, surely at present, is far less egregious on the very worst recounting of it than the story I just told.

When we do that latter unwinding, we likewise see that, though some of them may do wrong or commit atrocities in combat, *most do not*, nor are they any more predisposed to study "murder as a fine art" than normal people engaged in commerce are given to criminal deception and fraud. A soldier is not identical to a murderer or a terrorist, any more than a business "man" is automatically to be equated with a common criminal. The lines demarcating one from the other, on some rare and troubling occasions, may not always be as clear as we might wish, as my case demonstrates. It is the job of the educator, the teacher, to help demarcate those lines more clearly and help students of both professions remain on the proper side of them. And, one might add, it is the job of anthropologists, in particular, to use their expertise to help guide both soldiers and policymakers away from policies or military tactics that might harm precisely those whom the policies and tactics aimed to help. Their expertise is sought instead to assist both military and government personnel in gaining sufficient cultural and regional knowledge to formulate policies more wisely, and to avoid tactics and behaviors that foster hatred instead of cultivating goodwill, greater tolerance, and mutual respect.

It is, in addition, a profound anthropological question to ask what sorts of people, with what sorts of "character" and inclinations, are drawn to professions like the military, and how they are educated and socialized, how they interact with one another, face danger or withstand crisis, and how they manage so consistently (but not unfailingly) to keep themselves and their comrades on the right side of that line. Unlike the research agendas of Project Camelot and the AIR in Thailand, these are anthropological research questions, the answers to which might go far toward helping ensure that the right sorts of individuals gravitate toward or are encouraged to take up these careers, and perhaps help improve the education and the cultural environment that makes them suitable to undertake them. If so, MA_1, the study of the military, and MA_3, the education of soldiers (and sailors and Marines) is not simply "morally permissible." Both, more strongly, constitute *moral obligations* in which every citizen in a democracy has a profound stake, and a corresponding duty to encourage and support.

Notes

1. I have referenced specific instances of these accounts, including those from the specific list of publications above, in earlier citations and below. The episode of *The Diane Rehm Show* on Wednesday, October 10, 2007, titled "Anthropologists and

War," featured guest host Susan Page of *USA Today*, together with anthropologists David Price and Montgomery McFate, reporter David Rohde of the *New York Times* (who wrote the article on "Tracy" and HTS team in Afghanistan, discussed in detail in chapter 5), Col. John Agoglia, the director of the U.S. Army Peacekeeping and Stability Operations Institute, and, via satellite phone, an Army lieutenant colonel who was, at the time, serving as military leader of the 2nd Brigade Combat Team, 82nd Airborne Division Human Terrain Team in Iraq. I will take up the substance of this discussion in chapter 5. It may be accessed in streaming audio from WAMU Public Radio archives at http://wamu.org/programs/dr/07/10/10.php.

2. The details of Kilcullen's career experiences are taken from his own Power-point lecture notes at presentations made at the Marine Corps University and at the U.S. Naval Academy, "Counterinsurgency in Iraq: Theory and Practice, 2007."

3. David Price complains, however, that Nuti is not an impartial or fully reliable source for this, as his own primary responsibilities for the AAA are helping to facilitate increased "contract" work for anthropologists from government and the private sector.

4. The AAA website describes the Executive Board's positions in varying terms, from "opposing" to "strongly disapproving" of HTS as a violation of the AAA Code of Ethics.

5. The full text of this report is available on the AAA website: http://www.aaanet.org/pdf/Final_Report.pdf. A helpful schematic of the variety of types of engagement with MIS can be found at p. 13.

6. This equivocation over what is and is not being proscribed is endemic to the debate, despite repeated attempts at clarification. For example, the Network of Concerned Anthropologists (NCA), including both Price and Gonzalez, has circulated a "Pledge of Non-participation in Counter-insurgency" (NCA 2007) stating that "anthropologists should not engage in research and other activities that contribute to counter-insurgency operations in Iraq or in related theaters in the 'war on terror.'" Denouncing what the statement describes as a "brutal war of occupation which has entailed massive casualties," they go on to clarify their stance: "We are not all necessarily opposed to other forms of anthropological consulting for the state, or for the military, especially when such cooperation contributes to generally accepted humanitarian objectives." They confess, however, that on even this point: "A variety of views exist among us, and the ethical issues are complex." Work that might gain approval includes anything that contributes to "generally accepted humanitarian objectives—e.g., briefing diplomats or working with peacekeeping forces," while that intended to be proscribed includes "work that is covert, work that breaches relations of openness and trust with studied populations, and work that enables the occupation of one country by another." The CEAUSSIC report, by contrast, is considerably less definitive or judgmental about these and related forms of engagement with MIS, preferring to leave that to the professional judgment of anthropologists, as guided by the core precepts of the AAA's Code of Ethics (CEAUSSIC 2007: 26).

7. The report was careful to distinguish two quite different senses of "secrecy": protecting the confidentiality of human subjects, which the AAA Code of Ethics requires, and withholding vital findings from public and scholarly scrutiny for purposes of national security, of which the commission took a dim view, for reasons described earlier in this book. (See my earlier distinctions in chapter 1 regarding secret research projects, secret results, and transparency in conjunction with anonymity, confidentiality, and the principle of informed consent.)

8. This is not a quote, but a feeble attempt at summary of a complex position. What Geertz himself says is: "The concept of culture I espouse . . . is essentially a semiotic one. Believing, with Max Weber, that man is an animal suspended in webs of significance he himself has spun, I take culture to be those webs, and the analysis of it to be therefore not an experimental science in search of [covering] law [n.b., philosopher Carl Hempel's then-standard definition of a "science"], but an interpretive one in search of meaning [n.b., something more akin to Wilhelm Dilthey's *Geisteswissenschaft*]." Geertz goes on to define his "culture concept" as denoting "an historically transmitted pattern of meanings embodied in symbols, a system of inherited conceptions expressed in symbolic forms by means of which men communicate, perpetuate, and develop their knowledge about and attitudes toward life" (Geertz 1973: 5, 89).

9. The evidence for this kind of prejudice against scholars who, in the CEAUSSIC report's own language, "[engage] with the military, intelligence, defense, or other national security institutions or organizations," from which the commission sought to distance itself ("nor do we endorse positions that rule such engagements out a priori"), is admittedly hearsay. Anthropologists who work with or for the military, including Selmeski and Fosher, routinely report being the objects of such negative prejudice from their colleagues, but they may be simply overly sensitive about the nature of the work they do. Obviously, no responsible scholar is willing to go into print with such views. Hence, the strongest evidence for this problem is that the commission found it necessary to introduce these distinctions, and specifically exonerate what I have labeled MA_1 from any distinctive moral opprobrium. There would have been no need to do this were there not some confusion among the wider AAA membership over the issue, and that is all I am trying to establish.

10. Quotation from e-mail in response to my query (September 20, 2008); used by permission. Henk's colleague at the Royal Military College in Canada, anthropologist (and former U.S. Army officer) Brian Selmeski, offers a detailed portrait of the "cross-cultural competence" concept in his white paper "Military Cross-Cultural Competence: Core Concepts and Individual Development." *Centre for Security, Armed Forces & Society Occasional Paper Series*, No. 1. (Kingston, Ont.: Royal Military College of Canada, May 16, 2007), 42 pp.

11. This, it seems to me, accurately describes the set of background assumptions in David Price's massive project to document, not merely the "persecution" by the FBI and CIA of anthropologists who were social activists, but to "expose" those an-

thropologists who worked for such agencies, their predecessors, or the military itself during the past century.

I have cited selections from *Anthropological Intelligence* (Durham, N.C.: Duke University Press, 2008). Price's third volume in the works is tentatively titled *Buying Anthropology: The CIA and Pentagon's Uses of Anthropology during the Cold War*. He offers an account of the overall project on his faculty webpage at St. Martin's University: http://homepages.stmartin.edu/fac_staff/dprice/CW-PUB.htm.

What would decisively falsify my characterization of his work, however, would be the inclusion by Price, in this third volume, of case studies of anthropologists who engaged in such collaborations with heroic and morally praiseworthy results, serving their nation, upholding international law, and perhaps protecting basic human rights in the process. Other members of our nation's (and quite a few other nations') military and intelligence forces have been able to achieve just such accomplishments, certainly during World War II, and even during the Cold War. I have no doubt that anthropologists in their service could do so as well. It would be interesting to hear their stories.

12. Thus, in the radio talk show interviews cited above (Rehm 2007), Col. John Agoglia of the U.S. Army's Peacekeeping and Stability Operations Institute pleads with Price to acknowledge that the U.S. military has learned from its mistakes made in the Vietnam era, and continue to engage with military and intelligence forces, rather than boycott HTS, in their current efforts to employ anthropological expertise to help, rather than harm, victims of war and violence. Price, in this interview, is deeply concerned with those past abuses, but agrees that there are prospects for more positive and constructive engagement in the present.

13. (CEAUSSIC 2007: 9). The main item of professional ethics that emerged in this context was whether or not such individuals would be permitted to carry out unfettered and uncensored scientific research and publication.

14. Interestingly, in his portrait of civic decay during the French Revolution's Reign of Terror, Hegel refers to "culture" as the realm of "self-alienating Spirit," and seems perfectly to capture the poisonous spirit of guilt merely by association. He writes "*Being suspected*, therefore, takes the place, or has the significance and effect, of *being guilty*; and the external reaction against this reality that lies in the simple inwardness of intention, consists in the cold, matter-of-fact annihilation of this existent self, from which nothing else can be taken away but its mere being. . . . The sole work and deed of universal freedom is therefore *death*, a death, too, which has no inner significance or filling, for what is negated is the empty point of the absolutely free self. It is thus the coldest and meanest of all deaths, with no more significance than cutting off a head of cabbage." (Hegel 1807: 360)

15. Or maybe not! Conservative columnist Charles Krauthammer, writing in opposition to the funding of broader access to higher education included in the FY2010 Obama fiscal stimulus plan, clearly does fault higher education (if not professors of accounting specifically) for this fiasco. Lack of college graduates is not our main

problem, he writes: "Indeed, one could perversely make the case that, if anything the proliferation of overeducated, Gucci-wearing, smart-ass MBAs inventing ever more sophisticated and opaque mathematical models and debt instruments helped get us into this credit catastrophe." See "The Great Non Sequitur," *Washington Post* (March 6, 2009), p. A15.

CHAPTER FOUR

Ethics and the "Human Terrain"

Writing against Culture

Anthropologists occasionally engage in a fascinating debate over *essentialism*, a term with a number of distinct meanings. In this case, what is being disputed is the validity of using of a set of generic or commonly shared properties to characterize all the individual members of a set. For anthropology, the "set" is a society or "culture" whose members are the distinct and unique individual human beings who comprise it, and the generic properties are those common elements abstracted from particular narratives, cases, and individual experiences.

The first question a critic of essentialism might ask is whether this inference—from particulars to a small set of generic properties that are thought to characterize or apply somehow to each of these individuals—is a valid inference. This is especially problematic if we relate the question as it arises in anthropology, concerning individuals and their "culture," with the way the problem of essentialism is usually posed in philosophy itself, in terms of otherwise arcane and highly abstract debates in logic about "individuation" and the "identity of indiscernibles." The starting point, at which we group or classify otherwise unique individual entities seems straightforward enough. Individual entities are thought to constitute "members" of a "set" if and only if they share a number of common properties or attributes, the "essential properties" or characteristics defining the set. But if those essential properties define the set, in what sense do they also "define" or characterize each of its individual members? How can those members be distinct "individuals" if they are "defined" merely by their essential properties? This posed the problem of "individuation" in ancient and medieval logic, and in response, the German mathematician and philosopher Gottfried Leibniz eventually reasoned that no two objects (individual entities; unique "substances") can have exactly the same properties.

That principle is known as the identity of indiscernibles, and has come to play an important role in the philosophy of quantum mechanics, while discussion of the "principle of individuation" has enjoyed a renaissance in contemporary continental philosophy and philosophy of psychology. But such otherwise abstruse considerations obviously play a vital role in anthropology as well, as we ponder the relationships between a society or culture (a set defined by its essential properties, shared in common by all its individual members?), and individuals in that society or culture, none of whom (on Leibniz's principle) are exactly alike. How then do we study and characterize them when undertaking ethnographic field studies? What do we write about, what ought we to record?

We determine, as did anthropologist Napoleon Chagnon, for example, to live among, and study the Yąnomamö in the Amazon basin of Brazil and Venezeula (Chagnon 1997).[1] After a period of many months or years of observation, we find ourselves impressed by "the importance that aggression played in shaping their culture," and try to interpret in our ethnographic field notes how the resulting "chronic state of warfare is reflected in their mythology, ceremonies, settlement patterns, political behavior, and marriage practices." Can we reliably do this? And to what extent will the resulting portrait we may sketch of their "society" or their "culture" prove accurate or applicable as a portrayal of the individuals whose "culture" this is? In particular, suppose that the generic features (such as "aggression") that we seem to discern as properties of the group are, in our subsequent writing about them, privileged, "forefronted," and otherwise presumed to "characterize the essentials" of the broader culture to which the original (and actual) individuals and specific situations supposedly belong. Have we, in fact, merely described them, or have we created or manufactured something distinct from them, something perhaps not fully "real" or validly representative? To what extent do our descriptions (in this case, of aggression and its impact on other Yąnomamö "cultural practices") constitute a meaningful definition or description of the "culture" to which the individual members are thought to belong?

According to practitioners of cultural hermeneutics, such as Clifford Geertz, capturing such essentials in anthropological narrative is precisely the aim of field research. His "Notes on a Balinese Cockfight," for example, is a piece of ethnographic writing that appears in virtually every introductory course in anthropology.[2] In the various vignettes so vividly presented therein, Geertz seems to aim at revealing a number of essential features of Balinese culture that lie hidden in this interesting practice, and which it is the task of the field anthropologist to "unmask" through observing and writing about them. We could describe this as "writing culture" (Clifford and Marcus, 1986).

Critics of such cultural ethnography (such as Edward Said 1978, or Lila Abu-Loghad 1991), however, question whether "culture" might well be created—in a sense, "manufactured"—by writing about it in this fashion. The antidote, according to Abu-Lughod, for example, is to balance the macro-accounts of generic social, economic, and political essentials with "relentlessly local ethnography," or what she terms "ethnographies of the particular," using "stories about particular individuals in time and place" as a means of understanding the implicit roles played by power and structure in our wider understanding of "culture" (Abu-Lughod 1991: 149–56). The wonderfully rich field notes that these (and like-minded) anthropologists offer deliberately resist "lifting" the essentials out of their individualized, spatiotemporal context. Field notes become biographies, and sometimes even (as with Mehdi Abedi 1990) autobiographies. We might begin to wonder at this juncture, however, whether the resulting "micro-anthropology"[3] has ceased to be a distinctive discipline (let alone a "science") at all, but has instead collapsed into history, or even literature.

"Essentialism" in the "Human Terrain"

While the nascent philosophical issues in this debate are indeed intriguing, the methodological debate itself among anthropologists is rather clearly one of those "expert issues" that is, by definition, out of my domain. I invoke this debate among specialists in the present context (even thought it is a subject that a nonspecialist probably cannot fully understand or describe accurately), precisely because one might well be led to wonder whether something like "essentialism" or the "writing of culture" is in fact going on in anthropologists' debates with one another over the moral dilemmas of HTS. We saw earlier that this was a problem for the program itself, in the questionable activity of "boiling down" (as I put it) the essentials of complex cultures to a list on a so-called smart card for use by military troops on deployment abroad. It seems, at least, a fair question to raise now, and to invite the experts themselves to consider: is there, in the end, anything like the generic portrait of a "culture" of practitioners aimed uniformly at undertaking activities solidly at odds with the core principles of the anthropologists' Code of Ethics, or has this culture been "created" or manufactured by writing about it? We might ask, along with anthropologist Brian Selmeski, "Who *are* the 'security anthropologists'?" (Selmeski 2007a). The answers are often both different and far more prosaic than the present controversy over this issue seems to imply.[4]

I will leave that intriguing question for the specialists and professionals to ponder, and observe only this: if the methodological controversy itself has any purchase in the discipline, then it might behoove us to take special care to ensure that there are, in the end, *actual individuals*, or *discrete practices*, that correspond to the generic features we have fastened on as characterizations (and condemnations) of them. We would do well in particular to take care to distinguish discrete practices, and the life histories of individuals engaged in them, before reaching a conclusion as to the probability or improbability of such individuals' professional probity or moral rectitude. Just as we discovered that Project Camelot involved no actual project, we might discover in the present case that the hypothetical objections and concerns raised, in principle, against "military anthropology" or "security anthropology," also, like that infamous project itself, indict no actual anthropologists.

What I propose for the remainder of this chapter is to confront that problem as moral philosophers frequently do: by considering hypothetical or "imaginary" cases of anonymous individuals engaging in different variations of the practices in question (such as those characterized in the CEAUSSIC report). This approach allows us to examine whether, in each distinct case, we are able to discern the performance of activities that either violate specific provisions of the AAA Code of Ethics, or that violate broader norms in moral philosophy arising from a consideration of what is known as "just war theory." Frankly, this methodology is less perverse than it might seem since, technically speaking, we discovered above that any general characterizations based upon the behavior of individuals that is not limited to their specific individual biographies are "hypothetical" rather than actual, according to the accounts of this problem offered by anthropological critics of "writing culture." Obviously, such critiques make it well neigh impossible to characterize the behavior (let alone to evaluate the moral rectitude or professional probity of that behavior) of any "actually existing individuals" (as Kierkegaard might put it) solely through reference to properties or characteristics of that behavior that pertain only to their group or society.

Perhaps this is meant as a *reductio* of ethnography generally (at least, of all ethnographic writing that is not either biography or autobiography). In all seriousness, however, I take it as at least a cautionary tale that we might be engaged in a fruitless exercise when we try to describe and either approve or condemn "military anthropology," or "security anthropology," or even something more specific like the Human Terrain System (HTS). Instead, in order to draw any meaningful conclusions, we need specific accounts of "Professor Smith," employed as a military anthropologist at a defined location undertaking "the following specific activities," or "Dr. Jones," deployed as an anthropologist with an HTS team in a specific location, engaging in certain specific activities. And, I must repeatedly stress, we have no such accounts. If there is anything truly substantive about the interesting methodological debate in anthropology over essentialism and "writing against culture," then surely we ought not to do unto our own colleagues what we would never for a moment consider doing to other subjects of routine anthropological research.

The Use and Usefulness of Hypothetical Cases

If one were to search the copious literature concerning the methodology and practice of "applied ethics," it would be a safe generalization to observe that hypothetical cases are extensively used. These cases can constitute an extremely useful analytical tool, provided that they are appropriately constructed out of useful and relevant abstractions from the actual world. Elsewhere in this book (and in other writings cited) I have compared them in this sense to so-called thought experiments in physics, which are carefully constructed abstractions from nature, designed to capture and focus on essential features of a theory. In philosophy, as in physics, these "ideal experiments" are often used to develop consequences which are testable and falsifiable in principle, if not in fact, precisely in circumstances in which actual experiments are difficult (if not impossible) to perform and "actual facts" are, as yet, hard to come by. Such cases also allow us to focus on one issue at a time, in lieu of actual accounts in which complex and morally problematic issues may be hopelessly intertwined.

Such hypothetical cases, or "thought experiments," have additional useful features that I will take up in a moment. For the present, this seems a good approach to follow in discussing HTS, largely because "essentials," or hypothetical practices, alongside deeply flawed and badly misconstrued historical accounts, are (so far at least) primarily what have been invoked as morally problematic about military anthropology in general, and about the HTS program in particular. While opponents and proponents of these practices may, on occasion, display anger toward one another, unlike the case of Napoleon Chagnon among the Yąnomamö or even Oscar Lewis and the Sanchez family,

conspicuously absent so far from the controversy over military anthropology gener-
ally is "finger-pointing," or the testimony or complaints of alleged victims. There
are no specific accounts of individuals allegedly engaged in wrongdoing, nor
are there any concrete accounts of what such individuals did that might constitute unacceptable professional behavior. This is puzzling, even astonishing,
especially for scientists. How can one conduct a meaningful discussion of
charges of professional impropriety or misconduct in the absence of any specific details? I will attempt to address this problem in the next chapter.

In the previous chapter, I laid the foundations and provided the conceptual framework for a thoroughgoing description and detailed moral evaluation of the several dimensions of the Human Terrain Systems (HTS) project
(MA_2), in contrast to other, perhaps less controversial forms of "military
anthropology." I propose that we now explore hypothetically, and in principle, the pitfalls that anthropologists "embedded" with military forces in
combat zones might encounter, and explore the professional probity of what
they might conceivably be asked or expected to do. We can then examine
these problems against the wider backdrop of other sorts of "military anthropologists," working, for example, to provide "cultural orientation" to military
forces as part of the troops' education and training prior to deployment.

Once again, the fractious (and sometimes fratricidal) debate about these
activities in the present actually entails the two distinct lines of moral debate
that we unmasked in our earlier consideration of "Mead's Dilemma" during
World War II, and even more markedly in the counterinsurgency projects
proposed or sponsored during the era of the Cold War and Vietnam. Recall
that these two distinct lines comprise:

1. "Professional" ethics, invoking questions about the propriety and moral
   responsibility of practitioners engaged in field research that are not
   limited solely to anthropologists' involvement with military, intelligence, and security forces.
2. Classical "just war" arguments, in which the legitimacy of outsiders
   collaborating with the members of the military turns in large part on
   whether or not a wider public moral discourse concerning the actions
   in which that military is more generally engaged has deemed those
   activities morally or legally legitimate.

The details of anthropology's conception of "professional ethics," as
enshrined, for example, in the AAA Code of Ethics (1998; revised 2009),
might seem fairly straightforward. We have seen, however, that the current
CoE is highly controversial, especially for its omission (prior to most recent

revisions of 2009) of any explicit reference to the need for transparency, or of language explicitly condemning "secret or clandestine research." We have considered ongoing efforts to revise that code by reinserting language from earlier versions of anthropology's ethical standards that explicitly prohibit such activities. Accordingly, I will provide examples and illustrations of how this contested professional code informs choices and behaviors in a number of different activities associated with HTS. In terms of the preliminary distinctions I drew in chapter 1, for example, we would surely want to know whether the undertaking of "clandestine research projects" constituted a component of the HTS work plan, and if so, whether the results of that research were merely "secret" in the sense of "proprietary,"[5] or whether they were being withheld from the wider public, including those upon whom the research focused, for nefarious purposes.

By far the more complex moral issue concerns item 2 in the list above, namely the wider public moral discourse about the legitimacy of war. In the opening chapters of this book, I endeavored to show how that wider moral discourse was reflected in the more focused and specific discussions of "professional ethics." We also saw how much more difficult the latter discussions became for a given community of professionals whenever the general public itself, within which the profession functioned, was deeply divided over the moral justification of military conflicts in which that wider society found itself engaged. As a civic society, as well as a community of practicing professionals, we were found to grant a far wider license, and offer a wider degree of professional circumspection, when military, intelligence, and security activities were deemed to be, on the whole, morally justified (as during World War II) than we were prepared to grant when our nation's struggles were, even for its own public, far more morally ambiguous (as during Vietnam and the Cold War).

As an example of how this larger moral issue might affect our judgments regarding the proper structures of "professional ethics" in the present circumstances, we might find that our arguments over the legitimacy of cooperating with military efforts in Afghanistan is likely to differ substantially (perhaps by offering more professional latitude) from the evaluation of cooperating with the "illegal" war in Iraq. These, in turn, will likely differ substantially from our assessment of the professional appropriateness of collaborating with military forces engaged in humanitarian interventions (e.g., in Rwanda or Kosovo), or in drug interdiction in Latin America, or in aiding the democratically elected government of a country like the Philippines in dealing with a very limited and unrepresentative Islamic insurgency. The result is that it will prove difficult to formulate a professional stance that is likely to cover all these instances without ambiguity and disagreement.

The use and construction of hypothetical examples in this chapter also differ markedly from those offered toward the conclusion of the CEAUSSIC committee's final report. Accordingly, after finishing with the analysis of hypothetical cases here, I will turn in the next chapter to a consideration of the committee's own ruminations on this problem, and also to actual "real world" cases and conundrums, insofar as these can be found. Using what I believe we will have learned from the present chapter, we will then subject each of the CEAUSSIC examples, and the "real-world" alternatives, in turn, to its own examination.

Examinations of the limited "real-world" variety turn out, even as hypothetical cases do, to have surprising results. Just as our cross-examination of the historical background evidence for anthropology's "litany of shame" did not yield evidence that unequivocally supported that customary litany, so the examination of what is in fact transpiring under the rubric of HTS does not unequivocally support the general disapproval of it. Instead, it reveals new and different problems that demonstrate an urgent need for a method of review and redress that I believe the profession itself must finally adopt. I call that method or approach "anthropologists without borders," and liken it to the international organization of physicians that provide medical care in desolate and desperate areas of the world, without presuming to pass judgment on the wider issues that generate the deep human need to which their organizations' members provide merciful response.

I think, finally, that anthropologists may need to do something similar: to make their expertise available without being beholden to, or sitting in judgment of, any of the parties to the conflicts that generate the human suffering that only they can help alleviate. In procedure and practice, the case made for such anthropological intervention in particular zones of conflict will, in turn, require evaluation and review by something equivalent to an anthropologically oriented institutional review board, in which a diverse jury of peers (perhaps not limited solely to anthropologists) reviews requests for assistance (such as HTS specifics), or job offers, or any other specific proposal to employ anthropological expertise, in order to assure that such proposals meet the requirements of the AAA Code of Ethics, and conform as well to the broader mandates of moral justification. For the moment, we will allow such proposed solutions to await a more detailed evaluation of the specific problems requiring redress.

Contending with the Human Terrain

In table 3.1, I followed the order and distinction of the CEAUSSIC report in distinguishing various kinds of military anthropology. I reserved the label

MA$_2$ to designate their treatment of the "use" of anthropology and ethnography by military forces in the field of combat to improve their knowledge of human or cultural terrain. In marked contrast to their other distinctions of military anthropology, MA$_1$ and MA$_3$, discussed in the preceding chapter, here members and constituent societies of the American Anthropological Association (AAA), and other scholars concerned with the kinds of precedents likely to be set by such work, are certainly correct to worry that the use of anthropology by the military in various guises might invoke a range of serious conflicts of "professional ethics." In light of the functional distinctions we have employed between "ethics" and "morality," however, it does not now follow from their ethical concerns that the activity of providing such assistance is also morally objectionable.

Our wider *moral* evaluation of such practices would instead depend upon *what purposes informed their use, and whether those purposes were aimed at morally worthy or morally abhorrent objectives*.[6] Indeed, such moral arguments might just as well reflect badly on the incompleteness or inadequacies of "professional ethics" in this instance. If the newly revised CoE, for example, were now found to prohibit or exclude activities which are either morally benign or, more seriously, to prohibit activities that are otherwise morally obligatory, then the fault would lie with the code, and perhaps with its sponsoring organization, and not at all with the alleged "ethically wayward practitioner." All of this needs to be thought through carefully in the present context.

To that end, once again I think it helpful to consider yet another of what Clifford Geertz described condescendingly as "those little stories that Oxford philosophers like to tell themselves." And, once again, not everyone will agree with this move. One reviewer of an earlier version of my project denounced my introduction at this point of what he characterized as fictional "straw man" arguments as "bizarre." "Why do this," that reviewer complained,

> when there are so many historical examples (with native Americans, Lansdale, Leach, etc.) that could use documented historical outcomes rather than philosophically constructed relationships to make the author's political point? It is much easier to make such points because *the artificial world constructed for the argument doesn't have to collide with problems of real history*."[7]

These are, in a sense, valid objections, although I have shown that some "real" historical worlds that anthropologists think themselves to inhabit are likewise artificially (and very poorly) constructed. There are two formidable problems with following this reviewer's advice. First, the concern in this book is with a present practice, not these well-known historical abuses. To examine the present through that particular lens on the past begs the very question at issue, by assuming these present activities are already what we wonder them to be: examples of collusion with dark powers with malevolent intent. It is precisely this suspicion that the present-day security anthropologists and their military and security employers are denying as unfounded in fact. Thus, the specific comparisons this reviewer proposes would be hopelessly circular, and not of much use in untangling the present controversy.[8]

Of course, this reviewer's objection would make more sense if it were a demand for examination of genuine examples of present practice in the programs at issue: examples of behaviors by anthropologists working to educate military personnel who then made malevolent use of this information, for example, or examples of anthropologists collaborating with military forces in the hunting down and execution of civilian suspects, or aiding or abetting illegal interrogation of such suspects (through the use of torture). I would be happy to replace hypothetical examples with real-world cases, if any could be found. But, as we will discover in the next chapter, when we turn to present-day case studies of actual practices, there is surprisingly little of substance with which to work. Again, as in the historical case of Project Camelot, we have an extraordinarily large plume of smoke with which to contend, but a rather small fire.

Precisely because the historical accounts on which anthropologists routinely rely (and which this reviewer seems to prefer) are themselves so disputed and so politicized, it turns out that the philosophical methodology of "counterfactuals" proves useful in moral casuistry. Employing this method aids in moving a highly charged and emotional debate like this beyond the "collision with problems of real history," in order to construct a situation whose artificially constrained boundary conditions permit it to contain just precisely, and only, the specific moral dilemma we wish to isolate and examine. It is not impossible to do this with history, but it is exceedingly difficult when that history itself is under emotionally charged interpretive dispute. Whenever and wherever possible, however, I will attempt to point out the close resemblance of fictionalized cases with actual historical examples.

Case 1: Government with Malevolent Intent

To begin, then, let us imagine that a malevolent government wishes to displace a "troublesome tribe" from their ancestral land, so that the majority population can settle on the tribe's territory or mine and sell oil and other natural resources located there without obstacles or resistance. Something like this actually transpired in Burma, in which the government of "Myan-mar" sought to build a pipeline from the rich Yadana natural gas field off its coast to customers in Thailand. The pipeline traversed ancestral lands of an ethnic minority in the country, the Karen, whose members (according to accounts issued by Human Rights Watch and Amnesty International) were brutalized and enslaved by the ruthless Burmese regime to build the pipeline through their land.[9]

In our hypothetical case, by contrast, we will suppose that there are reasons why the government doesn't wish to appear ruthless, or cannot afford to do so (e.g., because its own citizens wouldn't stand for it). So, it employs anthropologists to engage in HTS-like ethnographic survey. These fictitious anthropologists are deployed (like Theodore Downing actually was among the Pehuenche) to study and observe the local population secretly, covertly, on behalf of the government's military and intelligence forces. The aim of this clandestine research is to uncover some vulnerability that would enable the government to manipulate them into appearing to vacate voluntarily.

In our hypothetical case, the government in fact does not care in the least about the welfare or interests of "troublesome" tribe members; it just wants them to vacate without incident. Like the infamous Stasi (Ministerium für Staatssicherheit) in former East Germany, this government finds the use of such "soft power" more effective in achieving and enforcing its edicts than "hard power."[10] HTS researchers discover that troublesome tribespeople are deeply afraid of evil spirits manifest as clumps of bloodied chicken feathers. Upon receiving this intelligence from its HTS researchers, the malevolent government adapts a strategy borrowed from the popular horror movie *The Blair Witch Project* and orders the anthropologists in its employ to place clumps of bloodied chicken feathers covertly, where they will certainly be discovered by troublesome tribe members in numerous, seemingly random lo-cations throughout their territory. Terrified at the sudden appearance of these strange omens, the council of tribal elders meets and advises its members to migrate at once away from the calamitous area to other sites (conveniently provided by the government), thereby achieving the government's morally illicit aims.

This case is a straightforward "con," and the HTS researchers are com-plicit in the government's immoral scheme of fraud, deception, and theft of the tribe's property. The anthropological research in question is clearly secret (either unknown or not fully disclosed), and also clandestine (sneaky, decep-tive, underhanded, and oriented toward nefarious purposes). Such research should be prohibited by the sponsoring profession's code of ethics, because it is clearly immoral: it engages in deception with malevolent intent. The secret research undertaken is morally objectionable, not simply because it is secret, but *because it is concealed precisely in order to enable the doing of harm to the research subjects*. The intent of this project from the outset is to victimize the research subjects (by denying them any compensating benefits, and without their knowledge or consent) by violating their privacy, abrogating their liberty and right to self-determination, and presumably also violating their collective (if not their individual tribe members') property rights.

Such research would have been unethical under the AAA's earlier Principles of Professional Responsibility (1971), but it is important to note that this egregiously immoral scheme was also unethical and unprofessional under the terms of definition of the 1998 version of the CoE, violating explicitly paragraph III (A), provisions 1, 2, and 4 as earlier worded: that is, failing to avoid harm or wrong, and failing to "respect the well-being" of the research subjects (#1); failing to do everything in the researcher's power "to ensure that their research does not harm the safety, dignity, or privacy of the people with whom they . . . conduct research, or perform other professional activities" (#2); and by failing to "obtain in advance the informed consent of the persons being studied," and offering full disclosure of the nature of the work being conducted (#4).

This case is a perfect (if hypothetical) representation of the sort of research that critics imagined Project Camelot to be, and that, in the hands of personnel like Professor Nuttini, it might have become. In that case, however, and despite the international furor that erupted at the time, no activities analogous to what is described above were envisioned by its directors or staff, nor specified in its plan of work, nor was the project itself or its specified activities secret or classified. In sharp contrast, the AIR's project in Thailand appears to have constituted something very closely analogous to this hypothetical (and also nefarious and clandestine) research project. Even worse, the AIR's project proposed to use "hard" as well as "soft" power to manipulate the local populace.

The corresponding suspicion regarding HTS is that all such projects with MIS involve, intend, or ultimately will aim at conducting sorties of the Thailand affair type. If this hypothetical example accurately captures the essential features of actual HTS requirements and practices, then HTS would rightly fall into the category in which it has provisionally been placed, for example, by the AAA Executive Committee resolution of October 31, 2007: namely, as a "problematic" and finally as "an unacceptable application of anthropological expertise" (AAA 2007). It remains for us to consider, in the next chapter, what actual HTS projects actually propose, and how they are actually (as opposed to hypothetically) conducted.

Case 2: Illegal Military Intervention

In order to see how background moral considerations affect our professional judgment, we consider a second hypothetical example. In this instance, we suppose that the large and powerful military forces of one nation invade another sovereign nation without bothering to obtain the authorization required under existing international laws and treaties that govern the very limited conditions in which such interventions may be conducted. The leaders of these military forces now wish to eliminate armed resistance to their illegal occupation, and preferably, to capture, disarm, or kill the members of the opposing militia or insurgency embedded in the local population until the insurgency is put down. The invading force employs scholars for HTS research, in order to help it sort out key identifying characteristics of insurgent forces in a manner that will render them relatively transparent and easy to spot, without their knowledge, or that of the local populace. This makes it easier for the invaders finally to defeat the insurgency.

By intention, this second example hits closer to home. It could be taken to represent the U.S. war of intervention in Iraq. As we will see, however, it can be made to represent a number of other historical cases. No matter what historical examples one perceives mirrored within it, given the boundary conditions described, there would be, quite properly, a strong "hermeneutic of suspicion" about this military expedition, and certainly a reluctance on the part of social scientists to cooperate in carrying it out. Even in this instance, surprisingly, we can clearly demonstrate that the cooperation of anthropologists with the invading military force through various sorts of HTS activities is not, simply as a matter of principle, either unethical or immoral. Instead, the ethical and moral legitimacy of anthropologists participating in this invading military's HTS efforts would depend critically upon the following factors:

1. The *moral* legitimacy of the invasion or intervention (given that, in this hypothetical case, it is technically in violation of international law)
2. A corresponding moral evaluation of the legitimacy of the insurgency
3. The aims or objectives for which the "anthropological intervention" (e.g., HTS efforts themselves) are being carried out.

Rather than being automatically "off limits" to anthropologists, in this instance there is clearly an enormous burden of proof that must be met before anthropologists could legitimately take part in HTS. We might begin by using a distinction introduced in earlier chapters, and saying that there is a strong prima facie ethical duty for anthropologists not to collaborate with the invading forces. Specifically, there are objectives described in this example, similar to the AIR's project in Thailand, that no anthropologist should propose, and in which no anthropologist should participate, such as helping the military to identify and kill enemy insurgents. This would be the case even if the targeting and killing of the insurgents could be morally justified as an otherwise legitimate military objective. That wider moral justification does not translate, in anthropology's case, into a professionally legitimate ("ethical") objective.

In this case, the overall burden of proof falls heavily upon the governing authorities on whose behalf the invading military forces are carrying out their intervention, because it is unauthorized by the legitimate forms of authority set forth in international law.[11] The first two of the three criteria listed above that the military forces would have to meet in this case are *moral* criteria. They pertain directly to what we earlier (in chapter 1) labeled and described as "just war doctrine," or just war "theory." It is according to these first two criteria alone that the overall operation of invasion or intervention, as well as the general participation of military personnel and insurgents engaged in it, will be evaluated.

The third criterion, by contrast, pertains only to anthropologists in this instance. It invites the application of the anthropologists' own professional code of ethics to the specific activities in which they are asked to engage in support of the (justified or unjustified) war. All this follows, and in a sense explains, the pattern of guidance offered in the CEAUSSIC commission report. Judgments reached according to this third criterion are limited in jurisdictional authority. They do not, in contrast to judgments employing the first two moral criteria, help us whatsoever in determining the morality of the war of intervention itself, nor reach a moral evaluation or judgment of the military personnel, insurgents, or others participating in it. Judgments of "ethical" or "unethical" behavior according to the third criterion above pertain only to members of the profession.

What this jurisdictional distinction entails, for example, is that it would be quite possible to discover that the war of intervention was morally justified (even if illegal), but that it would still be "wrong" in the sense of "unprofessional" (i.e., a violation of some provision of the profession's code of ethics) for anthropologists to participate in it. Conversely, it would also be possible to discover that the war of intervention was immoral (morally unjustifiable) as well as illegal under international law, and yet still discover that it *would* be acceptable for anthropologists to collaborate with one side or the other, depending upon the circumstances and on what they were being asked to undertake. Such is the nature and importance of professional jurisdiction. Thus, the only condition under which this last eventuality could be absolutely ruled out would be under what we might term the "Turner" condition: that is, the case in which any and all forms of collaboration of any sort, under any conditions, with military, intelligence, and security personnel were ipso facto prohibited in the profession's written code of ethics.

It is critical to keep these distinctions and questions of jurisdiction firmly in mind. It is quite easy, if utterly invalid, to stray back and forth from one to the other. In our first case, for example, the government's (and military's) larger objectives were immoral, and also we discovered that the collaboration of anthropologists in those activities would be unethical. In contrast, we might find it morally justifiable to, say, pursue terrorists or maritime pirates and employ deadly force against them if necessary. That is one question. A separate question would be whether an anthropologist's disciplinary expertise could be enlisted in those efforts. In terms of these distinctions, for example, the anthropologist, like a medical doctor or a psychologist, might be able to say without contradiction: "I approve *morally* of your pursuit of terrorists or pirates. But I am prohibited *ethically*, as a member of my profession, from bearing arms, or from materially aiding you otherwise in this pursuit." The doctor or psychologist could, of course, provide life-saving medical or psychological care for the military, provided such care was also available to any terrorists or pirates they might apprehend, and provided they were not asked to assist directly and materially in using force against or otherwise harming the pursued individuals (such as aiding in illegal interrogation or torture of captured suspects).

With respect to the first criterion applied to our second hypothetical case of illegal intervention, however, we might think that the moral burden of proof could not possibly be met by the invading government, simply because this invasion entailed a violation of what are termed the "bright line" or "black letter" statutes of international law. That position, known as "legal positivism" (the law simply is what the legislators, and the statutes they legislate, say it is), does not work very well in international law. International law is composed of roughly three parts: the specific written statutes and treaties (according to which this hypothetical invasion is illegal); what is known as *ius gentium*, the habits and customs of civilized nations and peoples; and thirdly, what are termed "tolerated practices," something analogous to the role of "precedent" in domestic law (Arend 1999). Sometimes the written statutes codify and clarify the other two, as in the landmark "Lieber Code" (1863),[12] and the subsequent formal treaty protocols of the several Hague and Geneva Conventions pertaining to the conduct of war and protection of war's victims. But in other instances, different sources of law may conflict. There is no founding document, like the U.S. Constitution, or other "grounding document" or set of fundamental principles from which to resolve conflicts between practices sanctioned from these distinct sources. It is thus possible that even clear violations of specific statutes might be offset by the remaining factors—as in the case of NATO's attacks against Serbia in the Kosovo war, which were deemed by British lawyers at the time "illegal, but necessary."[13]

The second factor, the legitimacy of the insurgency itself, seems to bear an inverse relationship to the first: that is, if the invasion or intervention is not morally justifiable, then, at least prima facie but not necessarily or inevitably, the insurgency is morally justifiable. We will test this assumption further, below.

The third "professional" criterion (item #3 in the list above) is not only limited in jurisdictional authority. It is also not specific to Iraq, or even to assisting invading military forces in hypothetically illegal situations. Instead, as we have seen, that "professional ethics" criterion calls attention to questions that must be asked with respect to any sort of intrusion or intervention by an anthropologist into a host culture (as, for example, the intervention by anthropologist Napoleon Chagnon in the Ya̧nomamö "culture"): for the sake of what, or whom, is the cultural intervention taking place? In all anthropological research, including that undertaken for or under the sponsorship of MIS (as the CEAUSSIC report makes clear), the project must, at very least (1) avoid deliberate doing of harm to the subjects studied; and (2) where possible, carry out the research for their benefit; and, in any case, *maintain transparency and informed consent, and avoid resort to secrecy* for any purposes other than to protect the privacy and confidentiality of research subjects.

It may seem at this point that we are proceeding too cautiously. After all, the second example sounds very much like Germany's invasion of Poland in 1939, or Japan's invasion of Manchuria in 1931 (or, closer to home, the U.S.-led coalition invasion of Iraq in 2003). And weren't all these wars of intervention patently unjustified?

Once again, the value of those "little stories" that philosophers tell themselves is that, in direct contrast to ethnographic accounts like Geertz's, these "stories" are intentionally devoid of specific cultural or historical content. That does not render them empty or useless. Instead, they allow us to examine the formal structure of certain circumstances and helpfully vary the boundary conditions, making them temporarily independent of terribly confusing cultural specifics. And nothing could be more apt than to describe the cultural specifics, in the case of Iraq in particular, as confusing. So let us proceed to vary or tweak those boundary conditions in three distinct versions of this second case, and determine what results from those thought experiments.

Case 2, Variation 1: Germany's Invasion of Poland

We begin with an easy example. We proceed to fill in the cultural and historical blanks in the formal, structural case above with Nazi Germany as the invading force and Poland in 1939 as the sovereign nation invaded. None of the three criteria for HTS legitimacy cited above could possibly be met. The invasion itself is immoral by conventional just war doctrine, as well as illegal under international laws and treaties in force then and since. Reciprocally, the status of any corresponding insurgency that might arise as resistance to tyranny and as a defense by the victimized population of its liberty and the basic human rights of its citizens is, rather clearly, morally justified. Hence any efforts to subvert it using social science are illegitimate, regardless of any enhanced scientific understanding that might result, simply because in this historical case, the anthropologist's collective professional criteria of ethical behavior, including "do no harm, avoid secrecy, and try where possible to benefit," also could not possibly be met.[14]

Case 2, Variation 2: The Rwandan Genocide

But now (by way of sneaking up on Iraq) let's try a harder case. This one is still at least partially "counterfactual," that is, it is not a historical case, but a hypothetical one based upon history. Imagine that the tragic Rwandan genocide of 1994 had unfolded in a slightly different fashion than it actually did. Rather than sending a paltry undermanned peacekeeping force as the U.N. initially did, imagine instead that the U.N. Security Council, faced with that impending crisis, had done absolutely nothing but stubbornly uphold the baseline principle of sovereignty and territorial integrity. Imagine that representatives of the Security Council's member nations had refused to intervene, upholding (as they often do) a contemporary variation of what philosopher John Stuart Mill denounced in his day as a "morally shabby refrain": to wit, that "none of our member-nations' interests are involved."[15] Imagine likewise that, for a variety of reasons, the Belgian government, mortified by these consequences of its colonial legacy, assumed full responsibility for the impending tragedy as stemming from its own earlier policies in the region. Accordingly (in our counterfactual variation) Belgium unilaterally decides to send an invading military force to quell the violence, but *without either U.N. authorization or invitation from the recognized local government.*

In this admittedly hypothetical and decidedly counterfactual case of an unauthorized humanitarian intervention, quite different from the historical Rwandan genocide, I think it is pretty obvious we are faced with a very difficult moral dilemma. For starters, Belgium has no "right" to enter or invade Rwanda with a military force. For it to proceed to do so anyway, without U.N. authorization, would constitute a clear violation of the "bright line" statutes of international law. The Belgian government offers a different defense, flung, appropriately, "in the teeth of the law" (to use Father Daniel Berrigan's phrase). *The Belgians argue that they have a moral responsibility to come to the aid of potential victims of genocide*, especially because their earlier colonial policies had helped bring these conditions about. So they argue that their intervention, while illegal, is nonetheless "morally necessary" or obligatory.

This is not such a farfetched scenario, since members of the international community argued along these lines with respect to Kosovo in 1998, and are doing so in the early 2000s with respect to the civil strife in Darfur. The arguments are, in effect, that *the provisions of international law are not sufficiently robust to address the moral responsibilities* befalling members of the international community to come to the aid of victims of genocide. With respect to the second criterion, pertaining to the legitimacy of the "insurgency": I think it would be difficult to conclude that the marauding Hutu Interahamwe (the youth militia, or "civilian defense force" founded by Rwandan president Juvénal Habyarimana),[16] as a kind of "insurgency," were morally legitimate in their intention to slaughter rival Tutsi as well as any of the intervening Belgian soldiers they could capture, merely because the Belgians were not legally entitled to intervene to prevent this.[17]

Now let us focus further on some essential features of this decidedly counterfactual case. Recognizing the enormity of the impending problem, in our hypothetical case *the Belgians deploy anthropologists in HTS teams* to discover, if possible, ways of heading off the impending genocide. Let's just say, for the sake of argument, that they find subtle cultural inroads that, when effectively deployed, have the effect of defusing the crisis. As nonspecialists, the Belgian military (like myself) has no idea what these "cultural inroads" might be, or whether there even are any. That is why they employ the anthropologists as subject-matter experts.

Our hypothetical Belgian HTS anthropologists, thankfully, *are* subject-matter experts. They discover vital "cultural" information that, when properly used, helps defuse the crisis. Some Tutsi are regrettably killed by Hutu militia, but not nearly as many as might have been otherwise. Regrettably, also, the invading Belgian military forces incur some casualties of their own, and kill and wound some Hutu, and capture and imprison (but, importantly, do not torture or mistreat) others. It was no part of the intention of HTS anthropologists to aid and abet this unfortunate killing on both sides; indeed, quite the opposite.

This is quite problematic, I admit; but I would submit that in this instance the third criterion above, the one specifying the baseline duties of the profession itself in such instances, is fully met. *This HTS project is not only morally permissible, but praiseworthy.* As to the unintended negative consequences that did ensue, our anthropologists, at very worst, find themselves in a situation similar to that of the hypothetical accounting professor in the previous chapter. They are accordingly not guilty of any moral or professional wrongdoing or liability for these deaths. Indeed, in this instance, what is known in moral philosophy as the doctrine of double effect (DDE) specifically comes to their rescue, clarifying that the legitimacy and praiseworthiness of their actions are not compromised by the secondary effect of some of the "insurgents" in this case being killed, wounded, or captured.

Here is how the DDE itself works. Recall, first, that it is a violation of the professional code of ethics to deliberately aid in targeting and killing enemy insurgents. In this case, we have stipulated that it was not part of the anthropologists' intention to engage in, aid, or abet such killing. Quite the opposite. We believe intuitively that they cannot and should not, therefore, be held morally liable for these unfortunate occurrences, and indeed that they deserve thanks and praise for helping ensure that the crisis (and the killing) was not much worse. Thomas Aquinas would account for this intuition by saying that the decision to deploy anthropologists in this campaign had "two effects," one deliberately intended and morally legitimate (helping to defuse the genocidal crisis), the other entirely unintended, even though it is, strictly speaking, "morally evil" (that is, by aiding and supporting the overall intervention, the anthropologists also, strictly speaking, aided in bringing about the deaths of Hutu, Tutsi, and even some of the Belgian soldiers who did end up dying).[18]

As common sense would also seem to dictate in this case, we do not blame the anthropologists for these unfortunate side effects of their primary activities. Nor do we accuse them of having somehow violated the ethics of their profession for having participated in the limited and specific way that they did in helping to limit the carnage, merely because some people ended up getting killed despite their best efforts to prevent this. Likewise, even if it was not fully possible to obtain informed consent, we may safely presume under the circumstances that they had the required consent of the victims, and that the consent of the perpetrators of genocide was, in this instance, irrelevant. More important, the anthropologists acted throughout to obey what we might term the "prime directive" of their professional code: to employ their knowledge and expertise to the benefit, and not the harm, of those whom they "studied."[19]

This variation of our second case, it seems to me, applies equally well to the role of anthropologists participating with U.S. military and security forces on HTS teams in Afghanistan and Iraq. Whether those anthropologists are violating professional canons and codes of conduct, let alone whether they are morally blameworthy, will depend specifically upon what they are asked to do while deployed. They are not acting unprofessionally or unethically, let alone immorally, simply by agreeing in principle to assist with limiting the harm done to local populations by the military intervention in these cases.

While this conclusion may seem clear to some, others will remain suspicious, and we should attend carefully to those suspicions. In particular, even if I am right about the analogy with Afghanistan, how can this judgment of nonculpability extend to aiding the military in its war in Iraq, whose legal status is virtually beyond question and whose moral legitimacy (to put the matter politely) remains sharply disputed? Let's proceed to find out.

Case 2, Variation 3: Intervention in Iraq

To explore these questions, consider a third variation of our second case, in which the moral legitimacy of the military invasion is initially in heated dispute, and *subsequently turns out to be insufficient* (or mistaken). The moral legitimacy of the insurgency, however, is mixed at best, and is certainly not like our first variation, a clear case of insurgents resisting aggression and defending the homeland's liberty and the rights of its citizens. Instead, it is more like the second variation just concluded, in which the insurgents are taking advantage of the breakdown of law and order caused by the questionable invasion, in order to avenge long-simmering ethnic, racial, or religious divisions and hatreds, or as in the case of Al Qaeda in Iraq, foment dramatic, politically charged mischief.

Interestingly, in this third case, the role of HTS anthropologists comes centrally to the fore. The invading force, seeking to minimize the impact of its mistakes, implores social scientists for help to defuse the insurgency, stop the killing, restore order, and extricate themselves from the mess they (or rather, their government) made. Again, in this instance, and providing the overall "professional" criterion (item #3 above, adhering to the provisions of one's professional code) has been fully met or is being fully met, the participation in HTS projects is morally justifiable. Note that such HTS projects cannot be directed toward interrogation or torture, nor can their intent, consistent with criterion #3, be to aid the invading force to capture or kill insurgents. Instead, their intention and objective is to assist the invading force to halt violence, restore order, make and keep peace, and get out and go home. To clarify: HTS team members cannot justifiably help the invading forces to capture, "illegally" interrogate (i.e., torture), or kill insurgents. Rather, their work is to understand and enlist the aid of the local population for its sake and safety to restore order, avoid violence, make peace, and establish the rule of law.

Naturally, it would require considerable vetting by the anthropologists' professional organization in order to ensure the full compliance of its participating members with these principles and constraints on what could and could not be undertaken. How that might occur, or how such safeguards might be organizationally implemented, I will address in my final chapter. At this point, it is difficult to speculate on the substantive features of peer review, absent some better understanding of just what HTS teams are asked to do and how that is actually translating from policy and plans into concrete action in combat zones.

Summary of Results

For the moment, where do these hypothetical examples and variations leave us with the AAA and its problem with HTS in Iraq and Afghanistan? That depends upon whether either of those two wars, and the proposed role of HTS anthropologists in each, is more like variation 1 (Nazi Germany), or more like variation 2 (Belgium in Rwanda), or variation 3 (similar to Iraq). Now, of course, these two actual wars are like none of those three cases, but I will argue that the current war in Afghanistan at least is vastly more akin to the second case variation than the first, and Iraq is even more akin, by design, to the third case variation (which is itself a slightly more morally ambiguous variation of the second). And in variations 2 and 3, the matter of anthropologists serving on HTS teams is not automatically proscribed in principle (as the AAA Executive Committee originally proposed), but is critically dependent upon the outcome of the larger, just war argument. That is: in this case (and, I suspect, in most cases) the appropriateness of social scientists aiding and abetting government projects like HTS is critically tied to the moral legitimacy of those projects and, if those projects be wars, including wars of humanitarian intervention or wars of counterinsurgency to topple tyrants or combat terrorism, then the moral legitimacy of HTS becomes inextricable from the larger "just war" debate about those conflicts themselves.

To summarize the argument and its provisional conclusions: we considered two distinct cases, and gave three variations of the second. Case 1 was designed to look like what Project Camelot was (mistakenly) thought to be, and what the AIR's project in Thailand surely seemed to be. In that case, we had little difficulty discerning that the activities and proposed activities of the anthropologists in question were a violation of professional ethics, both because any reasonable code of ethics would prohibit such activities and because the specific activities were also not morally justifiable. That was fairly straightforward, and helped us discern that at no point did the relevant issue ever turn on involvement in "secret or clandestine research," but instead turned entirely on the underlying intent of such research to gather information, covertly or otherwise, and use it to harm the research subjects without their knowledge or consent.

The initial broad and nonspecific outline of the second case was far more morally ambiguous: postulating an "unauthorized" war of intervention with an accompanying request for anthropologists to assist in carrying it out. To help clarify the nature of the moral ambiguity, we considered three distinct variations of this second case. Variation 1 removed the ambiguity by identifying the intervening force as Germany in Poland in 1939, an illegal and morally unjustifiable intervention, and the intent of the invading force to crush and destroy any insurgency and kill the insurgents. Such activities were clearly a violation of professional ethics; they were also morally unjustifiable because the activities themselves were prohibited by the profession's code and the war in which these professional activities were to be undertaken was itself illegal and immoral.

These conclusions, even granting the same formal structure of case 2, did not carry over to the second variation, however, which involved a hypothetical "unauthorized" intervention by Belgium in Rwanda to halt an ensuing genocide. The provisions restraining anthropologists from deliberately engaging in research in order to do harm (such as helping to kill insurgents) were likewise not lifted in this case. But because there were no explicit provisions of the intervention aimed at such illicit activity, and indeed, since the overall intention of the "illegal" intervention was to safeguard potential victims of genocide, the intervention proved to be morally justifiable and the involvement of anthropologists in it professionally sound and morally praiseworthy, even though some members of the warring factions, and the intervening army, did end up getting killed. They were not killed by the activities of the HTS anthropologists assisting the intervention, but in spite of them. The anthropologists, by assisting the intervention, did not intend anyone's death; indeed, they intended the opposite. That they supported and assisted in an illegal intervention in which military forces, "insurgents," and other partisans ended up nonetheless getting killed does not itself, under these conditions, impugn either the professional probity or the moral rectitude of the anthropologists.

Finally, for the sake of thoroughness, we constructed a third variation of case 2 in which the intervention was illegal and was also undertaken for reasons that were less morally straightforward and praiseworthy than the hypothetical Belgian intervention in Rwanda. By design, this final variation was constructed to resemble the U.S.-led invasion of Iraq. In this instance, the evaluation of professional conduct of HTS anthropologists was found to depend entirely upon what they intend to do and what they are specifically asked or expected to do, provided that the background intention for involving them was as described. That is (as with the counterfactual Rwandan case), the purpose of the anthropologists' involvement must be to avoid casualties, restore trust and security among local populations for their benefit (and presumably with their consent), to extricate the intervening troops from the problematic conflict, and withdraw as quickly as possible. Once again, the matter of "secret or clandestine research" did not play a role in reaching these conclusions. What did play a role, and should actually play a role in real-world deliberations, however, is independent oversight and peer review of these projects, and sustained monitoring of the activities in question. We should identify this requirement as tied to the principle of transparency, and we will take up these vital, procedural matters in the concluding chapter.

For the present, I believe that the conclusions drawn from the preceding examples are valid, inasmuch as they seem to follow or represent the proper inferences to be drawn from the specified boundary conditions. They are also "sound" in that they are grounded in the factual details stipulated. Nevertheless, these conclusions—based on abstract principles, formal codes of conduct, and hypothetical cases—are sharply at odds with conclusions reached within the American Anthropological Association (AAA) itself about the professional inappropriateness of HTS projects in particular. My analysis in this chapter suggests that those AAA conclusions, insofar as they are grounded in speculation about facts or reflection upon principles alone, were and are badly mistaken. But of course, I could be mistaken in this conclusion. That is for the profession itself to decide.

What I think the preceding account demonstrates most clearly is how professional judgment about ethics can be clouded by moral controversy. The controversy in question concerns the moral legitimacy of this nation's wars "against terror" in Afghanistan, and even more especially in Iraq. Against the backdrop of public controversy of this magnitude, it is quite easy to lose sight of one's professional bearings. There is no great shame in that, but it is now time for the profession to do a much better job than it has thus far in examining these questions. In particular, what I hope colleagues will recognize is that, absent concrete examples of specific individuals (such as Oscar Lewis or Napoleon Chagnon) whose behavior we can evaluate, or of specific incidents or affairs (like El Dorado, the Sanchez affair, or the AIR's research proposal in Thailand) whose structure we can scrutinize, it is very easy to be led astray and to draw invalid, mistaken, and often irrelevant conclusions about what might constitute the limits of acceptable professional practice.

Notes

1. The following account and quotations come from pp. 5–31. I am not planning specifically to revisit the controversy that surrounded the exposé, *Darkness in El Dorado* (Tierney 2000). I am more interested in reflecting on what Carolyn Fluehr-Lobban's careful analysis of that case revealed about what actually happened, rather than on what was initially alleged (Fluehr-Lobban 2003b), and about what the controversy and Chagnon's study represent for anthropology's historical litany, particularly with respect to the clash of otherwise defensible research methodologies and the principle of informed consent.

2. "Deep Play: Notes on the Balinese Cockfight," (Geertz 1973: 412–454).

3. This is my term to capture Abu-Lughod's contrast, analogous to the practice of distinguishing micro- and macro-accounts in economics. Abu-Lughod seems to imply that something similar might be at stake in anthropology, and expresses strong preference for those micro-accounts. In economics, by contrast, both are accorded validity, although both methodologies and modes of analysis are quite distinctive in the the two realms and the causal connections are often unclear. What one might cite in support of Abu-Lughod's preference is that, in some instances, it constitutes a critical blunder to mistake the domain to which a phenomenon might properly be said to belong. Occurrences of regional famine, for example, were long thought to be properly understood as macroeconomic phenomena until Amartya Sen demonstrated that they are much more accurately understood as microeconomic phenomena. See *Poverty and Famines: An Essay on Entitlement and Deprivation* (Oxford: Oxford University Press, 1981), the work which earned Sen the Nobel Prize in Economics in 1998. That example dramatically demonstrated that it is important to know in *which domain* one is properly working, rather than merely to dismiss one or the other as irrelevant.

4. This brief editorial plea for tolerance and understanding, incidentally, offers evidence of some of the shocking prejudice referred to earlier, in chapter 3. Selmeski describes comments like "scum with Ph.D.'s who stand beside torturers," and "rogue anthropologists" aimed at persons who are involved primarily in higher education in federal institutions.

5. David Price offers this distinction, with wider latitude granted to the former, in "Anthropology Sub Rosa," (2003: 29–30): "Secret or covert research is research in which an anthropologist does not disclose the true nature of his or her research to participants, or is research in which findings are made available only to a select body that does not include research participants. In principle, proprietary research differs from secret research because anthropologists engaging in proprietary research are unlikely to mislead research participants and the results of their research are often to be made available on a designated later date." Clearly, to his credit, Price is bending over backwards to be fair to proponents of "practice anthropology," which entails "proprietary" research, since he recognizes that this, too, could easily collapse into simple deception for inappropriate ends, as threatened, for example, in the case of the World Bank and the Pehuenche in Chile in 1998.

6. So, for example, it would likewise matter for what purposes military force was deployed to keep order and enforce the law: would this preference for law and order merely serve the interests of an imperial power, or would it truly be intended for the purposes of peace-keeping, security, and protection of the innocent from threat of harm? Those radically different intentions would make a significant moral difference in evaluating what otherwise would appear to be indistinguishable military actions (Rubinstein 2008: 146).

7. These are quotations from a review by an anonymous anthropologist of my original article for the *Journal of Military Ethics*, dated May 10, 2008. I have endeavored to address these deficiencies and omission in preceding chapters in the present work, although interestingly, neither of the names he cites figure strongly or consistently as figures or references in other historical accounts by anthropologists of wanton abuse and unprofessional conduct. This merely proves my point, made earlier, that the specific selections of incidents outside the mainstream moral history of the discipline is a matter of personal interpretation and not of settled disciplinary perspective. The practice of anonymous peer review, incidentally, constitutes another widely endorsed and approved example of "secrecy" that is neither clandestine nor deceptive (at least not necessarily or in principle).

8. That circularity is apparent in the radio discussions among anthropologists and military officers on *The Diane Rehm Show* (October 10, 2007). Professor Price persistently referred to the sorry history of such collaboration during the Cold War and Vietnam, without offering specific indictments of any present practices. Likewise, Dr. McFate and her Army colleagues persistently claimed that they had learned "hard lessons" from that prior history, and that HTS activities were utterly unlike any of those that Price condemned. The program may be accessed at http://wamu.org/programs/dr/07/10/10.php.

9. An excellent account of this case can be found in Manuel G. Velasquez, *Business Ethics: Concepts and Cases*, 6th ed. (New York: Pearson/Prentice-Hall, 2006), pp. 119–122. Astonishingly, after I cited this relatively obscure case in Lucas (2008) and in the first draft of this book, a new "Rambo" movie (starring Sylvester Stallone re-

prising his aging hero living out his life as a boatman and snake-catcher in Thailand) was released, in which the plight of the Karen (who happen to be largely Christian) became the focal point for intervention by the movie's hero.

10. This distinction between coercive and persuasive power was first introduced in international relations in the 1980s by Joseph Nye, a former dean of, and now professor at, the Kennedy School of Government at Harvard University. See *Soft Power: The Means to Success in World Politics* (New York: Perseus/Public Affairs Books, 2004).

11. Article 2(4) of the United Nations Charter prohibits the use or threat of force against the territorial integrity or political independence of any state. Article 2(7) extends this prohibition to the collective action of the U.N. itself, granting full domestic jurisdiction to member states and prohibiting the supranational body from intervening in matters "which are essentially within the domestic jurisdiction of any state," save in the case of collective self-defense as determined through an appropriate deliberative body of the U.N. (such as the Security Council), as described in Article 51 and Chapter VII. It is as straightforward as such matters can be that none of these conditions pertain to, or were satisfied by, the international deliberations leading up to the most recent war in Iraq, for example.

12. This is the shorthand name for one of the founding sets of "bright line" statutes of international law, known formally as General Orders 100, promulgated by U.S. President Abraham Lincoln on April 24, 1863, and prepared for that purpose by a German-American lawyer and professor of jurisprudence, Francis Leiber. The statutes govern conduct by military personnel in combat, and were subsequently taken up as guidelines for the Prussian army, and ultimately formed the cornerstone for provisions in the Geneva Conventions on the Conduct of War. The "Lieber Code" in a text from 1898 is available from the Avalon Project at the Yale University Law School: http://www.yale.edu/lawweb/avalon/lieber.htm.

13. This interesting phrase gained currency through use in a committee report for the British Parliament: see Patrick Witnour, "MPs Say Kosovo Bombing Was Illegal but Necessary," *London Guardian* (June 7, 2000). For a broader discussion of this dilemma, see Anthony C. Arend and Robert J. Beck, *International Law and the Use of Force: Beyond the United Nations Paradigm* (London: Routledge, 1993). Indeed, some international relations scholars argue that international law governing the resort to force had either broken down or had been effectively rewritten through practice, in the wake of Rwanda, Bosnia, and Kosovo: see, for instance, Michael J. Glennon, *Limits of Law, Prerogatives of Power: Interventionism after Kosovo* (London and New York: Palgrave Macmillan, 2001).

14. Robert Rubinstein poses an interesting question in this case: while the anthropologist clearly should not work for the morally illicit intervening military force, could he or she legitimately work for the insurgents fighting *against* this unjustifiable intervention? I suspect I would have Margaret Mead's concurrence in suggesting "yes." But I can see how others might disagree in principle, since this collaboration

with the resistance might involve their implication in secrecy or the doing of harm. Happily, insurgents in this case probably don't need anthropological expertise, since they're in their own country, so it is likely a moot point, although they would need the anthropologist merely as citizen to help fight against the invasion.

15. John Stuart Mill, "A Few Words on Non-Intervention" (1859). Reprinted in *Dissertations and Discussions: Political, Philosophical and Historical*, Vol. 3 (London: Longman, Green, Reader and Dyer, 1867), p. 158.

16. It is not at all my intention to analyze further the actual historical events leading up to this well-studied disaster. For details of the Rwandan case, see Lucas and Tripodi 2006.

17. Nota Bene: There was widespread confusion over this matter during the Rwandan crisis, in which leading diplomats assiduously avoided use of "the G-word" in order (so they apparently thought) not to incur a political obligation to intervene. The U.N. "Genocide Convention" of 1948, however, neither authorizes nor obligates nations to undertake military action in response to such emergencies. That, in turn, is because there are no substantive procedures defined or set forth in that document that would automatically be set into motion by calling an event a "genocide." We can usefully compare U.S. State Department official Madeline Albright's concern over this during Rwanda, with the repeated invocations by U.S. president George W. Bush and, earlier, by Secretary of State Colin Powell, all using the "G-word" regarding Darfur and Sudan, *to utterly no avail*. The 2004 report of the United Nations High Level Panel on Threats, Challenges, and Change invoked a "responsibility to protect" [R2P] citizens from civil violence of this sort, but this report, coming a decade after Rwanda (and not mentioning the Genocide Convention specifically) simply illustrates and laments the problem of a current absence of any meaningful institutions or procedures for dealing with such violence at the international level, although proposals to remedy this glaring deficiency abound.

18. This principle, like the use of anthropology by governments and their militaries, has a long and somewhat troubling history. Aristotle suggests the rudiments of the doctrine in the *Nicomachean Ethics*: that a moral agent cannot be held morally blameworthy for the consequences of actions that are the unintended secondary result of an otherwise morally acceptable action. One of its earliest formulations is found in St. Thomas Aquinas, *Summa Theologica*, Part II, Vol. II, Q. 64, Article 7, invoking this Aristotelian principle to examine an action of killing in self-defense: "Nothing hinders a single act from having two effects, only one of which is intended, while the other is beside the intention. Now moral acts get their character in accordance with what is intended, but not from what is beside the intention, since the latter is incidental." The so-called doctrine of double effect (DDE) became a familiar instrument in medieval moral casuistry, especially concerning actions during wartime. For example, in his sharp criticism of the practices of Spanish conquistadores, Dominican Francisco de Vitoria admits that the accidental and unintended killing of civilian noncombatants in an otherwise legitimate act of warfare may be "occasion-

ally lawful" if it is truly by mistake: *de jure belli*, Q3, Article 3 (Vitoria 1539/1557: 314–17). As this insight was later codified, DDE requires that: (1) a moral agent's primary action be morally permissible; (2) that any negative consequences be entirely unintended; which entails specifically (3) that the negative or morally objectionable results *cannot be the means through which* the desired end is obtained; and also (4) that the good end be such as to vastly outweigh the inadvertent harm done (this is sometimes called "the principle of proportionality"). All four conditions of the DDE are fully met in the foregoing example.

19. I believe this reasoning likewise exonerates anthropologists who might collaborate with insurgents resisting a morally unjustified military intervention in Rubinstein's example (see note 14, above).

CHAPTER FIVE

⬥

"CEAUSSIC Park"

From Principles to Case Analysis

On October 5, 2008, an anthropologist working on a Human Terrain System (HTS) team in Iraq posted a blog of his impressions after two months in the field. "The best description," he wrote,

> is that it's like, well everything in life. I get excited about the work, I get discouraged. I feel like I am doing things that can have long term value and I wonder what the hell I'm doing in this screwed up place. I have learned that the backs of my ears may never be clean again, the ex-pat life agrees with me, I miss beer and sushi, and now I know what it feels like to take pictures of young men that die two days later.
>
> Depending on the day you ask me, I will say that the problems with the entire HTS program are so insurmountable it should be started over from scratch, and on others, I see progress. We focus on being as much help as we can to our brigade in their efforts to help improve living and security conditions for local people as best we can. . . . I go from wanting to quit to wanting to stay here for at least a year because there always seem to be another interesting project we can do.
>
> In other words, it's a job just like jobs everywhere.[1]

Well, not quite. In May 2008, social scientist and HTS team member Michael Bhatia, working in eastern Afghanistan, was killed in an improvised explosive device (IED) roadside attack. The Taliban claimed credit for both this attack and the attack on Paula Loyd described in the preface. Setting women on fire is often inflicted as a punishment for immodesty. Immodesty,

131

however, was probably not the crime of HTS social scientist Nicole Suveges, killed in Iraq in July 2008, along with 11 others, when a bomb detonated inside the Sadr City District Council building in Baghdad. These deaths and injuries top the list of grievances of critics of the program. Journalist John Stanton writes:

> According to sources, United States Army brigade commanders privately believe that the US Army's TRADOC Human Terrain System (HTS) program is a "joke" and completely unnecessary. The HTS program is publicly supported by brigade military commanders, and Secretary of Defense Robert Gates, only because it is a "pet project" of the currently politically popular US Army General David Petraeus.
>
> BAE Systems, the prime contractor on the project, has repeatedly been pressured by the HTS program manager and his staff to hire individuals who are not field-experienced ethnographers/anthropologists, but rather Google-fed political and social scientists. In two cases, pre-security clearance award investigations revealed that one candidate recommended for hire by senior staff was a felon. The other candidate had health problems that would have compromised the functions of a deployed Human Terrain Team (HTT). BAE Systems has been the punching bag for the poor decision-making of HTS program managers and advisors.
>
> The tragic deaths of two HTS members—HTT IZ3 Nicole Suveges and HTT AF1 Michael Bhatia—came amidst program management's confusion over roles and missions, ignorance of threat situations, even dress code problems. Key questions remain open. What's the role of a civilian ethnographer/anthropologist working with the military in a combat zone? Is a civilian trained to respond to a threat without threatening the life of the team? Should they carry weapons and wear military gear? Are they there to enhance the kill chain, organize and facilitate sporting events, or examine trash dumps for behavioral patterns? What kind of data do warfighters and negotiators really want? What happens when the HTT leaves the site of success? What's the historical experience of the US military with human geographers?
>
> Whether all this mattered in the deaths of Suveges and Bhatia is utterly debatable. But according to sources, Suveges was a no-show at many training sessions at Fort Leavenworth and not properly trained for work in a combat zone. She was sent initially to the United Kingdom to recruit there for the HTS program and then afterwards was ultimately deployed to the volatile Sadr City in Iraq where three weeks later she met her end. One insider had predicted prior to her death that "someone was going to get killed."[2]

Who are we to believe? The fieldworker, on the one hand, working "first-person" and "onsite," but on the other, possibly laboring under the bias of a lucrative salary paid for his risky work? Or should we believe the critics and journalists back home, dependent for their evidence on secondhand sources (such as disappointed HTS team members, recently dismissed from the program) who seem eager to discredit the program?[3] In sharp contrast to Stanton's derogatory report on Suveges in particular, and on the lack of training and appropriate expertise of HTS team members generally, *Wired* reporter Noah Schachtman comments favorably on the most recent HTS victim, Paula Loyd:

> Lloyd [sic] knew Afghanistan well, having worked there previously for the State Department. She visited [the village of] Maywand several times and was "very popular there. She was accepted very positively throughout the village," one program official says. The man who attacked her was "from all appearances a non-belligerent." (Schachtman 2008a)

From Principles to Practices

This problem illustrates a glaring defect in the entire discussion of military anthropology to date. The defect is this. Thus far, that public debate about the moral legitimacy and professional propriety of HTS (reflected in my account and analysis of that controversy in this book, up to this point) has been *a debate about principles*—either disagreements about what moral principles might be placed in jeopardy by HTS, or about basic canons of professional practice that might be found at odds with the demands placed upon the likely activities of HTS teams. It has not, however, been a debate grounded in specific evidence, or widespread experience. When we move from principles to practice, for example, we might wonder more about the moral dilemma of putting lightly trained social scientists (along with embedded journalists) at risk in combat zones. Do they constitute a danger to themselves or to military personnel assigned to protect them, for example? Are the risks to themselves and the liability to others that they represent by their presence worth the benefits they might provide to those same military personnel in carrying out their stability and peacekeeping operations?

To be sure, the debate about principles *is* extremely significant. Would it, for example, be wrong "in principle" for an anthropologist (particularly a member of the American Anthropological Association, subject to its Code of Ethics) to work for or collaborate with military forces, especially U.S. forces in Afghanistan or Iraq? Are there conditions under which such work would serve generally to undermine the basic identity, autonomy, or integrity of the discipline itself? Would it not clearly be wrong, in any case, for an individual anthropologist to engage in work for an organization (like an intervening military force) that interferes with scientific transparency, imposes inappropriate requirements of secrecy, or demands the withholding of ethnographic findings deemed "highly classified?" What about principles like "informed consent," deemed essential for any kind of human subject research? Would not the very conditions of employment envisioned in HTS render such basic principles—alongside others, such as the rights of privacy or confidentiality of individual research subjects—impossible in principle to uphold? And if so, would this not, in turn, render this sort of engagement of anthropologists or other social scientists with the military illicit from the start, as critics like David Price, Hugh Gusterson, and Roberto Gonzalez hold?

These are challenging questions, to be certain, and (as we discovered in the preceding chapter) they constitute a substantial burden of proof that defenders of this form of public or government engagement would be obliged to meet. In one sense, it is appropriate to address hypothetical questions about principle with hypothetical cases designed to elicit and test the application of those principles. The CEAUSSIC report itself offers, in its conclusion, a list of hypothetical situations that an anthropologist might face—instructive or "illustrative examples" of anthropologists engaging with military and security forces, together with tentative conclusions about the professional probity of each, based upon application of specific provisions of the 1998 version of the AAA Code of Ethics as a guide to practice in such cases.[4] So, for example, the report's authors ask:

A) Should anthropologist A take employment with a form of direct engagement (e.g., HTS program)?

This "engagement" can take several forms, which are not further enumerated in this example. The response offered by the report's editors is not very specific, but cautions that such "direct engagement" in HTS-like operations is the sort of activity most likely to run afoul of AAA guidelines. They do not offer specific advice on which activities and which guidelines would be found in jeopardy. Instead, the report's editors opine:

This form of engagement, which falls into the "operations" category, requires careful assessment. On the one hand, some argue that direct engagement offers the most immediate results, including possible benefits to local populations (e.g., by mitigating conflict). On the other hand, this form of engagement is unlikely to accord with the ethical provisions of the AAA CoE. The anthropologist has an ethical and professional responsibility to make sure that basic human subjects and AAA ethical requirements are fully addressed. If these requirements are not fully addressed, then professional anthropologists should decline to participate in the project.

In the preceding chapter, we discovered that the presumption that "this form of engagement is *unlikely* to accord with the ethical provisions of the AAA Code of Ethics" (in either its 1998 or 1971 versions) is simply incorrect. Instead, what we discerned was a substantial burden of proof placed upon such projects to show how they would conform to the provisions of either set of professional ethical standards. In light of the varied accounts by both supporters and critics of what anthropologists might be expected to do specifically, if assigned to one of these HTS teams deployed in a combat zone, it would be well to refine this description further. We will do so with due attention to job advertisements, position descriptions, and descriptive accounts of concrete field practice. We will return to this formidable problem in a moment.

The CEAUASSIC report's next example is of a quite different sort:

B) Should anthropologist B teach cultural understanding to members of a military platoon slated for deployment in Iraq?

Here we have a straightforward case of MA_3, which, as we saw earlier, is a form of "anthropology *for* the military" altogether distinct from HTS, and already discussed in chapter 3. As we discovered therein, there is no obvious reason to oppose such work on ethical grounds. The report's editors seem to agree, if somewhat reluctantly, with this finding, observing, in effect, "yes,"

if this occurs in a way that does not violate the tenets of the CoE or other grounding human studies documents, such as the Belmont Report or the Helsinki Declarations.[5]

The references here to the two major protocols for biomedical research involving human subjects is somewhat puzzling, as neither document specifically pertains to teaching and education, and certainly not in anthropology. Their provisions apply more obviously to the work envisioned in example A, and would pose serious questions for such research. I cannot see how "teaching culture" to any audience, including career military personnel, would invoke these protocols, unless the subject-matter specialist knew in advance that his or her students harbored specific, malevolent intentions toward members of the society or culture, for example, studied in the anthropologist's course. Otherwise, the situation would be very much the same as that of an anthropologist teaching what the report calls "cultural understanding" to members of a police force assigned to duty in an ethnic-minority community.[6] Such knowledge might, on occasion, be misused by the student, but the presupposition (and the underlying intention in teaching these subjects to such audiences) would be exactly the opposite: to *improve* local community policing. We have explored this problem at length already in the "accounting professor" case at the conclusion of chapter 3, and perhaps no more need be said about it, other than noting how the occurrence and phrasing of the question and response unwittingly betray the implicit and unflattering background attitudes and presuppositions about anything pertaining to "the military," as likewise recounted in that chapter.

The commission goes on to ask:

C) Should anthropologist C do organizational studies of the military?

This, too, we have already covered in more substantial detail. It is MA_1, or "anthropology of the military," again discussed thoroughly in chapter 3. It is interesting that the commission chose, in responding to this example, to hold forth on the importance of transparency and protection of human research subjects (in this case, presumably, members of military organizations). To question C they answer:

> Yes, but with consideration of the impact of publication and classification restrictions on the research, and keeping in mind that classified status of findings may violate AAA's transparency tenets. Once again, we call attention to the importance of protecting human research subjects. Anthropologists must always ensure that their sponsoring institution is willing to let them adhere to basic human subjects protections, and must develop a rigorous protocol prior to conducting research. In addition, all anthropologists should seek venues for openly publishing their work, and should negotiate openness and transparency in research before work commences. Many anthropologists who work in restricted access environments (e.g., government classified and proprietary industrial) are able to publish their research findings and we applaud their openness and encourage others to follow their example.

While the concerns expressed are entirely appropriate, with the exception of transparency they seem to pertain more closely to the obstacles anthropologists would encounter in example A, when working in HTS. It is true, regrettably, that private and public organizations of all kinds seek to suppress evaluations that portray them in an unflattering light, but the problem of "suppression" of data in this case would seem more a problem in true biomedical research (e.g., in a pharmaceutical firm's desire to suppress unfavorable trials of a new drug) than in social and behavioral research, in which the "unflattering" or uncomplimentary nature of findings often lies more in the eyes of the overly sensitive organization than in the eyes of the wider public reviewing the findings. In any case, it is never wrong to remind all participants in human subjects research of their duties to share findings openly, while also protecting the privacy and dignity of individuals studied—just as true, if no more true, in military anthropology of the first kind (MA₁) than in other social and organizational research.

The CEAUSSIC report's remaining two illustrations deal with forensic studies of victims and the on-site preservation of cultural patrimony. The former seems a bit far-fetched: skill in physical, let alone forensic anthropology would most likely fall outside the areas of expertise in cultural anthropology, required for serving as a social scientist on an HTS team. But certainly if a cultural anthropologist also happened to have a specialty, skill, or experience in physical or forensic anthropology, then that individual, if requested, would be *obligated* (not merely permitted) to pursue what might well become the military investigation of a possible war crime with all due diligence.

Oddly, the advice the commission proffers does not recognize this, and indeed, seems to shrink from this responsibility. The commission notes, "In this case the interaction between anthropology and the institution in question would seem to reverse the expected power dynamic," a decided understatement, the implications of which (if I've even understood the phrasing here) are likely that no such request for assistance would likely be forthcoming. But if it were, the commission correctly notes, the consequences might be "of [the diligent practice of?] anthropology leading to sanctioning or worse of the military unit(s) involved." Here the commission's nuanced "doublespeak" seems to be envisioning a role in the investigation of noncombatant deaths. If so, the commission strangely concludes: "In this form of engagement, as with the others, anthropologists must be careful to adhere to the tenets of the Code of Ethics; for example, reflecting on any harm anthropological work might produce."

That hardly seems the relevant standard. In such a forensic investigation, the principals are charged with determining, with all due diligence, how the deaths were caused, and by whom—and if by U.S. or coalition forces, were these truly noncombatants? If so, were their deaths a tragic, unintended, and unavoidable accident (and so subject to limited liability under the doctrine of double effect)? Or did they result from carelessness, lack of due care, or even criminal negligence, let alone (as in a very few, widely publicized incidents) deliberate and intentional targeting in violation of the rules of engagement and provisions of Geneva Conventions protecting noncombatants from intentional injury or death? If any of the latter, then such deaths would constitute a war crime, subject on site to investigation and possible prosecution. NATO and U.N. forces in Afghanistan, and U.S.-led coalition forces in Iraq, have been diligent for the most part in pursuing these investigations, compensating survivors of accidents, and prosecuting individuals guilty of negligence or worse (Orend 2006). One would have likewise preferred the CEAUSSIC commission's vigorous and unqualified endorsement of these relevant provisions of international law, in lieu of "reflecting on any harm anthropological work might produce" (whatever on earth that could possibly mean in a situation like this).

Likewise, concerning their final example of the responsibility for preservation of "cultural resources" (cultural patrimony), the commission seems to believe that an anthropologist could (and perhaps should) work toward cultural preservation "so long as cooperation with the parties involved is transparent and otherwise adheres to Code of Ethics guidelines." I am hard pressed, despite some experience with hypotheticals and counterfactuals, to wonder from whence the commission's apparent caution stems in this final example. I try to envision how, for example, warning troops about the need to avoid damaging a historic and culturally prominent mosque or (even more dramatically) lobbying during the early days of the war for a military guard to be placed around the Iraqi National Museum, would *ever* run afoul of the principle of transparency and the AAA CoE! I suppose the example would have to involve the anthropologist participating in, rather than lobbying to prevent, the looting of cultural artifacts, but such a transparent outrage is not, to put it mildly, "ethically interesting." More helpfully, the commission's concluding advice to its membership on this point is that

> anthropologists, particularly archaeologists, might work with the International Committee of the Blue Shield (ICBS) to protect the world's cultural heritage by coordinating preparations to meet and respond to emergency situations (e.g., establishing training manuals, maintaining lists of resource personnel, advocating in public forums, etc.). Anthropologist E might participate in ICBS activities such as public education about damage to cultural heritage; providing training in military situations or to prepare for natural disasters; identifying resources during times of emergency; and advocating for cultural heritage in different venues. (CEAUSSIC 2007: 28)

These CEAUSSIC examples or "illustrative cases" are not, of course, actual cases, but are presumably based upon culturally "thin" accounts of testimony offered to the commission itself regarding what HTS researchers specifically, as well as other military anthropologists, are actually being called upon to do. These examples were surely intended in good faith to suggest the moral and professional challenges that would arise in each instance. My objections are that the instances selected are not very clear nor representative, let alone fully and properly differentiated. And the advice offered in response is quite often largely irrelevant to the type of example considered, or else it is hopelessly vague and abstract, or otherwise disappointingly "limp-wristed" in light of the degree of controversy surrounding these issues. These shortcomings demonstrate not merely that little of substance can be accomplished by committee, but that the commission in this case was operating far from its comfort zone of expertise in grappling with substantive questions of ethics.

Typology of the "Human Terrain"

Following the methodology of previous chapters, we will begin first by setting aside the two examples (B and C) already identified and analyzed as forms of military anthropology other than HTS, and then sorting out some of the different types of HTS activities embedded in the remaining CEAUSSIC illustrations. We will then be in a position to evaluate the ethical compliance and moral probity of each.

I will start with HTS_1, the activity of engaging in strict cross-cultural translation. Team members talk to villagers and then pass along their interpretation of what villagers say to members of the military. What they learn is for immediate and local consumption, guiding the actions and reactions of civil and military forces in zones of conflict.[7] This is what the "embedded" military anthropologist Mark Dawson, quoted at the beginning of this chapter, describes himself primarily as doing as part of an HTS team. It seems pretty clear that this is the activity that Paula Loyd was engaged in when she was brutally attacked. This is one possible meaning of the CEAUSSIC report's example A above, and, from all the limited accounts to date, appears to comprise the bulk of HTS activities carried out by anthropologists who are deployed and embedded in combat zones.

On a live radio interview in October 2007, for example, Lt. Col. Edward Villacres, a Middle East historian from West Point deployed at the time to command an HTS team in Iraq, described to anthropologists David Price and Montgomery McFate how his four-person team (consisting of an adjunct professor of anthropology from California State University, East Bay, a junior officer fluent in Arabic, and a civil affairs specialist who is an Army staff sergeant) attempted to "enhance the ability of ground forces to make good decisions" (Rehm 2007). He recounted how rival tribal leaders in war-torn areas have a specific cultural "formula" for reconciliation negotiations following a conflict. It is imperative to be aware of, and to subscribe to, the rituals of this formula in order to conduct effective negotiations and help the warring factions make peace. It was the HTS team's job to interpret these vital cultural data to the American troops engaged in peacemaking in contested areas of the "Sunni triangle" in Iraq.[8]

Not coincidentally, this is the kind of HTS activity regarded with the greatest suspicion by critics of military anthropology, and by the CEAUSSIC commission itself, as fundamentally incompatible with the AAA Code of Ethics. Price, on the same program, reiterated the results of his own historical research on the military's use and abuse of social scientists during World War II and the Cold War. He complained about one Pentagon official who had compared HTS favorably with the "civil operations revolutionary development support" (CORDS) programs undertaken during the Vietnam War.[9] That effort, Price explained, helped identify Vietnamese communist insurgents and Vietcong collaborators. It entailed Army Green Berets (Price alleged) "illegally" translating into English a detailed ethnography of Highlanders in Vietnam by a French anthropologist, Georges Condominas,[10] and then using the insights gained from this work to target and assassinate Vietcong collaborators. He acknowledged that he himself was not charging that such things are taking place now in Iraq and Afghanistan, but he understandably found it "troubling that a Pentagon spokesman would make such a comparison."

The foregoing discussion suggests further distinctions, such as HTS_2, in which the anthropologist gathers information to populate databases located back in the U.S., accessible to analysts who are not anthropologists. These databases are proprietary to the military but not classified, so that results can be accessed and used by other anthropologists engaged in legitimate scientific work. In her account during this radio interview, anthropologist Montgomery McFate described how she had originally proposed something like this as the main activity of HTS when she was first approached to undertake this new task in 2003. The Army, however, wanted something different, what she described as "an angel on the shoulder"—that is, HTS_1, mediated by a real person and not merely a database, and "there" (meaning in the field) rather than "here" (in the U.S.).

The oft-voiced concern about "clandestine research" (or the misuse and misappropriation, without knowledge or permission, of prior anthropological research, like the fieldwork of Condominas), however, would constitute something different from HTS_2, something more akin to genuine espionage or "intelligence gathering" than legitimate anthropological research. We might label this HTS_3, in which the primary activity of the anthropologist (or those purloining the results of anthropological studies) is to gather information to populate classified databases (see table 5.1). As illustrated in Price's comments, this concern constitutes a holdover from the days of Vietnam, Project Camelot, and the Thailand controversy.

On the one hand, this third category appears to encompass the recent allegations of the Zapotec in Mexico, who allege that a geographer and anthropologist from the University of Kansas solicited their consent, under false and deceptive circumstances, to engage in an ethnographic mapping of indigenous communities. They claim that, unknown to them at the time, his research was partially funded by the Foreign Military Studies Office of the U.S. Army, which maintains a proprietary global database used in the Human Terrain Systems project. [11] On the other hand, as we note below, there are no reports of job openings for, or other reports apart from this allegation, of anthropologists engaging in HTS$_3$, the most explicitly problematic of these three activities from the standpoint of professional ethics. HTS anthropologist Mark Dawson does not acknowledge engaging in such activities. When they were injured or killed, neither Bhatia, Suveges, nor Loyd were engaged in such clandestine activities. No published or broadcast accounts document instances or even suggest that such clandestine activities are part of this program. At best, as seems to be the case with Price, this concern constitutes a kind of historical anxiety through which lens one refracts the prospects for commission of such abuses in the present.

In fact, however, the preponderance of work to be found, apart from working on education, doctrine, and training back home, is for HTS$_1$, as we will note below. It is possible, but not confirmed, that some of the data and experiences gathered will find its way into proprietary but unclassified databases back home. HTS$_2$ does have a certain allure in holding out to Middle East regional experts the prospect of regaining access to regions of central Asia, such as Afghanistan, long off limits to them as zones of conflict. But populating databases is not the principal motivation for the HTS program itself. Rather, as we note in job ads and position descriptions, the prospect for ethnographic field research and data-gathering is part of the wider lure to research anthropologists, a potential "added personal benefit" of their HTS employment that (the job openings promise) will allow them to pursue their own scholarly research and publication on the people and "cultures" in which they are immersed during their deployment, *should they wish to do so.* That is what the job ads promise enticingly, and such a benefit is far from constituting the sinister or clandestine activity defined as HTS$_3$.

Indeed, a critic of a suspicious turn of mind might suspect that language in these position descriptions, offering HTS$_2$ as an added personal benefit to those who enlist in the program, has been inserted precisely to assuage critics, fulfill ethical and professional restrictions, and otherwise comply with AAA CoE provisions that those critics, and the CEAUSSIC commission, have identified as the chief obstacles to approval of the Human Terrain

Systems program overall. In any case, it would be vital to examine actual experiences of team members, to determine whether, under combat conditions, very much in the way of useful cultural data could be gathered and referred to "proprietary databases," whether classified (HTS_3) or not.

Finally, the CEAUSSIC illustrations suggest two other kinds of HTS embedded activities: HTS_4 (providing forensic advice or examining evidence of combat casualties in pursuit of war crimes), and HTS_5 (lobbying and, indeed, actively working for the preservation of valuable cultural patrimony that happens to be located in war zones). I have expressed skepticism about the likelihood of HTS_4, and, in any case, illustrated what would be the proper advice and concerns for engaging in it as a perfectly legitimate form of law enforcement.

HTS_5 (assuming the good faith and integrity of anthropologists on the project) is not a moral "problem" but a moral *obligation*: anthropologists (including archaeologists) are enjoined by the very nature of their discipline to refrain from damage or theft themselves, and to do all in their power to resist damage to or theft of valuable cultural patrimony, which is sacred to the people and cultures they study, and vital to the advancement of cultural knowledge worldwide.

No more need be said about these activities, save that it would be an unqualifiedly good thing (however improbable), never a bad thing, to have sufficient resources and personnel to ensure that both forensic anthropologists and archaeologists were available onsite in combat zones (or, at least, zones where combat was recently concluded) to ensure that HTS_4 and HTS_5, adequate forensic examination and protection of cultural patrimony respectively, were provided to local residents and citizens. I am mystified that anyone on the CEAUSSIC commission might have imagined otherwise.

Table 5.1. Forms of HTS Activities

Symbol	Description
HTS_1	Providing cultural advice and regional knowledge (including language skills) onsite to military personnel in combat zones
HTS_2	Populating nonclassified, nonproprietary cultural databases maintained in the United States
HTS_3	Cultural espionage; gathering clandestine cultural data for classified databases (Thailand affair)
HTS_4	Forensic anthropology; investigation of possible war crimes
HTS_5	Preservation of valuable cultural patrimony in war zones

Searching for Substance in All the Wrong Places

Ultimately, the questions of principle that remain pertain entirely to HTS_1 and HTS_2. These can be addressed only within the crucible of issues arising in actual attempts to engage in the practices under scrutiny. Put simply and starkly: *we need case studies* to consider and evaluate.

Rarely, in any profession or discipline, are abstract discussions of principles, or even past history alone, allowed to settle, and particularly to foreclose a priori an area of activity that might otherwise hold promise, especially if the nature of that promise, as formally presented, was to aid and protect vulnerable victims of war.[12] Instead, as in most disciplines, professions, and vocations, the genuine moral challenges are to be found arising in specific circumstances, in that crucible of issues that constitute case literature grounded in actual professional experience.

Indeed, we might observe that the entire course of this public debate over anthropology and its proper practice has followed a trajectory directly inverse to the norm in every other discipline, profession, and practice. Normally, moral concern arises in the aftermath of, and only when confronted with profound and disturbing evidence of, specific forms of malpractice, or else crisis stemming from harm to individuals engaged in certain activities (such as Bhatia, Suveges, and Loyd). Accounts of these tragedies filter through the profession or discipline as these are now doing, prompting comment and reflection. Ultimately (as happened with the gradual forging of the AAA's first Code of Ethics in 1971, for example), the reflection upon the most disturbing features of actual practice leads to a formulation of general principles to guide and restrain that practice. Professions like medicine and law, faced with their own moral challenges, quickly found it necessary to move from discussion of vague abstractions to the analysis and examination of such abstractions, including the provisions of their respective professional codes of ethics (including the Helsinki Declarations of 1964 and the Belmont Report of 1979). These biomedical codes pertaining to human subject research, for example, were forged in the context of experience and practice. Specific practices raised questions, posed problems, and even resulted in charges of malpractice to which the provisions of these codes were both answers and guidelines for future "best practice." The methodology of "professional ethics," as a result, has been from its inception grounded in the study and analysis of *concrete cases.*

To its credit, the AAA CEAUSSIC commission quickly came to recognize how thin and ultimately inadequate was the provisional guidance to members offered in the five hypothetical scenarios presented and examined in its initial report in 2007. In recognition of this problem, the commission issued a call for case studies in the spring of 2008, inviting its members who might have worked in or otherwise gained familiarity with HTS operations, to write up and publish these concrete accounts as a future guide to actual practice. This is a commendable effort, a valuable next step in the evolution of considered opinion that might be more properly grounded in so-called best practices (and also in the recognition and rejection of "unacceptable practices") in the actual experience of practicing anthropologists attempting to engage with military, intelligence, and security forces.

This new initiative, for its part, raises serious difficulties with case provenance and peer review. How will the case book editorial committee be constituted and convened? What areas of expertise and experience will be represented there? How will that peer review committee determine the validity of cases submitted? What documentary evidence will be required to verify case details? And given that the case book, like the commission's original report, will contain hypothetical cases, what are the parameters of suitability for these?[13] That is to say: in a debate driven largely by ideology and innuendo in the absence of concrete evidence, how will editors insure that the influx of "case studies" will not be redacted to fit a preconceived perspective on the moral probity of HTS_1 and HTS_2? These kinds of questions would not be quite as delicate, were the entire matter not so thoroughly politicized and rife with conspiratorial hypotheses from the opposing sides in the wider debate.

In the meantime, at the time of this publication, it is striking how little factual information, let alone well-organized case studies, are available either to support or refute the concerns raging in the discipline over HTS in any of the five forms here identified. The recently authored Marine Corps handbook on "operational culture," for example, features a variety of illustrations and case studies, drawn, as it claims, "from around the world," and based "on the research and field experiences of Marines themselves." Surprisingly, however, the handbook does not cite any specific examples of HTS activities from Iraq and Afghanistan. Instead, most of the teaching about the importance of "operational culture" invokes generalized or fictionalized experiences that emphasize the need for prudence and good judgment in the field, based upon adequate regional knowledge and mature intercultural understanding. For example, one reads this mildly interesting (but not very specific or instructive) case of French peacekeepers in Central Africa:

> In the Central African Republic, a French Marine lance corporal on patrol far from base had been instructed not to search clergy. When he encountered a

local missionary, not only did he refrain from searching him, but he initiated a rapport. This rapport yielded much intelligence about local networks of power and influence, and improved the unit's relationship with the indigenous people. If the LCpl had only been instructed not search the clergy, but was not informed that the clergy have important family, economic, and political relationships, he might not have established the rapport that benefited the entire company. (Salmoni and Holmes-Eber 2008: 262)

This case admittedly hints at the value of accurate knowledge of a local culture by individual members of an intervening military force. Nevertheless, even as a concrete case study, this account leaves a number of essential anthropological specifics undefined. We would surely want and need to know whether the "missionary" was truly a member of the local clergy, or someone from abroad—and if the latter, how reliable was his information regarding what the case describes as "the indigenous people"? Leaving all that aside, however, what is most striking about this manual is the absence of any specific cases set in Afghanistan or Iraq, even after several years of Marine Corps deployment in both nations. Why didn't the two staff anthropologists who coauthored this handbook avail themselves of anthropological field data on "embedded HTS" available, supposedly, since the deployment of the first five HTS teams in Iraq and one in Afghanistan, beginning at least two years prior to the publication of this essential guide to practice—and this in a military organization whose main challenges have, in this decade, come specifically in these two war zones (as opposed to Central Africa)?

The answer is twofold. First, HTS is primarily an "Army" program. Over several months, I have queried a number of Special Operations personnel (e.g., Navy SEALS) returning from both theaters. When asked about their awareness or observation of HTS, they drew a blank. Some Marines, by contrast, exhibit familiarity in a very limited degree, based on interaction with Army units that may have had an HTS specialist, but they are skeptical of the value of the program and express preference for the kind of "on the ground" intelligence about the locale that they get from "the local plumber or electrician who served as our unit interpreter."[14] This failure even to be aware of, let alone incorporate, experience or innovation across service culture boundaries is a fairly typical phenomenon, stemming from both lack of contact and traditional interservice rivalries. Anthropologists engaged in MA_1 can enlighten others on this curious (and, to outsiders, often surprising) state of affairs.

Second, and in any case, as persistently noted, there is very little in the way of concrete specifics available to discuss, either to explain or defend the essentials of the HTS team operation, or to support the allegations of critics opposed to it, other than largely unsupported accusations that anthropologists may have assisted or advised on interrogation techniques of suspected terrorists at the Abu Ghraib and Guantánamo Bay prisons.[15] Even these scant charges are worth a moment's reflection. Let us suppose we were able to support such claims with genuine evidence: that is, suppose that Laura McNamara *had* been able to confirm that it was true that one or more anthropologists worked at, or in support of, both of these controversial detention facilities. It would still be vital to know who did what, and to whom, and in what capacity.

Consider a straightforward and simple example. A staff anthropologist who advised officials in charge of detention facilities about the importance of showing proper respect for the Qur'an wouldn't prima facie seem to be even remotely involved in a violation of any existing statute in the AAA Code of Ethics. This would be so even if the motivation of that scientist's supervisors was to build greater trust or gain cooperation from imprisoned suspects so as to conduct a more successful interrogation. That is because any such respect shown to authentically valued and significant elements of an individual's culture is, ipso facto, a good thing, no matter what the underlying motivation for it. Anything that can be done, *ceteris paribus*, to increase understanding and respect for essential features of another person's culture might be said to have moral worth, even if that other person is an enemy prisoner, or suspected "illegal combatant," providing that such understanding and proper respect were the intended result. Thus, by way of contrast, if the information provided by the anthropologist about the Qur'an, for example, were then used by its recipients to knowingly desecrate so sacred a symbol in order to cause anger, pain, shame, or humiliation—in effect, to inflict harm—in order thereby somehow to "soften up" the subject for interrogation, then the anthropologist should not comply. The anthropologist would not become guilty of unprofessional conduct or moral wrongdoing, however, simply by providing such information or even by aiding in legally sanctioned interrogation of suspected terrorists generally. Such charges would be valid only if that individual intended or knew in advance that the information provided would be used to do harm to those prisoners.

In the above case, our evaluation of the anthropologist's behavior would presumably be much different from that of a staff psychologist who advised just how to attack a prisoner's physical or psychological vulnerabilities so as to cause extreme discomfort or pain as a prologue to interrogation. The anthropologist would be attempting to foster humane treatment and appropriate respect for imprisoned suspects, while the psychologist would clearly be complicit in their unlawful interrogation and abuse. In any case, *it would be the differing circumstances of those cases*, not the background debate about principles, that would decide the morality of the matter.[16]

Not surprisingly, commendations from practitioners and supporters appear likewise vague and unsubstantiated. In discussing and defending the Minerva Consortia, for example, Secretary of Defense Robert M. Gates launched into a defense of HTS as a positive example of greater collaboration between scholars and the military generally. While admitting (without specifics) that the program had "growing pains," he reportedly argued that "the net effect of these efforts is often less violence across the board, with fewer hardship and casualties among civilians as a result. One commander in Afghanistan said last year that after working with a Human Terrain Team, the number of armed strikes he had to make declined more than 60 percent."[17] Perhaps, but we might have cause to doubt this, and in any case, how would we know?

Job Hunting in the Human Terrain

None of this, pro or con, is particularly informative or helpful. Suppose, instead, that we grant a conclusion about anthropologists that may be fairly derived from the arguments of the previous chapter: namely, that it would not be wrong, prima facie or in principle, for an anthropologist to accept the job in variation 3 of the second of the two cases we sketched there. Recall, in that hypothetical third variation of case 2, that the government of a nation has embarked upon a preventive war of dubious justification, gotten itself into quite a mess, and now realizes it needs to change course, patch up the damage, and leave. Its military now finds itself enmeshed in a nasty and seemingly intractable counterinsurgency, and reaches out to anthropologists to assist with greater understanding of the regional culture in order to provide effective and workable solutions toward political stability, get the local populace working together to rebuild their civil infrastructure, reintroduce reasonable security under the rule of law, and then pack up and go home.

In the preceding chapter, we concluded that in such an instance our hypothetical anthropologist would not automatically be forbidden, ethically or morally, from providing such assistance. Specifically, providing such assistance would not constitute a violation of the AAA Code of Ethics, provided the motivations for this engagement were as described and the constraints on allowable activities that these motivations imposed were indeed met. What is problematic about this hypothetical case is not the conclusions (even if some are displeased with them), but the lack of material and cultural substance in the example.

"The military," for example, is not a single monolithic entity that enter-tains objectives or even goes out and hires employees. There are competing military services, with complex internal service cultures and subcultures and conflicting chains of command. "The military's objectives," like those of a nation, may reflect the fundamental proposals of some governing elite, but that does not automatically translate into compliance up and down the chain of command, even granting basic "buy-in" and good faith in carrying out those objectives. There are political factions within each service, and within the Department of Defense, vying for power and influence.

Typically an influential member of the governing elite, a figure like General David Petraeus in the Army, for example, formulates the idea that "the military mission" in a nation like Iraq or Afghanistan (however that mission itself is, in fact, generally characterized) might be more effectively accomplished with the help of anthropologists, who might bring an enhanced understanding of the "cultural terrain." This proposal automatically becomes the brainchild or pet project of one faction of that branch of the military services, perhaps shared or agreed to by others, and largely ignored, or even actively opposed by yet others as a "waste of time and money," or unworkable.

Even apart from such political fragmentation, there are practical questions that bear heavily on the actual practice proposed as a remedy. For example, who will recruit and hire these scholars? How will they be oriented to the rigors of this particular kind of fieldwork (largely unlike any most will have encountered before)? How will they be organized, deployed "into country," commanded, even evaluated? To whom will they report, and to what uses will their information finally be put in the field, far from the headquarters of those leaders whose brainchild their inclusion in these delicate, fragile, and (as we now see) risk-fraught military operations was in the first place?

Given all the assumptions packed into the hypothetical cases in the pre-vious chapter, we would need some rather robust assurances that practical and procedural questions like these would admit of some decidedly positive answers, in order to address the manifold and substantive concerns of critics of this program. Instead, the scanty evidence we have in fact ranges from random and anecdotal testimony (such as the remarks of HTS anthropolo-gist Mark Dawson, cited at the opening of this chapter), that the record of accomplishment is decidedly mixed (with some positive results, and no dilemmas of "professional ethics"), through rosy accounts of success from the secretary of defense, all the way to increasingly exaggerated accounts of death and injury, and journalistic (but unsubstantiated) charges that the actual, functioning HTS program is, on balance, an unmitigated disaster, "in total disarray," and largely amounts to a useless waste of time and resources.

Just as important, as I have suggested heretofore, we would want some kind of external oversight and evaluation of these ongoing arrangements, so as not to have to rely solely on the reports of the individuals hired, or heads of organizations hiring them, let alone of journalists and bloggers transparently fronting for critics of the program.[18] All these are now involved in an inherent conflict of interest that might cloud their own evaluations of the successes or failures, as well as of the professional probity and moral rectitude, of their activities. We would need, as military officials themselves often say, "to trust, but verify."

Let's begin with the matter of recruiting and hiring. For many years, the military has been divesting itself of the principal responsibility for hiring civilians. Using the image of their overall operations as an effective "guard dog," the policy question has been how most effectively to invest personnel and resources between "tooth" and "tail." The primary, combat-ready aspects, the "tooth" in this metaphor, are the responsibility of men and women in uniform. Their job is to "take the fight to the enemy." The logistical and support activities necessary to mobilize and sustain those combat missions (the "tail" in this metaphor) have been increasingly divested and subcontracted to private military contractors (PMCs).[19] This encompasses everything from preparing and serving food, to maintaining barracks, showers, and latrines, to providing troop transport and supply convoys, to maintaining shipyards and motor pools. All the noncombat activities that used to fall to "Beetle Bailey" or "Sergeant Bilko" are now performed by civilian contractors. Recruiting, assembling, training, and deploying HTS teams is a noncombat logistical enterprise and, as such, is the sort of thing done by PMCs.[20]

Until 2009, the principal responsibility for recruiting, hiring, training, compensating, deploying, and ultimately evaluating "social scientists" hired to serve in various components of the Human Terrain System project was delegated via competitive bidding to a private firm, BAE Systems, Inc.[21] With operations in five continents and customers in more than 100 countries worldwide, BAE Systems is a private military contractor that describes itself as "one of the world's foremost providers of advanced aerospace products, intelligent electronic systems and technology services for government and commercial customers." The firm, formerly known as British Aerospace, employs nearly 100,000 personnel worldwide, reports gross annual income of nearly $30 billion, and (as its original name implies) is based in the U.K. In its early years, British Aerospace largely exported military aircraft, armored vehicles, and other war-fighting equipment. BAE Systems, Inc. now describes itself, however, as involved increasingly in the "integration" business, rather than merely in hardware and platform provision. The company has major offices in South Africa, Sweden, Saudi Arabia, Australia, and the United States.[22]

For the record, the United Kingdom's Serious Fraud Office has for several years been looking into suspected bribery payments by BAE Systems to members of the Saudi royal family in connection with a huge contract known as al-Yamamah, an enormous purchase of fighter aircraft (Tornados, Hawks, and, later, Eurofighter Typhoons). The Saudi family recently pressured the Tony Blair government to abandon the investigation without issuing findings. Because BAE has offices in the U.S. and at least some of the alleged bribes may have been exchanged there, the U.S. Department of Justice has taken up the case (Wrage 2007). This, then, is the private contracting firm that won the bid to advertise for, interview, hire, train, and ultimately deploy HTS teams.

The job descriptions below were posted in the recent past on BAE's non-classified public website, soliciting anthropologists to work on the Human Terrain System. Positions include openings for social scientists, research managers, HTS "analysts," and team leaders.[23] The positions include an initial training period, typically of four months duration, at the company's facility in Fort Leavenworth, Kansas, "including orientation to the military/deployment environment, in-depth country briefings, and multi-disciplinary social science concepts and methods." Training and orientation are followed by deployment to Iraq and/or Afghanistan, typically for six to nine months. This is how a prospective applicant would initially be introduced to the program as an opportunity for his or her prospective career:

The Human Terrain System (HTS) is a new Army program designed to improve the military's ability to understand the local socio-cultural environment in Iraq and Afghanistan. *Human Terrain Teams help military commanders reduce the amount of lethal force used, with a corresponding reduction in military and civilian casualties* [my emphasis], allowing the commander to make decisions that will increase the security of the area, allow other organizations (local and international) to more effectively provide aid and restore the infrastructure, ensure that US efforts are culturally sensitive, promote economic development, and help the local population more effectively communicate their needs to US and Coalition forces. HTS teams act as advisers to Army Brigades and Marine Corps Regiments. [An HTS Team] will not engage in combat missions, nor does it collect intelligence. [An HTS] team will [typically] analyze data from a variety of sources operating in theatre (e.g., conventional military patrols, non-governmental organizations, international organizations, civil affairs units, special forces). Working as a social scientist on a Human Terrain Team offers a rare and unique opportunity to help reshape the military's execution of their mission by offering them a much greater appreciation of existing socio-cultural realities and sensitivities in the countries where they are operating. This position also offers an opportunity to develop new methods for data collection and analysis. *Social scientists will be able to write about their experiences and otherwise contribute to the academic literature in their field after participation, subject to standard security review* [my emphasis].

The characterization of the work offered by the hiring entity corresponds closely with the morally benign parameters of the final hypothetical case variant in the preceding chapter. Indeed, the overall description of the team's work seems meticulously crafted to meet the requirements of AAA Code of Ethics restrictions, including even language reintroduced by the Turner amendment designed to promote "transparency" and inhibit "secret research." The ad deftly addresses suspicions or reservations about the nature of the work the recruited candidate might finally be asked to undertake, or the restrictions under which he or she might finally be forced to work. As we have seen, however, living up to the requirements or restrictions of that CoE will likely prove to be the least of a job applicant's legitimate worries.

Job applicants in this instance are required to hold U.S. citizenship, and to hold or have the ability to obtain and maintain a security clearance. The jobs also require a Ph.D. in anthropology or in a "related field such as sociology, political science, history, theology [sic], economics, public policy, social psychology, or area studies."

Despite reports of salaries in excess of $20,000 per month during deployment, these positions are not for just anyone. In fact, one of the main criticisms of the program is that (apart from the fictional Hollywood character Indiana Jones) few if any persons are likely to possess the entire skill set required. As if this weren't enough, the BAE Systems advertisements also warn that successful candidates must be able to endure rigorous conditions and physical hardships of the sort that would lead even the "early," let alone the "later" Indiana Jones to complain, including:

- Adverse battlefield conditions
- Heat well in excess of 110 degrees in the summer, cold and freezing conditions during the winter
- Rough terrain, requiring the climbing of rocks and mountains and fording bodies of water
- Hostile environment, including persons, that may cause bodily harm, injury, or loss of life
- Required to work at times with little sleep or rest for extended periods of time while producing both physically and mentally challenging projects

- Extended travel by foot, military ground vehicles, and air transport into mountainous regions for extended periods of time
- Sleeping on the ground in environmentally unprotected areas
- Required to lift 40–75 pounds of equipment and personal gear including protective equipment several times a day
- Required to carry 40–75 pounds of gear and personal protective equipment for 10–16 hours a day while walking in rough terrain.

Finally and not surprisingly, the ads suggest that preferred candidates will have experience living or working in the Middle East and possess language skills in Arabic, Pashtun, or Dari.

Assuming that BAE contract staff are fortunate enough to locate and recruit interested individuals with these impressive skill sets, what positions might they occupy? Typical positions include HTS team leader, analyst, research manager, and a more general "social scientist." Here is where the nature of the team structure and organization come into play. The "Human Terrain Team Leader" requires *prior substantial military experience* as a brigade staff officer, at the rank of O-5 (i.e., lieutenant colonel or Navy commander) or above, and preferably, graduation from a Staff and Command College or its equivalent. The HTS team leader (the BAE job advertisement states), "will lead the Human Terrain System (HTS), which is a team that will collect and analyze data from the Brigade Combat Team (BCT) and Regional Combat Team (RCT) to obtain cultural and political awareness in order to sustain and foster stabilization. The HTS project is designed to improve the *gathering, interpretation, understanding, operational application and sharing of local population knowledge* [my emphasis] at the BCT and RCT and Division levels. The Human Terrain Team Leader will be the BCT commander's principal human terrain advisor, responsible for supervising the team's effort and *helping integrate data into the staff decision process.* The key attribute of the HTT team leader is the ability to successfully integrate the HTT into the process of the BCT in an effective and credible manner and become a trusted advisor to the BCT commander."

An HTS analyst is also required to have prior military experience, preferably with intelligence debriefing. The analyst "will be a part of the Human Terrain System (HTS), which is a team that will collect and analyze data from the Brigade Combat Team (BCT) and Regional Combat Team (RCT), once again, *to obtain cultural and political awareness in order to sustain and foster stabilization.* The Human Terrain Analyst will serve as the primary human terrain data researcher. He/She will participate in debriefings, and will interact with other target area organizations and agencies." Yet another position, the "Human Terrain Research Manager," must also have some prior military experience, preferably in HUMINT (human intelligence), and is expected to integrate the team's findings into a broader regional context "to obtain cultural and political awareness in order to sustain and foster stabilization."

The "social scientist" position as a member of the HTS team is *the only position that does not require prior military service*, and which emphasizes in particular the skill set acquired in earning a doctorate in anthropology. "The Social Scientist will provide local interpretation of socio-cultural data, information and understanding of local and regional culture. The Social Scientist will work closely with and possess similar skills as the Cultural Analyst, but with more focus on the larger region in which the target area is embedded." Note that this last was the position that both Michael Bhatia and Paula Loyd apparently held in their respective teams in Afghanistan. Lt. Col. Edward Villacres, with the 82 Airborne Division HTS team in Iraq, was the "HTT team leader," while Nicole Suveges, also in Iraq, was an HTS analyst. Both these individuals had prior military experience at the officer and enlisted level, respectively.

There are a number of grave problems with these job descriptions, most of which are not the "questions of professional ethics" envisioned by the HTS program's critics back in the United States. But those problems are formidable nonetheless, and may raise a host of moral and ethical questions in their own right. Note, for example, that all members of the proposed HTS team except the subject-matter expert in social science must have substantial prior military experience. Thus, the abilities and training in surviving wartime conditions that might be envisioned, and even the ability to work cooperatively with brigade and regional combat forces, are likely to be handled by those with prior experience in such operations, with the academic anthropologist "tagging along." Both HTT IZ3 Nicole Suveges and HTT AF1 Michael Bhatia, for example, were not neophyte anthropology scholars lured in by high salaries, or minimally trained at Fort Leavenworth, and then released recklessly into a combat zone, as was erroneously reported at first. Instead (although this does not mitigate the tragedy of their loss), both (as their enlisted ratings suggest) were either prior military (Suveges, Loyd) or civilians with substantial experience in counterinsurgency and post-conflict interventions (Bhatia). They are the ones whose job it is to liaise with brigade and regional commanders, coordinate embedded team activities with combat and security operations, and, in all likelihood, keep their less-well-oriented academic "SME" (subject-matter expert, the "adjunct professor of anthropology" from Cal State, for example) from getting his or her head blown off (or, just as seriously, causing others to get their heads blown off by being in the wrong place at the wrong time).

This is not an ideal working relationship. Military commanders in the field with some experience of these kinds of arrangements opine that the likely problems with HTS teams is not that they will provide "critical or clandestine intelligence" about local populations (which might better be obtained from the brigade's assigned native translator), let alone that they will be asked to collude in doing harm to locals. Rather, having all these "noncombat personnel" wandering around in a combat zone is a dangerous distraction for all concerned. Journalist Stanton's hearsay report of opinions that "someone is likely to get killed" over HTS pertains more to that problem than to the alleged lack of training of the prior military personnel who form the bulk of the team.

The risk might be worthwhile, if the subject expertise that the academic social scientist could bring to bear on brigade operations were substantial and accurate. But, as the BAE advertisement suggests, there is very little likelihood of that. Given that all these regions have been in a state of armed conflict for over two decades, it is extremely unlikely that any scholar who is not native-born (and perhaps a refugee from the violence) would have found the opportunity of acquiring remotely the diverse kinds of skill sets requested. Bhatia and Loyd were notable and commendable exceptions in this respect. As the BAE advertisement also makes clear, the hiring contractor has adopted (shall we say) a rather ecumenical, eclectic attitude toward relevant subject-matter expertise: if the candidate lacks a degree in anthropology, then a degree in theology, economics, or (only slightly more plausibly) social psychology will suffice.

Where's the Outrage?

Once again, most of the AAA debate has focused on the principled outrage within the discipline of anthropology occasioned by such ads, and by the revelations that programs like HTS and companies like BAE Systems are recruiting academically trained anthropologists for such work. Is the concern warranted? Is there, finally, any good reason, in principle, why an anthropologist should not accept these jobs?

On one hand, I'm inclined at this point to conclude that the answer to that question, grounded in principle, and based upon the foregoing job descriptions, is simply no. On the other hand, from the foregoing accounts, this does not seem to be quite the right question, not at least for HTS team members engaged in HTS$_1$. The proper question is, *could* anyone hired through such a process meet these requirements successfully? Would their brief four-month orientation at Fort Leavenworth be enough (absent a prior career either in the military itself, or as a field anthropologist under the most demanding of circumstances) to prepare them for the risks and rigors they would face? Would they end up proving an asset, or a liability, even to their HTS team members, let alone to the military forces they are trying to assist? Would the rewards they might bring in protecting human subjects and lowering the incidents of conflict or mistaken resort to deadly force be worth the risks they would incur to themselves, let alone worth the implicit threat that all noncombatant support personnel pose to military units when deployed in a combat zone? That is to say, the real problems, including true moral dilemmas or conflicts of professional ethics, likely arise in filling these positions, providing the promised training, and delivering on the promises contained in the description of the overall HTS mission.

At present, we rely for our evaluation of such important questions entirely on the scattered reports and rumors emanating from the field. As noted, the scant factual reports vary widely. In the fall of 2007, with the first HTS team initially deployed to Afghanistan and five presumably embedded in Iraq, a Pulitzer Prize–winning reporter, David Rohde of the *New York Times*, featured interviews with the participating anthropologists and their military supervisors, praising the program. The article reported on the experiences of a "soft-spoken civilian anthropologist" named "Tracy," and the evaluations of her supervisors and chain of command:

> Tracy, who asked that her surname not be used for security reasons, is a member of the first Human Terrain Team, an experimental Pentagon program that assigns anthropologists and other social scientists to American combat units in Afghanistan and Iraq. Her team's ability to understand subtle points of tribal relations—in one case spotting a land dispute that allowed the Taliban to bully parts of a major tribe—has won the praise of officers who say they are seeing concrete results.
>
> Col. Martin Schweitzer, commander of the 82nd Airborne Division unit working with the anthropologists here, said that the unit's combat operations had been reduced by 60 percent since the scientists arrived in February, and that the soldiers were now able to focus more on improving security, health care and education for the population. "We're looking at this from a human perspective, from a social scientist's perspective," he said. "We're not focused on the enemy. We're focused on bringing governance down to the people."
>
> In September, Defense Secretary Robert M. Gates authorized a $40 million expansion of the program, which will assign teams of anthropologists and social scientists to each of the 26 American combat brigades in Iraq and Afghanistan. Since early September, five new teams have been deployed in the Baghdad area, bringing the total to six. (Rhode 2007)

That report, as of this writing, is nearly two years old.[24] As we noted, other, more recent reports have been less flattering. Some tell of malfunction rather than abusive practice. Others dismiss the entire project of HTS "teams" as a useless waste of resources, while the most recent have contained reports of the deaths of two and the serious injury of a third program participant (who subsequently died of complications from her injuries while hospitalized). In this respect, the testimony of our embedded anthropologist, Mark Dawson, blogging from Iraq, speaks forcefully, and seems sharply at odds with what both supporters and critics of the programs have attempted to project as its current condition. He writes:

> What's it like? The Army has been helpful, hospitable, arranged about any kind of fieldwork we wish to do. It should be no surprise that they were polite and helpful, but deeply skeptical over any real value we might add other than eating the food in the Dining Facility (DFAC). But now we have gotten a seat at the table, so to speak, people request our assistance on various topics. . . . Looking at the AAA controversy after two months actually in the field makes some of the issues laughable. This idea that Human Terrain Teams are involved in gathering intelligence for example (we'll ignore for the moment the error of jargon people make: you don't "gather" intelligence). I have seen this written about as if there are people in trench coats and dark glasses hovering by the HTT door just dying for a chance to peek at our work! Lord what a load of nonsense. I don't know how many times this can be said, no . . . we don't, ever. They don't even want us to. Why, because it's not our jobs, and they have professionals for that. [Instead] we look at people in transition from jobs in one sector to another, how effective governance is in areas, issues of economy. The meetings I sit in are about building schools, putting in water purification facilities, trying to help local governments get more support for their communities from the Iraq national government, understanding complex issues related to agriculture and the economy . . . any anthropologist involved with development work would be pretty [much] at home here.

Once again, it is important to stress that this account, while it may count as "field notes" of a sort, is the report of a single individual. Despite the preference of anthropological critics of "writing culture" for such reports, this one may not be representative of successes or failures of the program as a whole, let alone of the adequacy with which this kind of program is administered by the private sector in the midst of combat. What is telling, and what rings true on the basis of the testimony of myriad others with onsite, on-the-ground experiences of this sort to report from their deployment in both Afghanistan and Iraq (including skeptical journalists embedded with combat troops) is what follows:

I think what has struck me the most since I have been here are the relationships that the military have built with their Iraqi counterparts helping them [in] creating their own local governmental structures. Most of these young women and men have been trained to lead tanks and infantry companies. They showed up in Iraq and someone told them to establish security in an area and help the local population create an effective structure for representation to the provincial and national level. I have done part of my fieldwork in these meetings all over our area of the country. It's amazing and impressive. They have made it happen with no training and little support. It's fragile, rough, does not work always the way it should, but it's indeed on the way. These military people figured out how to make it happen simply because they had no other choice but to try. *They have all told me they wish anthropologists and governmental experts had been there to help them 12 months ago* [my emphasis].

This recent account squares, in its mixed assessment and moral ambiguity, with similar accounts of progress or its lack from military personnel rotating in from the field. Surface Warfare officers with degrees in oceanography find themselves detailed to disassemble improvised explosive devices (IEDs) in the Sunni Triangle, while P-3 pilots and submariners "I.A'd" ("individually augmented," in military-speak) to Afghanistan, command special forces units in rebuilding schools, roads, hospitals, and constructing wells and water treatment plants while fending off Taliban attacks against the villagers in their regions. "It's okay, sir," one Navy captain joked recently, during a video teleconference from Kabul with the U.S. president, secretary of state, and secretary of defense. "I spent the night in a Holiday Inn Express."[25]

Dawson's description also aligns with the earlier accounts of independent news reports, like that of David Rodhe in the *New York Times*, and also by the head of the HTS team attached to the 82nd Airborne Division in Iraq in the fall of 2007 on *The Diane Rehm Show*. In all instances, those reports are more detailed, nuanced, and usually at odds with the portraits painted by war's supporters, detractors, and also with the verbal snapshots obtained from conventional media sources.[26] The complexity of which this individual testifies, and the bureaucratic and logistical complaints he lodges, can be traced to a number of factors worthy of consideration because they have a substantial bearing on whether, on balance, the HTS program will prove effective, let alone morally justifiable, in achieving its aims.

Conclusions: The Need for External Program Review

What emerges as the principal moral (as opposed to ethical) dilemma on the foregoing accounts has less to do with "clandestine research" or malevolent covert actions than with safety and transparency. The HTS program is similar in many respects to the practice of embedding journalists, chaplains, and perhaps also medical personnel with combat troops. Such personnel can be tremendously helpful, but they also pose a grave danger to themselves and others. The kidnapping of reporter David Rohde and the serious injury and subsequent death of HTS team member Paula Loyd illustrate the problem of "forward-deploying" nonessential personnel in combat zones. The moral dilemma, as stated, is whether the benefits and rewards of doing so outweigh these risks.

It is impossible to answer that question, in turn, without a much fuller account of HTS activities than we are thus far able to give. These important questions of safety and cost-effectiveness can be addressed only through a full program review. It is high time that such a review is conducted. The Human Terrain System is, admittedly, a fairly new program with only a few units in the field, and there has been little assessment thus far of its overall effectiveness. That situation, in turn, owes much to the unusual requirements of the program, recruitment difficulties, and complexity of operation. This would be true even if the supervising PMC, BAE Systems, were able to retain the very best talent, and train and deploy individuals with the most exemplary personal character on all fronts. The problems would be magnified, quite naturally, if some of the personnel hired and deployed turned out to be unqualified, irresponsible, or incompetent, or if (as alleged) some BAE management staff themselves were irascible, difficult, or malevolent.

At present, however, there is no reliable system for external program oversight, nor, just as important, for program review and assessment. This is unfortunately typical of government programs. Enormous energy and thoughtfulness go into their creation, but the government and military are far less effective when it comes to managing and evaluating the effectiveness of ongoing programs. Such concerns are often an afterthought in the planning stages, and are brought to the fore only by an internal crisis or by external criticism. To date, there is no evidence than anyone internal to the HTS program has provided procedurally for such program review and evaluation. We rely on endorsements from participants and advocates, or criticism from detractors, most of which consist more of rumor than of fact.

Program review and assessment, however, is a requirement for any government contract, in compliance with requirements of full accountability to Congress, taxpayers, and other relevant stakeholders. This is true of every single military, intelligence, or security program, whether classified or not, including all activities of the CIA. There are absolutely no grounds for deeming anything in this particular program area as "classified." Thus, in light of the questions and controversy surrounding this program, such a review is incumbent, and should be carried out as soon as possible.

The procedures for peer review are quite familiar to any who have worked on government-funded research or in the academic realm. An external team should be constituted, likely under the jurisdiction of the Government Accountability Office (GAO), and perhaps including some of those subject matter experts who have raised questions about the nature and effectiveness of the program. At least one member of the review team should, in addition, be familiar with government procurement policy in order to evaluate the role of the PMC.[27] A full review of program documents and records should be conducted, and site visits made to training facilities in the United States and to representative teams deployed in both war theaters. The questions concerning safety of team members, adequacy of training, suitability of credentials, performance of the supervising PMC (BAE Systems), effectiveness of HTS teams on deployment, and ultimately, of both risk to troops and cost-effectiveness of the program itself in terms of the benefits to deployed troops and the local populations affected, should be thoroughly addressed and explored. Any questions concerning disclosure and informed consent regarding the performance of HTS teams among local populations, such as those raised persistently by Professor Price, should also be addressed during those site visits. Indeed, Price himself should volunteer, and probably should be selected, to serve as a member of the review team. That is about as transparent as one can get, and the American public deserves nothing less.

In its magnitude, this requirement is a far greater problem in practical or applied ethics than any malevolent actions or intentions, or any "secret or clandestine research" in which participants may be engaged. We have, through this experimental program, apparently recruited some very decent and talented individuals, placed them in harm's way in the midst of combat, and asked them to "do some good." As with our military forces, to whom we gave essentially the same vague mission, we have provided no guidance, no framework for success, and no procedures to evaluate how well or poorly they are doing. Meanwhile, back home, uninformed pundits and state-side journalists spin dark tales of malevolent conspiracy, and rant ponderously and pompously about "secret research." Mark Dawson is right: it would all be laughable, were it not—as in the cases of Bhatia, Suveges, reporter David Rohde, and now Paula Loyd—so thoroughly tragic.

Notes

1. The blog from Mark Dawson can be found at http://www.ethnography. com/ (accessed October 10, 2008), and archived, along with similar accounts or responses from other HTS team members, on the site for subsequent reference at www.ethnography.com/index.php?s=HTS+Teams. The author is hardly an unbiased source of information on the program. It is clear from his remarks that he is contemptuous of the main groups of critics of the program "back home," and discouraged by the AAA's handling of the controversy. Also important, he does not identify himself as an academic or former academic anthropologist, but as a "practitioner," meaning one who has worked as an anthropologist in the private sector even before accepting a position in the HTS program. The responses to this and previous postings by this author on HTS, moreover, elicited a number of responses, some highly critical, and many raising legitimate questions about the accuracy or comprehensiveness of his account, or the moral probity of the terms of his employment and the working conditions he describes.

2. An earlier article, dated July 23, 2008, at the same hyperlink is the first of three published by this journalist, most simply repeating, updating, or amplifying the charges found here. Stanton describes himself as "a Virginia-based writer specializing in national security and political matters, and author of *Talking Politics with God & the Devil in Washington, DC* [n.d., n.p.]" He, likewise, is not an unbiased source, as most of his information for this article appears to come from Professor David Price's book *Anthropological Intelligence* (Price 2008).

3. Attributing the cause of death of the two HTS team members killed in action to their inexperience or inadequate training seems to be inaccurate. As the analysis (below) of the private military contractor BAE Systems and its hiring practices shows, these two team members either would have had to have been former U.S. Army personnel with prior experience and considerable training in counterinsurgency, or else have provided evidence of equivalent experience. Robert Rubinstein indicates that, although Michael Bhatia had not to his knowledge served in the U.S. Army, he had extensive experience in post-conflict interventions in Afghanistan and with the United Nations in East Timor. The charges in Stanton's *Pravda* article, above, have been, item by item, disputed or refuted by one of the principals named and criticized in it, Dr. Montgomery McFate. In particular, she points out that IZ3 Nicole Suveges was an Army reservist who had years of prior experience in combat zones in Bosnia and Iraq. See excerpts from her letter to the editor of *Newsweek*, offering a very different perspective on these same developments reported by Stanton and other journalists, who tend to cite sources from the Network of Concerned Anthropologists: http://www.ethnography.com/index. php?s=HTS+Teams.

4. The following five illustrations are found in the 2007 CEAUSSIC report, pp. 27–28.

5. References to these two sets of guiding principles occur repeatedly in the CEAUSSIC report without citation, source, or reference of specific relevant provisions. The "Helsinki Declarations" refers in fact to the World Medical Organization's "Declaration of Helsinki," first adopted in 1964, setting forth protocols for human subject research: *British Medical Journal* (December 7, 1996); 313 (7070):1448–1449. The "Belmont Report" is the short name given to the report of the U.S. Department of Health, Education and Welfare's National Commission for the Protection of Human Subjects of Biomedical and Behavioral Research in 1979, titled: "Ethical Principles and Guidelines for the Protection of Human Subjects of Research." The relevant provisions of both documents are largely incorporated into the AAA's existing (1998) Code of Ethics, insofar as these protocols extend to human subjects of behavioral science versus biomedical research. The documents collectively stress the scientific validity of research, the avoidance of harm, the necessity of obtaining the informed consent of research subjects, and transparency in conduct of the research and dissemination of results. The latter document is available online from the U.S. National Institutes of Health at http://ohsr.od.nih.gov/guidelines/belmont.html.

6. Recall that, in making just such a comparison, military anthropologist Kerry Fosher reports that a member of her audience likened such an effort to making a sympathetic study of Nazi concentration camp guards (Fosher 2008). It is symptomatic of the deeper underlying problem here that anyone could, with a straight face, liken an impartial study of one of our nation's domestic police forces, however flawed and morally imperfect one suspected their organizations of acting on occasion, to a study of Nazi concentration camp guards. And yet such virulent and uncritical prejudices seem to drive the argument.

7. Here I'm indebted to Anna J. Simons for originally suggesting this line of inquiry in her review and critique of my *Journal of Military Ethics* article (Lucas 2008). This, and some of the remaining descriptions of specific activities, follow from her suggestions.

8. "Anthropologists and War," (Rehm 2007). Guests included McFate, Price (via telephone from the West Coast), Lt. Col. Villacres (via telephone from Iraq), Col. John Agoglia, director of the U.S. Army's Peacekeeping and Stability Operations Institute, and David Rohde, a renowned reporter from the *New York Times*, whose article on HTS teams from the previous week is cited below. Rohde was kidnapped by Taliban insurgents on November 10, 2008 and held incommunicado for more than seven months. Though feared dead, he managed to escape safely and take refuge in a nearby Pakistani army base in northern Waziristan on Friday, June 19, 2009. See Keith B. Richburg, "Reporter Escapes Taliban Captors," *Washington Post*, June 21, 2009, A-1.

9. In Price and Gonzalez (2007: 3), this remark is attributed to David Kipp of the Foreign Military Studies Office at Fort Leavenworth, Kansas, who reportedly described HTS as "a CORDS for the 21st century."

10. The reference is to Condominas (1994). It is not clear why translating a published work into the readers' language is "illegal" unless the intent was to publish in violation of copyright. The point is, rather, that research results were being appropriated and used contrary to professional intent and the constraints of professional ethics.

11. It is unclear whether their objection is to the failure of full disclosure, including funding sources and purposes to which the ethnographic data will be put, or obtaining "informed consent" allegedly under false pretenses, or, as with David Price, fear of the eventual use to which such data might be put by researchers. See "Zapotec Indigenous People in Mexico Demand Transparency from U.S. Scholar," by Saulo Araujo of the Union of Organizations of the Sierra Juarez of Oaxaca (UNOSJO), reported on January 22, 2009 (http://elenemigocomun.net/2059). There has as yet been no verification that this research or the personnel conducting it were, in fact, connected to the HTS program.

12. One exception to this rule that comes to mind is the recent moratorium on genetic and stem-cell research, the former self-imposed by researchers on the basis of widespread, if somewhat anomalous, moral concerns. Given the nature of this research, many of those concerns (or fears of abuse) constituted speculations on matters of moral and professional principle that might be (but at the time, had not yet been) grounded in any actual negative experiences. But this moratorium was hardly a priori: indeed, it was imposed by researchers (and some would argue, forced upon those researchers by fears of the general public) after many years of breathtaking scientific discoveries and advances. The chief complaint about the moratorium was that it constituted unwarranted interference by nonspecialists in scientific and medical research activities that otherwise offered substantial promise of aid and protection to otherwise vulnerable victims (admittedly of disease or genetic defect, rather than of war). At this writing, the stem-cell research ban has been partially lifted by the incoming presidential administration; the wider voluntary moratorium on genetic research remains in place.

To put it mildly, this episode in human genetic research would be an odd precedent for anthropologists to invoke to defend their own a priori opposition to working with the military at the present time! Yet the association collectively does seem to be behaving in a fashion analogous to that of politicians and the public regarding genetic research. This is hardly a flattering comparison.

13. There is a kind of informal methodology for hypothetical cases, of which vexed anthropologists are not likely to be aware. A hypothetical case, for example, should never be constructed simply to demonstrate a form of disputed behavior, so as to "prove" that such disputed behaviors occur. So one would not, for example, construct a fictitious case in which the military and its anthropologists were simply engaged in illicit behavior: that would be question-begging. The question is instead whether any or all such forms of collaboration are illicit. Thus, as in the preceding chapter, one first identifies the abuses or problems with which one is concerned, and

then constructs a hypothetical case (a military, engaged in an illegal war of intervention, seeking the assistance of anthropologists, for example) in which such elements are present, so as to test whether or not they constitute abuses, or automatically result in the feared violation of professional codes of conduct. And frequently, these cases need to be nested and varied, as were the three main variations used in the preceding chapter, to determine where the precise problem in question is likely to arise. As with all kinds of thought experiments, this requires some practice, and perhaps some background subject expertise. The CEAUSSIC commission's own attempts at hypothetical case construction above do not inspire confidence in this respect.

14. There are more positive assessments from the Marine Corps perspective, though not necessarily from personnel returning directly from theater. See, for example, Sullivan (2009) for an upbeat internal assessment of how the insights of linguists and cultural anthropologists can "empower" Marine Corps personnel to function with greater effectiveness and moral probity in zones of combat.

15. Roberto J. Gonzalez (2007) alleges such behavior, and the charge is repeated in the "Pledge of Non-participation in Counter-insurgency" from the Network of Concerned Anthropologists (NCA 2007), which urges anthropologists to "refrain from assisting the U.S. military . . . through torture, interrogation, or tactical advice." These and similar articles in turn cite exposés of torture at Abu Ghraib (Hersh 2004, Packer 2006) as sources. The accuracy of these allegations, however, is disputed by New Mexican anthropologist Laura McNamara on the basis of an interview with Hersh and her examination of thousands of pages of Department of Defense directives obtained under the Freedom of Information Act (FOIA). She reports that there is no evidence of collusion by anthropologists in interrogation, or even in instituting improper detention practices (like taking humiliating photographs of prisoners) at either Guantánamo Bay or Abu Ghraib. See her "Interrogation Diaries," at http://interrogationdiaries.blogspot.com. Price, in *The Diane Rehm Show* interview (Rehm 2007), acknowledges McNamara's findings and concedes there is no evidence confirming anthropologists' participation in such activities. And though it might seem odd in the extreme for a philosopher to be pointing this out, McNamara's work is also significant in that it represents one of the few legitimate attempts to move empirical material into this debate.

16. These conclusions are thus similar to the results of an equally heated but far less public debate within the American Psychological Association over the professional probity ("the ethics") of psychologists serving at either prison. One might disagree with these conclusions, however, and argue that the moral predicament of both social scientists was equivalent: both are condemned "in principle," regardless of their specific duties or activities, because both were collaborating in illegal acts of detention. Such a conclusion seems to confuse the "ethics of the profession" with the wider moral argument over war and detention of suspected terrorists. In the latter instance, it is not the finding of any court, legislative body, or NGO "watchdog" organization regarding either detention facility that the original detention of suspects

was either immoral or illegal. The detention of suspects at both prisons was, instead, anomalous, inasmuch as the suspects were classified as "unlawful combatants." The extant moral and legal debate was thus not about their detention per se, but about the terms and duration of their detention and, even more, about the rights of suspects in custody (such as their presumed innocence, right to counsel, right not to be subjected to proscribed methods of interrogation and torture as POWs falling under the jurisdiction of Geneva protocols, or threatened with "rendition" to cooperating nations in which these constraints are not observed).

The recent closure of facilities such as the Guantánamo Bay prison are responses to allegations of improper practices of detention. So the anthropologist in the above case is absolved, while the complicit psychologist is condemned, not for their very presence at the detention facility or cooperation in the detention itself, but for their participation in proscribed activities directed against detainees that brought the detention itself into disrepute. Once again, the facts of the case, and not the political proclivities of opponents of the "war on terror," nor of opponents of detention of suspects in that "war" on principle, is what adjudicates the moral culpability of the individuals cited in these cases.

17. "A Pentagon Olive Branch to Academe," *Inside Higher Ed* (April 16, 2008), p. 2 (www.insidehighered.com/news/2008/04/16/minerva). Secretary Gates is apparently referring to an earlier remark made by Col. Martin Schweitzer, commander of the 82nd Airborne Division in Afghanistan, originally cited in Rohde (2007). One wonders, of course, how such statistical judgments are arrived at for purposes of comparison. Upon reading this claim, Price, whom we've identified as a prominent critic of HTS, requested supporting evidence for this claim of success via the FOIA. *Wired Magazine's* "Danger Room" journalist, Sharon Weinberger, reported that Price's FOIA inquiry had not uncovered any study or report to substantiate these numbers. Apparently this military officer's statement was more an enthusiastic appraisal than a careful assessment of the program. See "Military Research: the Pentagon's Culture Wars," in *Nature News* (October 1, 2008).

18. One such persistent critic is Maximilian ("Max") Forte, a professor of anthropology at Concordia University (Montreal, Quebec), who routinely posts articles with blog commentary and readers' replies on his website, Open Anthropology (http://www.openanthropology.wordpress.com). He describes himself as relentlessly opposed to "institutional and disciplinary anthropology, insofar as it has or may continue to support, justify, participate in, or abide by imperial projects." His perspectives on the discipline and its habits, as well as specific comments on the HTS project, can be found on his website.

19. There is an enormous and burgeoning literature on this phenomenon, and on its advisability. Probably the best-known work is Singer (2003/2008). For a somewhat different, and more positive account of the activities, quality of performance, and moral and legal questions involved in using such contractors in combat zones, see Carafano (2008). These two works adequately map the boundaries of highly disputed terrain over

this interesting development. There are troubling ramifications that we cannot explore in detail in this book, such as the increasing reliance on such contractors to make combat operations even possible to sustain, together with questions about whether such reliance makes it easier for democracies like the U.S., Britain, and Australia to pursue military options in foreign policy without the full knowledge and consent of the electorate, in violation of the classical just war requirement of "legitimate authority." As a professional matter, moreover, why should taxpayers pay private contractors three times the wages we pay military personnel to do the same job? What does this do to military training, professionalism, and morale? These issues are currently under scrutiny at the U.S. Naval Academy's Stockdale Center for Ethics and Leadership. The Executive Summary of findings and recommendations regarding PMCs from the Center's 2009 McCain Conference may be accessed at http://www.usna.edu/ethics/seminars/mccain.htm.

20. As this book goes to press, the Obama administration and Congress are instigating vigorous inquiries into the DOD's policy of heavy reliance upon private contractors for security and logistical support in combat. See Tiron (2009).

21. In January 2009, partly as a response to the problems documented in this chapter, the BAE Systems contract was terminated and the HTS program directly subsumed under TRADOC, the U.S. Army's training and doctrine command. The new regime may be studied at its website, established January 15, 2009, at http://humanterrainsystem.army.mil. The job advertisements and position descriptions detailed below have been largely transposed intact to this new site. However, the positions are now standard civilian DOD positions in the U.S. Civil Service, rather than PMC positions. With those changes, most of the remainder of the present analysis remains intact.

22. This information is from the company's website: www.baesystems.com.

23. These position descriptions have been migrated largely intact, and are now posted at the HTS TRADOC website: http://humanterrainsystem.army.mil/employment.html.

24. Some readers might also note the additional oddity that all the credible journalistic reports thus far seem to cite the Army's 82nd Airborne Division. Lt. Col. Villacres of the 2nd Brigade Combat Team of the 82nd Airborne Division, on *The Diane Rehm Show* in October 2007, telephoned from Baghdad. *New York Times* reporter David Rohde, author of the account cited above, was also present in the WAMU studio in Washington, D.C., at the time. But his report, written only a few days before, is situated in Afghanistan and quotes Col. Martin Schweitzer, also from the Army's 82nd Airborne Division. One wonders how thin this particular division is stretched.

25. That story was related during a brief furlough in the United States by Captain Scott Cooledge, USN, commander of a provincial reconstruction team in Gahzni Province, Afghanistan, the keynote speaker at the Stockdale Center's semiannual Ethics Essay Award banquet on September 17, 2008. Secretaries Gates and Rice, he reported, were somewhat mystified by his reference to a U.S. hotel chain in Afghanistan, but President Bush got the joke.

26. For more nuanced background accounts of Iraq in particular, readers might wish to consult the reflections published in the November 27, 2008, edition of the *Washington Post*, by Captain Giles Clarke, USMC, midway through his third tour of duty since 2003, with a personal investment of more than nineteen months in that country (Clarke 2008).

27. Inasmuch as that dimension of the program has now been discontinued, it would no longer be absolutely necessary to have a defense procurement or contract specialist on the team. All the remaining questions about staffing, administration, and competent performance are still appropriate as described for program review and assessment.

CHAPTER SIX

"Anthropologists without Borders"

I conclude this inquiry[1] by both summarizing what we've learned so far, and proposing some strategies that anthropologists might wish to consider for engaging appropriately with military forces. As we summarize the findings of these several chapters, it might be good also to offer concrete recommendations for reflection and action by anthropologists and their professional associations on how they might serve reliably as resources and guides to best practices for the engagement of their individual members in various forms of military anthropology.

It is appropriate to reflect, as well, on how those associations might establish procedures for the institutional review and support of these efforts that will be less prone to inherent conflicts of interest and unhelpful politicization than the present ad hoc arrangements. The role of formal, published Codes of Ethics or guides to professional best practice should play an important but not a determinative role in these institutional procedures. Placing too strong an emphasis on establishing ironclad guidelines, even if these are only advisory, may have unintended consequences. This can be demonstrated by first returning briefly to the past debates about secrecy and transparency in the evaluation of "practical" or "practice anthropology." Recall that many, at the time, regarded those outcomes as highly unsatisfactory. That dissatisfaction reverberates in the present "Turner amendment" (see chapter 1), which has occasioned the need for even further deliberations on this vexed question.

"Clandestinity"

Anthropologist Gerald D. Berreman reflects with evident bitterness on the aftermath of the Thailand affair, and the subsequent deliberations over the lessons it enshrined about "secret and clandestine research." He expresses moral indignation, even outrage, over the gradual weakening of explicit language contained in the "Principles of Professional Responsibility" in 1971, leading eventually to omission of that explicit language in the current American Association of Anthropologists' (AAA) Code of Ethics by 1998. In particular, he focuses his criticism on the proposal, by the AAA's president-elect in 1985, June Helm, to come to terms with the emerging needs of practical or "practice" anthropology by distinguishing more carefully between "secret" and "clandestine" activity, and by proposing to eliminate the latter term as pejorative. "Why?" he asks.

> Was it that, although "secret" and "clandestine" mean the same, they are after all necessary activities in the minds of some practicing anthropologists, and "clandestine" just *sounds* worse? . . . It seems that *secret* is to be the word for approved clandestinity; *clandestine* will be the word for disapproved secrecy or . . . the "pejorative" word for secrecy. . . . I regard this as abject surrender of principle to a misguided practicality; a sacrifice of public interest to misperceived self interest, replacing ethics with greed. (Berreman 2003: 67–68; author's emphases)

He proceeds, by way of contrast, to cite his own conclusions about "secret research," offered at the annual meeting of the Association for Asian Studies in 1970, at the height of the unfolding professional crisis and debate about Thailand.

> There is no scholarly activity any of us can do better in secret than in public. There is none we can pursue as well, in fact, because of the implicit but inevitable restraints secrecy places on scholarship. To do research in secret, or to report it in secret, is to invite suspicion, and legitimately so *because secrecy is the hallmark of intrigue, not scholarship*. (Berreman 1971: 396; my emphasis)

There is much else that earns Berreman's ire about the way anthropologists, in his estimation, gradually undermined their sense of disciplinary ethics and professional responsibilities over the ensuing years. He rails against the influence of "Reaganethics" in the 1980s, for example, and laments the gradual loss of a strict sense of accountability for one's professional actions, and even more what he perceived as the downgrading of what had once been anthropologists' explicit and "paramount" commitment to the welfare of those they study.

But it is secrecy and "clandestinity" to which he persistently returns in this essay, and for which he reserves his greatest sense of indignation over what he perceives as the discipline of anthropology's increasing tolerance, under the presumed influence of practical and applied (nonacademic) anthropology, of secrecy and intrigue. "To tolerate secret research is to sacrifice the credibility of anthropology as a research discipline and a humane science," he fumes. "So much for secret and/or clandestine activity as excusable, much less legitimate, by anthropologists, and so much for an ethics that permits it."

It is well to recall this eloquent, impassioned, and high-minded indictment of anthropology's alleged erosion of conscience, for Berreman evidently captures the sentiments of many in the profession, even as his ruminations reflect the discipline's widely shared understanding of its recent past. As a victim of the vicious intrigue of his own colleagues, moreover, one can understand the personal anger, as well as the professional indignation, that infuses Berreman's rhetoric and strengthens his commitment to what he evidently sees as the highest possible standards of ethical conduct and professional principle.

One can surely understand and sympathize with such sentiments. I would argue, however, that *we must not, in the end, agree*. For, though eloquent and unquestionably high-minded, Berreman himself, and colleagues who may yet agree with him on these matters are, in a number of important respects, gravely mistaken.

In an editorial for the *Chronicle of Higher Education*, published only a few days prior to the AAA's 2008 annual meeting (at which these very matters would once again become the object of heated discussion), Professor Carolyn Fluehr-Lobban offered an equally eloquent, if far less impassioned plea for a more profound understanding of these underlying problems than Berreman's essay affords. Her editorial's subtitle revealed this intent: "The Terms 'Secret Research' and 'Do No Harm' Need to Be Clarified." More than any other, Professor Fluehr-Lobban has proven herself the conscience of her profession, and her long record of service to the discipline in these respects, including her many other thoughtful and reflective essays on professional ethics, have earned her the right to be heard respectfully by her colleagues.

I have found her work particularly instructive for this project, in large part because, unlike her colleagues who are otherwise equally committed to a principled discussion of the ethics of the profession, she has taken the time and trouble to ground her reflections about anthropology in the wider public and professional discourse about such matters. That is to say, she has invested the necessary effort to make herself a subject-matter expert on relevant aspects of moral philosophy and professional ethics more generally.

It was from that resulting perspective, for example, that she was able almost single-handedly to transform the discipline's prior and otherwise unpardonable myopia regarding "informed consent."[2] I have argued in this work that anthropology's internal moral history, its "litany of shame," and its attitudes of antipathy toward the government and the military based upon suspicions regarding "secret and clandestine research" likewise require a profound reexamination and perhaps transformation.

For her part, Fluehr-Lobban never explicitly cross-examines or questions the accuracy of her discipline's historical consciousness on any issue other than informed consent. In this editorial, for example, she cites the recent controversy over HTS, and acknowledges the AAA Executive Board's admonition to scholars "not to participate in the Human Terrain Teams," citing the risk of erosion of scientific trust, the inherent contradiction in essential anthropological methodology, and even the personal worry that "several social scientists have been killed in these operations."[3] She likewise acknowledges that

> part of the work [that Human Terrain Teams] do unquestionably causes harm to some people—but it may prevent harm to others. In addition, we know so little about what the teams do, or the projects they are part of, that objective evaluation is impossible at present. (Fluehr-Lobban 2008)

I have likewise had occasion to note the problems with uncertainty about specific activities, lack of concrete evidence or cases, and the difficulty in assessing the effectiveness, as well as the moral and professional probity, of such activities in the preceding chapter. Specifically, in response to her most recent comments, there is no concrete evidence of any harm coming to anyone as a result of HTS activities, other than that sustained by the three HTS team members already cited. What Fluehr-Lobban appears to have in mind in this qualifying statement is not so much harm *known* to have been done by HTS teams, as the *prospect* of harm of the inadvertent sort, of the "double-effect" sort that we discussed in chapter 4: harm that might occur through misuse of the anthropologist's work, or else harm that could conceivably occur simultaneously with (but altogether independently of) their presence in the area.

In the face of persistent and sustained controversy, and in light of the underlying uncertainty about essential specifics, Fluehr-Lobban wisely advises her colleagues to do what any knowledgeable outside consultant would likewise recommend: to step back, find (or construct) an analogous situation, change the context (but not the terms) of the debate, and examine the disputed underlying principles at arm's length. She invites us to set aside HTS teams in Iraq, and instead consider anthropologists aiding the humanitarian intervention in Darfur.

She describes the conflict that Western and Sudanese anthropologists, working with humanitarian aid organizations in the region, encounter when assisting rape victims. The need, as well as the desire, is to document this heinous act with evidence and eyewitness testimony, in part to help build the case that such atrocities are being inflicted on innocent victims, and that assistance (including armed military assistance) from the wider international community ought to be forthcoming (even though thus far, for the most part, it has not).

That fully justifiable project, however, runs afoul of local customs whose sinister dimensions anthropologists, more than most, can fully appreciate and interpret to well-intended associates: the prospect of "honor killings" of the rape victim by her family, for example, or the prospect of igniting a violent and disproportionate armed retaliation against, not only the perpetrators, but any other individuals thought to be their kin. And so the necessity arises to keep such discoveries or research results "secret." Otherwise, she writes:

> a powerful, well-intentioned nongovernmental organization may inadvertently increase harm, while striving to lessen it. On the other hand, armed military units, often seen as causing harm, may in fact offer more real protection to potential rape victims and lessen harm in the course of their engagement. Thus harm is not an absolute concept; it is subject to cultural context. (Fluehr-Lobban 2008)

What is more, she concludes, "anthropologists make excellent brokers in such delicate environments, helping interpret and debate the issues with the people being studied."[4]

Fluehr-Lobban concludes her editorial by discussing and recommending some institutional arrangements and procedural guarantees that might help to adjudicate such moral and professional dilemmas more effectively. We will turn to these at the very end of this chapter, as we consider the ways in which anthropologists might, indeed, make excellent "brokers" of cultural knowledge who might help to defuse crises and avoid the doing of deliberate or even inadvertent harm to innocent victims of war and violence.

For the moment, let us examine her analysis of the concept of "secrecy." In large part, I believe we should not only concur with her astute observations, I believe also that we can commend them even further, on somewhat different grounds. From her example of anthropologists in Darfur, we discern that "secrecy" is not itself a moral (or rather, an immoral) policy, as Berreman mistakenly took it to be, nor does its pursuit automatically entail that other fundamental moral principles will necessarily be violated (as he and others in the profession likewise seem to believe). "Secrecy" is, rather, a method, or better, an essential part of an overall strategy. Secrecy is a *policy* employed in pursuit of certain strategic aims or goals, or in behalf of some set of underlying strategic intentions. We condone or condemn the policy of secrecy, accordingly, on the basis of our overall evaluation of these strategic goals and underlying intentions.

In this case, as Fluehr-Lobban notes, "If a woman who has been raped asks for anonymity, few scholars would consider it ethical to refuse her," even though honoring that request entails keeping the results of their "research" into rape, in this case, "secret." Why do we not condemn secrecy or (technically speaking) "secret research" in this case? I believe it is because, in this instance, we can discern that the underlying strategy, the intentions behind this policy of secrecy, are to respect the autonomy of those being studied, not only (as Fluehr-Lobban suggests) their "right not to be studied," but also *their right not to be harmed* or to be put at risk of harm. Most important, this is their choice to make, and their life to live (or lose), and not ours. Our policy of secrecy is thus part of an overall strategy that honors this fundamental "moral fact" about them. To act otherwise in these circumstances, as Fluehr-Lobban implies, would constitute an act of gravely unprofessional behavior. There is nothing inherently wrong, we conclude, with a policy of secrecy employed as part of an overall strategy aimed at respecting the rights and protecting the well-being of research subjects.

I hasten to add that neither my analysis nor (I suspect) hers are grounded in some sort of crass, utilitarian calculus of means and ends. It forms no part of my own argument on behalf of her observations to hold somehow that "transparency" and openness are principles we can override with a policy of secrecy merely whenever it is part of a strategy whose hoped-for results redound to the benefit of all concerned. One could, of course, make that sort of argument on behalf of the policy elicited in Fluehr-Lobban's example. It might seem that this is the overall strategy that anthropologists in Darfur, in this case, are employing. But I think there are good grounds for rejecting that as poor reasoning and a bad argument in this case, not the least because the resulting temptation to override important principles whenever it seems convenient to do so becomes overwhelming.

That recognition, I surmise, is what lay behind Berreman's denouncing his colleagues for having replaced "ethics with greed." This, I also suspect, was the strong but incompletely formed intuition that lay behind Franz Boas's denunciation of his colleagues for engaging in espionage. Utilitarian calculus, notoriously difficult to effect in the proper manner, quickly degenerates into a purely subjective calculus of expediency. The morality of expedience is, finally, no morality at all, as Berreman rightly suspected, and we are probably right to denounce our colleagues (or perhaps, more properly, ourselves) for stooping to it.

I would recur instead to the teachings of the German enlightenment philosopher Immanuel Kant on this subject. Surely a formidable (and, some would complain, unintelligible) philosopher in his own right, Kant was no partisan of either expediency or utilitarian calculus (which he held to be notoriously unreliable). He was, in point of fact, nearly as strong an advocate of acting purely "on principle" as either Berreman or Boas.

What rescues Fluehr-Lobban's example, on Kantian terms, is not the expected (or hoped-for) outcome, but the respect shown, in our policy of secrecy, for the rape victim's autonomy. The ability to act, choose, and decide on a course of life, our moral freedom and self-determination, if you will, is our most essential and (for each individual moral agent) most precious possession. We might rightly characterize this as a capacity for (moral) deliberation and consequent action. This is a capacity that every fully mature, fully developed and endowed human being possesses, regardless of his or her historical and cultural context, and so (Kant also thought) might "beings" of many other diverse sorts. Exploring the ramifications of that last observation constitutes a fascinating detour in itself that we shall not bother to pursue here, save that it led, in part, to his offering the first formal university lecture course (anywhere in the Western world, at least) on a subject he first labeled "*Anthropologie.*"[5]

In any case, the constraint Kant imposes as a matter of principle is that we cannot do things to ourselves or to one another that deprive ourselves or others of that capacity. He offers several different descriptions or accounts of this general constraint, or underlying "imperative," as a procedure for the assessment of the various strategies or "maxims of behavior" we might be inclined, from time to time, to consider or pursue. With what might politely be described as "varying degrees of clarity," those descriptions amount to this requirement: that, at minimum, the strategies we adopt in dealing with one another must never aim, either deliberately or even inadvertently, at depriving others of their autonomy. (Beyond the minimum requirement that we not undermine this capacity, this kind of "deontological" reasoning also demonstrates that we should, where possible, nurture and enhance that capacity in ourselves and others. But that is a topic for another conversation.)

Though it is admittedly anachronistic, the contemporary moral principle that this "Kantian assessment procedure" appears to enshrine most unambiguously is not transparency, prohibitions of secrecy, or, surprisingly, even the admonition to do no harm. Instead, all of these legitimate moral concerns, which customarily constitute a recognizable list of prima facie moral obligations, can be shown to emerge from considered reflection upon a broader and more fundamental principle that seems to encompass all that we have just summarized about morally right and wrong action: namely, *the principle of informed consent*. That is to say, if one wished to summarize in a nutshell the Kantian position on our moral obligations, it is that we have an overriding obligation *never* to act on strategies we formulate for dealing with one another, to which the subjects implicated in, or involved with those strategies could not *give their full and unqualified, voluntary consent when fully informed* about them. [6]

This may seem a surprising result, and not altogether a comforting one for a discipline that has had, until quite recently, so troubled a history with the principle of informed consent itself. I take this result, however, to be the thrust of Professor Louis Irving Horowitz's final evaluation of Project Camelot to the effect that "all of the questions raised by the birth and death of Camelot only push in a more agonizing *way the problems long raised by Kant in philosophy* . . . which continue to plague the social science world" (Horowitz 1967: 40; my emphasis).[7] Likewise, my foregoing account may serve to explain, in the ancillary moral codes from other professions that the CEAUSSIC report itself cites, why "informed consent," particularly in the Nuremburg Code,[8] occupies pride of place even above primum non nocere. Doctors, unfortunately, harm their patients inadvertently all the time, and sometimes perhaps deliberately, but are never to do either without the patient's knowledge of, and consent to the risks, usually (if not always) in the hope that the risks, or even the harm itself, will be properly encompassed within choices that those patients have willingly, knowingly, and voluntarily made for (and about) themselves.

There is, of course, a great deal of commentary on such matters, while the attempt to offer intelligible thumbnail sketches of a philosopher as complicated as Kant that are simultaneously comprehensive, complete, and unassailable has consigned many a scholar vastly more competent than I to an early grave.[9] But this, as well as any such sketch, captures what it is about the resort to secrecy in the treatment of rape victims in Darfur that makes that policy, in that instance, morally acceptable. It is not the (good?) results, but the respect for the autonomy of the victim—specifically, her right to know and give her consent to how information about her is utilized—that constitutes the morally salient feature of this example. Fluehr-Lobban's case entails *secrecy* and the concealment of research results but, importantly, it does *not* entail "clandestinity."

Informed Consent, Intrigue, and Espionage

Having criticized prevalent misunderstandings of adopting a policy of secrecy as part of a moral agent's underlying strategy in some cases, let me rescue what I think is the redeeming insight about such concerns. Professor Berreman had this, at least, right on the mark: promotion of suspicion and erosion of trust. If informed consent is the hallmark of our obligations to one another, it is quite appropriate to wonder how on earth it could ever be guaranteed if the research project itself, or the precise nature and conduct of it, are kept secret. How can one give knowledgeable consent to that of which one is totally unaware? Even worse, if we somehow become aware that something is "going on behind our backs," so to speak, isn't it reasonable to wonder whether that project or activity is being concealed from us precisely *because* we would never consent to involvement in it if we found out the true nature of the facts? If so, haven't we established Berreman's conclusion that secrecy is "the hallmark of intrigue, not scholarship," and thus its toleration and practice are bound to undermine anthropology as a science?

Certainly this suspicion is borne out by David Price's accounts, in *Threatening Anthropologists* (2004), of secret research carried out by the FBI and CIA during the 1950s and 1960s on the lives and activities of anthropologists who were also civil rights activists and antiwar dissidents. This research was sometimes done with the assistance of other anthropologists. These were, indeed, secret research projects. They were also "clandestine," that is, sneaky, deceptive, deceitful, duplicitous, and underhanded, involving intrigue, and aimed at doing harm to the reputations and careers, and sometimes even the "persons," of those studied. The harm done by such projects is manifold. Not only are the research subjects threatened with harm, but the very fabric of trust that must, to some degree, be presupposed among friends, neighbors, and fellow citizens, as well as between citizens and their government and its institutions, is shattered by such revelations.

Here it might be well to revisit some of the distinctions pertaining to secrecy and transparency with respect to research projects, as opposed to research results, introduced in chapter 1. My account of "informed consent" above can be shown to address all the various strategies thought to invoke a policy of secrecy, or otherwise attempting to legitimize secret or clandestine research, described in that earlier chapter: namely, anonymity and protection of confidentiality, the withholding of proprietary research results, as well as secret projects or undertakings themselves. The discussion of the underlying principle of informed consent, and of its overriding importance, likewise help us sort out the kinds of cases of secrecy in both senses offered by Price on the one hand and Fluehr-Lobban on the other. Her account of withholding the identity of rape victims in Darfur, for example, is a case of "secrecy" only in the sense of withholding research results. This is done, in turn, to provide anonymity to the victims in order to protect their confidentiality and to keep them from harm. As we saw, this is a strategy to which they, and we, when fully informed, can readily provide our consent. By contrast, Price's accounts are of research projects, the full dimensions and purpose of which were concealed from their subjects. These projects also invariably involved concealing the results of that research *from those subjects*, all in pursuit of purposes to which the subjects of that research did not and could not consent. These distinct strategies, each entailing a policy of secrecy, either succeed or fail the attempt to justify them morally, based, not merely on their reliance on secrecy per se, but rather on each distinct strategy's ability to pass (at least in principle) the test of informed consent.

Especially in light of Professor Price's research project (Price 2004, 2008), it seems appropriate to observe that this principle is even recognized in the so-called clandestine services, namely military and intelligence services like the CIA, which, in democratic regimes, are subject to peer review and oversight. The public collectively recognizes the need for a limited policy of secrecy in international relations, and consents to it to a certain degree as the price of their security. The result, however, is that the remaining features of informed "public" review and consent in this unusual case are deliberately delegated to elected officials who are appointed, in turn, to oversight committees that are specifically charged to review in confidence and approve or prohibit the actions of these agencies and their personnel on behalf of the electorate. In reminding us of this underlying constraint on intelligence and security activities, I certainly do not mean to claim that such oversight is routinely successful, beyond reproach, or even that procedures and institutions currently in place to handle this responsibility constitute by themselves an adequate safeguard of public interest and welfare. Those are all procedural, institutional questions for the public to debate and evaluate constantly, on the basis of evidence of performance.

Rather, my observation about accountability and the so-called clandestine services merely accounts for the very existence, as well as the ongoing commitment to the operation of forms of public oversight and accountability, and of procedures of institutional review, instituted precisely for the purpose of obtaining "informed consent" on behalf of the electorate in these exceptional instances. This observation, in turn, explains the importance of these oversight mechanisms, and of the need for them to function with integrity and reliability in the public interest. Historical studies and exposés of flaws and failures in the integrity of that system of accountability and oversight, like those of Professor Price, constitute an essential dimension of that oversight. So also is the willingness of scholars like Robert Rubinstein to engage with these agencies and their personnel, if only to break what he terms "the cycle of autistic hostility" (Rubinstein 2008a: 15–17). These institutions and procedures, and our willing engagement in the forms of public discourse they elicit, as John Stuart Mill so clearly and eloquently observed, constitute the foundations of civil liberty.[10]

What all this illustrates even further, however, is that "secrecy" itself is not automatically proscribed, nor is "transparency" always to be universally endorsed as settled public or professional policy, as critics like Berreman and Turner maintain. That inference is profoundly mistaken. Rather, both of these opposing policies, and the choice between them in specific instances, are subject to public peer review in the light of the underlying principle of informed consent.[11]

We might nevertheless conclude, in defense of Berreman and Turner, that as general practices, transparency and openness about one's activities (including one's anthropological research) are unlikely to undermine the autonomy of others. A general policy of transparency enables our projects, including research projects, to be easily reviewed and evaluated, permitting knowledgeable consent (or refusal) to participate in them without engendering suspicion and mistrust. That is why we tend to approve of transparency as the default policy in such matters. Secrecy, by contrast, is a policy or practice that can (and does, in the cases Professor Price documents) serve as a cover for activities that do undermine autonomy, intend harm, and to which the subjects or victims could not and would not knowledgeably and freely consent. That is why, all things considered, we tend strongly to disapprove of secrecy itself as a policy.

There are, however, other examples of such secret research, investigations, and deliberations that are nonetheless not ominous, and indeed where the policy of secrecy is not clandestine, or need not be, in part because the subjects implicated in it have given either explicit or tacit consent to the practice. The most obvious, if simple, example is that of "double-blind" experiments, such as drug trials in which participants are informed in advance of the risks and prospect of benefits, as well as of the overall experimental design and intent, but are asked willingly to "allow themselves to be deceived," that is, to forego knowledge of their own precise role in the trial itself—whether they get the drug, a placebo, or some other alternative. "Clandestinity," if you will, is eliminated from the policy of secrecy through the procedure of informed consent.

More difficult, even though otherwise familiar, are the cases of peer review of research proposals, scientific publications, and (even more germane) "secret" peer review in the process of application for tenure or promotion in academic settings. The first and the last come closest to representing a nonmalevolent form of the kind of espionage Price otherwise describes and denounces in his project. The line demarcating these benign practices from outright espionage is easily blurred, especially in situations of bad faith or malevolent intent. The huge difference between them is not "secrecy" but prior consent, which helps guard against (but does not guarantee, in these cases) an absence of "clandestinity."

Thus, in the case of domestic surveillance by agencies of the government, we would say that the citizens targeted as "research subjects" did not know about it, and would not have consented to it had they known, largely because the intentions were malevolent and prospectively harmful. By contrast, we do know in advance, and tacitly or explicitly consent to, the gathering of confidential information about ourselves, including evaluations of our past behavior, achievements, and professional conduct (much of which may never be known directly by us) for the purpose of assessing our worthiness to receive research support, or even a position or a promotion. Unlike domestic surveillance, however, we consent to this form of secrecy because we believe, on balance, that we benefit by the practice, and that (again, unlike domestic surveillance) it is carried out in reasonably good faith. We fret over it when subjected to it, or when engaged in it, because we know that, on occasion, that trust and good faith are abused.[12]

Make no mistake, such information is secret in all these cases of otherwise morally defensible practices. In fact, it is much easier at present to break the convention of secrecy through FOIA requests pertaining to domestic surveillance (and also, to a lesser extent, on federal grant-making decisions) than it is on one of the most sensitive and private areas of the scholar's existence, the evaluation by one's peers. That this is so can be demonstrated from recognizing that Price could not conceivably obtain anything remotely comparable to the information he successfully pried out of the U.S. government, even from his own institution, let alone from others, sufficient to permit him to write a similar study of the justice and probity of tenure review. If this does not constitute secrecy, absence of transparency, and carry us far from the practice of full and open disclosure, then nothing does. Yet we tolerate it, and generally approve of it. It is thus neither "secrecy," nor even "transparency" that differentiates morally between these practices. Instead, the bedrock moral principle at issue is prior, informed (even if tacit) consent.

Fluehr-Lobban is correct: we still don't have this right, and we need to get this right, if we are ever to hope to resolve the present controversy. There is something misguided, if not pathological, in anthropology's obsession with secrecy and transparency, and in the contrasting studied neglect (until she herself forced the issue) of informed consent. This is all the more so when we recall that secrecy and secret research were not even at issue in the vignettes from anthropology's moral history that are taken to symbolize these issues. Project Camelot, in particular, was unclassified, wholly transparent to the scientific community, and did not call in its proposed plan of work for any "secret," let alone clandestine, research. There were, however (Horowitz reports), concerns about whether the gathering of data and conducting of required field surveys would constitute legitimate research, or espionage (Horowitz 1967: 56).

It is espionage and accusations of espionage, not "secret research," that have long dogged the steps of anthropology's history. Franz Boas railed against it, and anthropologists are loath to be accused of it. Collaboration with the government, or with military, intelligence, or security forces will, they fear, undermine their reputations and get them confused with, and wrongly accused by the local populace and the subjects they wish to study as, spies. Fluehr-Lobban reports that, in places where America's image has been damaged and trust in it undermined, "Many anthropologists, myself included, report being thought of as spies, irrespective of their open presentation of themselves, their research objectives and methods, and sources of funds" (Fluehr-Lobban 2008).

Perhaps it is time for the discipline to confront and to deconstruct this pathology. Imagine Fluehr-Lobban's "ghost of Franz Boas," railing against social scientists engaged in "espionage," encountering the even more formidable ghost of Michel Foucault, who would most assuredly observe in response, "But, Franz! It's *all* espionage!"[13] Not just in Project Camelot, but in rural Mexico, among the Yąnomamö, and everywhere else that anthropologists have gone and not thought fit, in the past—not really thought at all, as Fluehr-Lobban phrases it—to make an "open presentation of themselves, their research objectives and methods, and sources of funds"—and I would add, the use to which their findings will be put, the likely beneficiaries, and the likely impact all of this will have on the subjects studied.

In the face of all this, the presence or support of MIS or governments is largely beside the point, as is the obsession with "colonialism." Oscar Lewis and Napoleon Chagnon did not work for or collaborate with military, intelligence, or security organizations.[14] They did not represent or serve colonial power. At worst, the presence or sponsorship of MIS, or the employment of anthropological methodology in the explicit service of colonialism, simply makes all the more evident the underlying bad faith and self-deception that I earlier posed as the inherent and inexpungable structural defect of the profession itself. "Espionage" is, as Foucault might say, a completely accurate act-description of its fundamental methodology. Anthropologists are as rightly anxious, if not fully or honestly self-conscious, about this fact as they are about other practices of espionage to which, on balance, the wider public gives grudging consent. Under the right historical circumstances, it is easier, more convenient, and psychologically more comforting to lance this particular painful professional "boil" by scapegoating government and the military for the sins of the profession. In truth, anthropological research has always been "secret," inasmuch as its true purposes and likely ramifications for the research subjects were seldom, if ever (until quite recently), fully disclosed. Likewise, such research has seldom been truly informed, nor can its subjects truly be said (again, until quite recently) to have given their consent to it.

With these somewhat unsettling considerations in mind, how might Fluehr-Lobban's counterexample help anthropologists think anew about secrecy and secret research, and also, as she urges, about how to understand harm and their "paramount responsibility to the people studied?"

First, her real-life case involving Darfur offers an assessment that both parallels and supports the one derived from the counterfactual variation of the Rwandan case, and even the "Iraq-like" case, in chapter 4. Both of those involved scenarios similar to the one Fluehr-Lobban paints: situations in which comfortable and conventional convictions about professional probity and moral rectitude are turned on their heads and are shown to entail little of the consequences we attribute to them. That, in turn, as I have rather unkindly insisted, is not because there is anything wrong with those convictions themselves, but because members of the discipline have consistently failed to think accurately or carefully about how those convictions are actually embodied and symbolized in anthropology's moral history, and about what inferences to draw from those convictions, as well as from the historical "litany of shame" they are erroneously taken to support.

In particular, the blind antipathy toward collaborating with military and intelligence forces, reflected in the recent official resolutions which Fluehr-Lobban now delicately suggests we repudiate, is simply unwarranted. Historically, the "bad episodes" never, in fact, proved nearly as bad as they were portrayed to be (Rubinstein 2008a), although they were bad enough, and also stupid enough, and certainly aren't now to be commended, even if they don't rise to the degree of gravity of Nuremburg, Helsinki, or even the background history that gave rise to the Belmont standards. The error then and since is not the collaboration per se, but the belief on the part of MIS that they (it) could purchase such needed, complex expertise off the shelf, like a commodity, without investing the time and patience and resources necessary to cultivate the needed expertise in its (their) own ranks. And the sin of the social scientists was in pandering to that expectation, which also coincidentally pandered to their hyperinflated opinions of their own importance at the time, as Horowitz so devastatingly observed.

The Nature and Limitation of Codes of Conduct

The Turner amendment, cited at the outset of this study, aimed at addressing all of these concerns principally by amending (yet again) the AAA's existing Code of Ethics (1998). As we saw in chapter 1, this was to be accomplished by reintroducing language from the 1971 statement of "Principles of Professional Responsibility" calling for "a strict ban on secret research" (Glenn 2009).

All of the subsequent discussion in this book, however, bears critically upon the questionable history and faulty underlying assumptions that went into those earlier efforts. The frustration encountered by members of the discipline who have since served on the AAA's Committee on Ethics, or as advisors or members of subcommittees tasked to write or review recommended changes to the existing code, testify to the difficulties of complying verbatim with the specific provisions of Professor Turner's motion. Their struggle does not stem from their incompetence or duplicity, nor (as Professor Turner unkindly suggests) do their proposed revisions merely reflect their persistent "waffling" or "agonized hypocritical twisting" (Jaschik 2009). Rather, in attempting to respond to his literal-minded and questionable claim that "classified work for the military is unethical . . . and the association should have the will and guts to say so," the members of the association are bumping up against the very limitations inherent in all such legislative projects themselves, of a sort well known to all who are acquainted with the history of jurisprudence.[15]

In chapter 1, we saw that the absence of any kind of formal written guidance whatsoever left individuals like Margaret Mead or Gregory Bateson on their own, wrestling with their conscience, and also with their sense of conflict among prima facie duties to their discipline and to their endangered civic society. In those instances, such individuals received absolutely no guidance on how to resolve these moral dilemmas apart from their own vague, unsettled intuitions and professional misgivings. A "code of ethics," or a list of generally accepted guidelines for best practice, serves to rescue individuals from the onerous responsibility of having to generate a full-blown set of moral or legal guidelines in each separate encounter with conflict entirely on their own.

To the weak of will or the deficient of character, absent (as Aristotle famously observed) even a "tincture of virtue," laws and codes offer ominous warnings concerning the boundaries of minimally acceptable behavior, and include stern sanctions for transgressing those boundaries. More often, however, formal codification offers struggling individuals a lifeline, connecting their individual dilemmas of agonized choice to the broader experience and consensus of a community of fellow citizens or (as in anthropology's case) of colleagues and like-minded inquirers. For this reason, as another ancient cultural tradition describes it, the wise and the righteous do not merely comply with the law; rather, they delight in the law, and "meditate on it day and night."

In practice, that "meditation" takes the form of a perpetual debate in forging the specific provisions of these codes. That ongoing debate is, to a point, a healthy exercise for the members of a profession, just as such debate about the law is formative and constructive for the members of a democratic polity. All are compelled to reflect together about the very meaning of their practices, about their essential identity and function as either citizens or "professionals," and finally about their common projects and their life together as a polity or professional community. From all of these reflections, their notions of the limits of acceptable practice, and aspirational guidelines for best practice, finally emerge.[16]

If this is the underlying nature and function of all such deliberations, however, it would be the height of folly to imagine that issues of the kind, let alone the complexity of those we have been considering in this book, are simply going to be resolved once and for all through legislative deliberation and codification. This would be as foolish and misguided an expectation as to imagine that a complete and unimpeachable legal code could ever be written—or that (in a more familiar setting) if only we could get the "right people" on the curriculum committee, we could design, once and for all, a core curriculum for our students that would forever hereafter address every need and rectify every intellectual shortcoming in our students, without either omission or need for revision. Such expectations miss the point of the exercise, which is to sustain the ongoing, thoughtful reflection, the civil discourse about civic responsibilities, which are, like the societies or associations that sustain them, living things in constant flux and development.

In fact, an overemphasis on the precise wording of the exact provisions of such codes introduces its own fallacies. First, influential voices within, and perhaps even the majority of the members of the community itself can simply be mistaken on specific issues. I believe I have provided substantial grounds for suspecting that influential voices in the AAA are, indeed, profoundly mistaken in their understanding of and attitudes toward secrecy and transparency, for example, in a manner likely to lead them to rigorously enshrine precisely the wrong principles and guidelines in their code. I take Professor Fluehr-Lobban, with much greater tact and diplomacy, to be advancing the very same concern.

Is it aimed to do this?

More likely, however, these attempts to nail down every ambiguity, or to circumscribe and prohibit every conceivable instance of ostensibly objectionable behavior, end up paradoxically generating a host of new exceptions and loopholes, within which new varieties of objectionable behavior are bound to flourish. One of the most compelling recent examples of this paradox in action, in my own opinion, was the International Convention against the Recruitment, Use, Financing and Training of Mercenaries, adopted by the United Nations in 1989.[17] The resolution was designed to confront the dangerous and destabilizing role of mercenary military forces in postcolonial Africa. Upon passage, it was invoked early on to condemn and finally halt the role of South African–based "Executive Outcomes" in Sierra Leone in the early 1990s. Critics and supporters alike believe, in that instance, however, that the government of Sierra Leone had little alternative to hiring the company in the absence of any military assistance from the U.N. itself, and that the company did succeed in reestablishing a reasonable modicum of law and order before being expelled (Singer 2003; Carafano 2008).

Paradoxically, however, these and other scholars (e.g., Avant 2002) note that the passage of this resolution coincided with the unprecedented rise in the number of, and in increased reliance by many nation-states on, private military contractors, especially during the current decade. Some even go so far as to fault the U.N. resolution itself for this development. Its very precise and specific language of condemnation and prohibition (with which it is hard to disagree) inadvertently provided legal guidance in constructing the loopholes within which private military firms (ranging from the infamous former Blackwater Worldwide, Inc., all the way to the private contractor that until recently hired, trained, and deployed HTS teams for the U.S. Army) conducted their controversial operations in perfect compliance with international law. In a similar fashion, I noted in chapter 5 how the position descriptions for these HTS positions appeared to have been carefully structured to comply not only with every restriction in the AAA's 1998 Code of Ethics, but with all the pending revisions of language contained in the Turner amendment as well.

Ole

Codes of conduct and guidelines for best practice are designed to guide thinking and to help shape what we might call "professional identity," the symbolic and aspirational image of the "ideal professional." They are not sub-stitutes for pure or practical reasoning. Finally, however, professional conduct in any viable professional organization or society must be shaped not merely by minimal compliance with laws and codes but by the behavior of mature, responsible individuals seeking to live up to their professional (or civic) iden-tity by exercising what Aristotle called *phronesis*: sound practical judgment.

On rare and unenviable occasions, as in the midst of a profound moral di-lemma or controversy, such routine practical judgment must be guided in turn by dialectic, the individual's or community's ability to reflect hypothetically (as we have done in our "imaginary" case studies) on the implications of principles whose precise meaning and significance are ambiguous, and whose application in concrete decision-making is inherently unclear. No substitute for this abil-ity of a profession's individual members will be found in tightly worded legal formulae, lofty and judgmental plenary resolutions, or simplistic algorithms for decision-making. Every attempt to capture the dialectic of reason in this fashion is not merely doomed to fail; worse, it is doomed to generate far more perverse conduct than it eliminates. The sin to be guarded against in such in-stances is self-righteousness and unwarranted self-certainty. Had the academic partisans at war with one another in the days of the Thailand controversy been more attuned to this problem, I am persuaded that the AAA would narrate a very different and less fractured disciplinary history than it now does.

Summarizing Lessons and Learning from Mistakes

In a larger sense, throughout this book we have discovered that the actual debate over military anthropology in general and the HTS problem in particular, especially in the context of the war in Iraq, is complicated by a number of issues. The first is a broad background tendency (which the CEAUSSIC report did much to define and rectify) to conflate the "human terrain" project itself (MA_2) with the remaining, diverse, and far less morally problematic forms of military anthropology. I specifically focused on MA_1, the anthropological study of military organizations, as a wholly different and fully legitimate scientific enterprise.

That in turn was distinguished from various kinds of educational undertak-ings (MA_3) pertaining to language competence and regional studies, as well as to routine and morally unobjectionable services provided by educators for student clients of all sorts, including military, intelligence, and security personnel. I discovered that this tendency toward indiscriminate conflation of these vastly disparate and morally distinctive activities could be traced to a widespread underlying ideological antipathy toward the military itself, manifest in the opposition of academics and scholars toward engagement at any level with the military. That deeply ingrained antipathy has its origins, and at least some legitimate roots, in the recent history of the discipline, as we discovered in the opening two chapters of this book. But it blinds adherents to the prospects for collaboration on more favorable terms that might well serve to redress some of the more urgent concerns they have voiced. Even more important, this steadfast refusal to consider working with military forces in the present robs the most vulnerable victims—in at least two different, morally distinct as well as culturally distinct, theaters of war—of assistance based on expertise that only anthropologists have, and that only they are in a position to reliably dispense. [18]

The second problem is conceptual. As demonstrated in chapter 4, critics of military anthropology, when they do focus exclusively on the Human Terrain System projects, have not fully appreciated that the debate about the moral legitimacy of these projects constitutes, de facto, a form of just war analysis. That means, at very least, that it would be a mistake to beg the question by presupposing the outcome of that analysis (as the AAA Executive Board did, for example, in its resolution of October 2007), or merely reduce it to a matter of compliance with international law. Instead, and in part because the autonomous sources of international law do not converge univocally on this matter, the larger debate about the justification of the war in Iraq surely must be enjoined.

When we enjoin that debate, moreover, with an eye to examining the moral legitimacy of participation by anthropologists in that war in particular, we discover that the formal, logical structure of that debate about what medieval scholars termed *bellum offensivum* (in this case, "wars of intervention"; see Lucas 2005) is invariant under transformations into three radically different historical and cultural contexts. The examples I constructed were Nazi Germany, Rwanda, and Iraq itself. As I tried to show in that chapter, the formal structure and principal categories of just war discourse alone do not, in and of themselves, fully resolve the debate over the legitimacy of HTS, at least not until we infuse each hypothetical instance of the application of those criteria with the cultural specifics of each of those three different situations. Importantly, those three variations are all variations of a hypothetical case concerning an "illegal" and unauthorized war of intervention, of the sort that would not be justifiable under application of just war criteria or under existing international law. Certainly, we presumed, it would therefore be unjustifiable for anthropologists to involve themselves in any of those wars.

When we infused the invariant formal structure of such offensive wars with specific historical and cultural contents, however, we discovered a very different range of answers than this blanket condemnation would suggest. As case variation 2 (Rwanda) demonstrated, there could wars of intervention in which the hypothetical war itself might be formally declared illegal under international law. Even so, the participation by anthropologists would be not merely permissible but possibly even obligatory, in part because the moral case for war under "just war" criteria quite clearly took precedence over the legal prohibitions against it. As case variation 3 (Iraq?) demonstrated, there could also be wars of intervention that might turn out both to be proscribed under international law and also fail to satisfy just war criteria. Yet even so, even in this "worst case," we discovered that it would be possible in principle for the participation by anthropologists in such wars to be morally justified, if that participation were aimed at what is increasingly termed *jus post bellum*: that is, if anthropological expertise were sought solely for the purposes of *minimizing casualties, ending conflict, restoring peace, and extricating the invading troops as quickly as possible* (Orend 2006, Lucas 2007). Provided no HTS projects were specifically intended for purposes specifically proscribed by provisions of the profession's own Code of Ethics (such as illegal interrogation or torture), then concepts like "moral responsibility" and the doctrine of double effect (DDE) otherwise limit the liability of anthropologists for the inadvertent sort of "harm" that (Fluehr-Lobban worried) might stem from their presence. In any case, these concepts certainly absolve the anthropologists for blame stemming from any "moral errors" made by combatants not under their direct jurisdiction.

As mentioned initially, anthropologists have in the past been charged with having consorted with colonialists and aided in the oppression, victimization, and forced migration or resettlement of indigenous peoples and cultures by powerful foreign elites. Once again, present-day anthropologists are quite rightly sensitive about such charges, and are determined not to be deceived into complicity with such atrocities again. Professors Price and Gonzalez, for example, are right to oppose any involvement of anthropologists with HTS projects aimed at coercive interrogation or torture of suspected terrorists or insurgents (although, in the course of this investigation, we failed to uncover any actual instances of such involvement). The AAA Executive Board, however, was simply mistaken to oppose, or even "strongly disapprove" in principle of the larger involvement of anthropologists with HTS projects, even in those instances when the moral justification for a war of intervention turns out to be seriously flawed or absent. Actual cases, we discovered, are substantially more nuanced than this initial resolution in October 2007 envisions.[19]

This illustrates a third problem: namely, the highly abstract and conceptual nature of this debate itself over both HTS and "military anthropology" more generally. There are no concrete cases of abusive practice upon which to forge some consensus about appropriate professional behavior. There are job openings in HTS, and as we've seen, job descriptions that accompany those positions that are troubling in many respects. There is ample historical precedent for such concern, but no actual instances to date that would justify a complete ban on HTS itself (*Nature* 2008), let alone justify the extraordinary suspicion and opprobrium heaped upon *all* military anthropologists in the sweeping indictment of the HTS program (Selmeski 2008).

Thus, when we turned in the preceding chapter to battlefield examples and specific case studies, we found the literature sparse, and the real-life cases (based in substantiated fact, rather than allegation) few and far between. The job descriptions for actual positions in HTS betrayed no overt signs of inviting anthropologists to collude in morally illicit or outrageous behavior. Quite the contrary, the descriptions aimed to inspire prospective job candidates with the promise of making a positive moral difference in the well-being of peoples to whose study and welfare they would have presumably already devoted their academic and professional careers. The advertisements also appeared to entice prospective recruits with the prospect of unfettered research and publication, as a side benefit, on peoples and regions in a specific area of the Middle East and Central Asia that, owing to its status as a zone of conflict and political instability, has long been off-limits to scholarly research.

The question, instead, was *how well did those actual positions deliver on those promises?* And that is where the gathering of real-life cases is vital. Anthropology, like medicine, business, or law, requires the development and subsequent study and discussion of a robust case literature, in lieu of the philosopher's hypothetical thought experiments, and in lieu also of the uninformed critics' wild speculations and unsubstantiated allegations. Nothing can substitute for the facts.

David Price's research admittedly shows how government, security, and intelligence forces in the United States harassed outspoken anthropologists for their political views, largely on race and segregation, during the McCarthy era. That, however, was half a century ago—a very long time ago (if I might say), in a galaxy far, far away. Anthropologists were hardly the only intellectuals, artists, or public activists to suffer during this disgraceful period. And that period and its practices have been relentlessly described and denounced ever since. It is fair to say that when a very limited segment of present-day government, intelligence, and security forces, under much different (and in many respects, more compelling) circumstances proposed a reversion to such policies, the reaction of the broader government, military, intelligence and security forces to such proposals and practices was and is

"Never again!" It was, for example, outraged military lawyers who first called attention to procedural abuses of detainees and to illegal methods of interrogation at Guantanamo Bay.[20] And at Abu Ghraib, an Air Force intelligence officer denounced the interrogations long before they became public, while it was a high-ranking Army general who risked his career (and was finally forced into retirement) in order to bring a full account of these abuses to congressional and public attention after an Army enlisted reservist blew the whistle on them.[21]

In these and other controversial policies and decisions relating to intelligence, interrogation, war-fighting, nation-building, and peacekeeping, it has been forceful elements within military culture itself, not watchdogs from the general public, who have protested the actions of their civilian leaders and brought these forward for public scrutiny.[22] This hardly conveys the impression of a monolithic organization relentlessly devoted to destroying freedoms at home or oppressing victims abroad. This is hardly surprising, since "the military" is as much a product of our recent history, including misfortunes like McCarthyism, Vietnam, My Lai, and Project Camelot, as is the general public that it exists to serve, and from which its membership is drawn. If it is claiming too much to declare that those lessons have been learned once and for all, it is admitting far too little to suggest that they have had no impact on military "culture" or military practice.[23]

Indeed, one of the virtues of MA_1, of "anthropology of the military," has been the achievements of scholars like Anna Simons (1997), Brian Selmeski, Robert Rubinstein, Kerry Fosher, Clementine Fujimura (2003), and a host of others in calling our attention to the extraordinary complexities, distinctions, and tensions within the variety of cultures that constitute "the military." Those who persist in simply denouncing or abhorring these cultures and their members uniformly as anathema are thus guilty of the worst excesses of essentialism, of the sort they themselves would not tolerate (let alone advocate) toward the members of other cultures. It is high time that such prejudices, wholly unworthy of scholars, be set aside.

Professional Jurisdiction: Friends, Colleagues, and "Bucket Brigades"

Toward the end of the previous chapter, we cited and explored portions of a three-part account of controversies swirling around HTS written by *Pravda* journalist John Stanton, alleging shortcomings and egregious deficiencies in expertise and training. The accuracy of his account is disputed by other anthropologists and by representatives of the HTS program, and the press credentials of the reporter are not unimpeachable. That does not mean that what he alleges might not in fact have occurred, nor that other situations similar to these might occur in the future. This is an entirely different sort of dilemma, one that remains even if the other, less relevant or just plain specious concerns are put to flight. How might we guard against this? How might we go about verifying such accounts? How might we work to prevent the sorts of abuses and deficiencies this one reporter alleges?

The first response is to settle in some fashion on a procedure to avoid what I termed, earlier in this book, the "jurisdictional fallacy." Time and again in this debate we witness anthropologists equivocating mightily between "anthropology" as a profession and a discipline, on the one hand, and "social science" on the other. Time and again we see these matters hopelessly confused and carelessly conflated, from Project Camelot to the present HTS program, including even the death or injury of some of its participants. It is not simply that we need to ask, with Brian Selmeski, "Who are the security anthropologists?" Even more, we need to know who are the actual anthropologists involved with these projects: we need a more precise definition of the boundaries and of professional jurisdiction.

Michael Bhatia, tragically killed in Afghanistan, was a political scientist who at the time of his death was working on a doctoral degree in politics and international relations at Oxford. He was in no conceivable sense an anthropologist. Lt. Col. Villacres, whose NPR interview from Iraq was quoted in the previous chapter, is a Middle East historian. Paula Loyd, the HTS team member burned in an attack by a local villager in Afghanistan, did hold an undergraduate degree in cultural anthropology from Wellesley, but her master's degree was in conflict resolution and diplomacy from Georgetown.

Likewise, Kalman Silvert, reporting "on the scene" from Chile about Project Camelot in the 1960s, was a political scientist. That project's directors and staff were principally sociologists, while the remainder were, for the greater part, political scientists and historians. The one and only anthropologist involved in that sorry affair wasn't even, strictly speaking, part of the project (although he foolishly posed as one).

Curiously, the professional society of anthropologists insists nonetheless in taking solely upon itself the responsibility, the blame, and, in its "litany of shame," a perverse kind of credit for spearheading these projects. The historical truth is, quite frankly, anthropologists as such have played no meaningful role in them whatsoever. An anthropologist is not a political scientist, nor a sociologist, nor a social psychologist, nor even (except for Professor Price, perhaps) a historian. Nor is someone properly labeled an "anthropologist" simply because he or she took a few undergraduate courses or even earned a master's degree in the subject.[24] This is every bit as absurd as, say, charging the fictitious "accounting professor" (in chapter 3) with the jurisdictional authority or professional responsibility for all the flotsam and jetsam that passed through his accounting class on their way to the destruction of the global economy. That, as we saw, is a ridiculous notion of moral (or ethical) responsibility, and to insist on it is to arrogate to oneself the responsibility for a moral debate that is more properly the purview of the wider public (or at least the academic public) generally.

In order to carry on this important debate regarding professional ethics, the serious equivocation between anthropology and "social science," and even sociology itself, requires a more effective jurisdictional clarification.[25] If it is, finally (as it seems to be) the latter, broader category at issue, then it is rather pointless for the AAA and its membership alone to address issues like HTS or accept blame for these matters unilaterally. Perhaps a coalition of relevant professional societies needs to act jointly on these matters, prescribing guidelines for all their members. Perhaps, instead, since "social science research" is implicated, the Social Science Research Council (SSRC) should be the jurisdictional authority, with anthropologists joining their colleagues from the other relevant professional and disciplinary organizations (e.g., the American Psychological Association, the American Sociological Association, American Political Science Association, and so forth) to lobby for a coherent, unified response to these ethical and moral challenges.

Beyond settling this procedural detail, I would suggest three responses: (1) a full program review of HTS itself; (2) the formulation of a wider institutional review board (IRB) of anthropologists to evaluate and advise (if not "rule") on the professional appropriateness of this and similar kinds of collaboration with MIS forces in the future; and, finally, (3) the creation of a discipline-sponsored and disciplined-sanctioned non-govermental organization (NGO) to serve as a source for and clearing-house of anthropological expertise in the future.

I commented in detail on the reasons, procedures, questions, and likely composition of a GAO-administered peer review of the HTS program in the previous chapter. That should be undertaken as soon as possible, and AAA and the Network of Concerned Anthropologists are well-positioned to lobby for this action, and even to participate in the peer review process itself. I would think it in the interest of members of Mil_Ant_Net and the CEAUSSIC committee to join them in lobbying for this measure. Like the $6 million initially appropriated for Project Camelot in 1964, $40 million in today's currency may seem little more than inconsequential "budget dust" in a DOD–sponsored program, but it is a lot of money for a social science project, equivalent to nearly one-fourth the entire annual budget of the National Endowment for the Humanities, for example. Taxpayers and the public, including anthropologists, have a right to know exactly what it is for, and how effectively it is being spent.

Professor Fluehr-Lobban (2008) has herself offered a version of my second proposal for an anthropological IRB, what she calls "Friends of the Committee on Ethics."[26] The particular virtue of this approach is that it avoids having the AAA Committee on Ethics itself lapse back into adjudicating the kind of ponderous grievance procedures that, on her earlier account (Fluehr-Lobban 2003a, 18) characterized and largely paralyzed its work prior to 1998. For her part, Kerry Fosher, in her account of her own work with the Marine Corps Intelligence Activity (Fosher 2008), describes how a similar informal process of peer review, what she terms her "bucket brigade," or her network of supportive colleagues, helps individual anthropologists calibrate and re-calibrate their own moral and professional sensibilities, and guards against lapsing too easily or readily into questionable or compliant practices that sponsoring, funding, or employing organizations might otherwise encourage. This is precisely the kind of civil discourse promoting mature judgment that I advocated above, and Fosher's most recent book provides an additional exemplary illustration of phronesis and dialectic at work within a domestic bureaucracy, guiding and shaping effective moral judgment in effecting public security policy (Fosher 2009).

My own proposal is slightly more formal, and would involve establishing institutional arrangements for submitting and reviewing projects, as well a forming a panel of scholars to conduct such reviews. Those institutional arrangements would need to define what sorts of projects require this review, how that review is to be conducted, and how, or in what sense, compliance with this "ethics review" requirement ought to be enforced. Those are admittedly delicate issues on which I have some vague thoughts but no clear proposals or answers at present. In theory, however, I liken this to an institutional review board, in which a diverse jury of peers (perhaps not limited solely to anthropologists) reviews requests for assistance or job offers from MIS sources, and possibly other questionable requests for specific employment of anthropological expertise to assure that those prospects or proposals meet the requirements of the AAA Code of Ethics, and conform to the broader moral mandates of justice and respect for human rights.

Finally, I suggest that the AAA consider creating an independent NGO sponsored, and perhaps operated by, the profession in lieu of the HTS program itself, both to avoid inherent conflicts of interest (such as those that the IRB "Friends" and "bucket brigades" help detect), and to avoid having the

HTS experiment itself merge into the morally murky world of private military contracting.[27] There is an enormous difference in the relationship to the deployed military forces, as well as in the moral and even the legal status, of a nongovernmental organization's relief workers, as opposed to the employees of a private military contractor. While their status under international law remains far from clear, employees of PMCs engaged in security operations in zones of combat are increasingly classified as "combatants" under the broadest interpretations of the Geneva Protocols.[28] In addition, American citizens, as well as foreign nationals employed by American military contractors working for the Department of Defense, have also recently been subsumed for jurisdictional purposes under the Uniform Code of Military Justice (UCMJ).[29] BAE Systems, Inc., has an office in the U.S. and is under contract to the U.S. Department of Defense. Hence its employees, including HTS team members, are (or, at least, were) subject to legal jurisdiction under the UCMJ. This can prove awkward for a number of reasons, including (for example) that certain widespread cultural practices, such as adultery, are specifically prohibited and subject to military court-martial under this code.

The abrupt transition in January 2009 of HTS program employees from the status of private contractors to civilian federal civil service employees of the Department of Defense only solidifies these concerns. DOD civilian employees are at minimum subject to the Military Extraterritorial Jurisdiction Act (MEJA), which extends the jurisdiction of U.S. federal law to U.S. citizens and employees living and working abroad. More important, such civilian support personnel may readily be considered combatants or legitimate military targets under international law, certainly if deployed with military personnel in combat zones, and either bearing arms themselves or accompanied by armed security personnel. Finally, such an arrangement does little to allay the fears of external critics over the possible compromises forced on practicing anthropologists who are employed inside the organization they hope to advise and (in some sense) restrain.

Representatives of NGOs, by contrast, are recognized in international law as noncombatants, present in combat zones to provide humanitarian relief and assistance, or to guard the basic rights and welfare of indigenous noncombatants, prisoners of war, and other victims of the conflict or of its consequences (victims of injury, disease, or famine in a war zone, for example). While there are tremendous logistical and jurisdictional obstacles to the smooth coordination of military forces and NGOs in combat zones, increasingly in the contemporary battle space there are even greater logistical and jurisdictional obstacles impeding the coordination and command of private military contractors, especially private security contractors (PSCs), alongside journalists and other professionals (such as anthropologists) "embedded" with military troops in combat zones. Quite unlike these more recent and problematic additions to the battlefield, however, there is ample precedent and considerable experience with the NGO model that would serve as an effective guide and would allow anthropologists to administer advice and assistance under conditions more likely to guarantee that such assistance is not subject to misuse or conflict of interest. And, of course, there is the added personal benefit that one's private life remains, for the most part, one's own.

Perhaps the most significant moral argument in favor of this alternative arrangement (legal and jurisdictional questions aside) is that compassionate humanitarian relief work of the sort that NGOs frequently carry out in troubled regions of the globe, often at considerable risk of harm to themselves, is precisely what dedicated individuals like Paula Loyd and Michael Bhatia had committed themselves to undertake. As the full life histories of both emerge into public view following their tragic deaths, it is quite evident that both were deeply committed to the welfare and well-being of the local inhabitants of the respective country in which they served and died, and that neither was involved in HTS simply for putative financial gain. Why not grant such individuals the legal and moral status, and the underlying forms of institutional support and approbation, that most closely adhere to their own understanding and description of their mission and purpose?

Les Anthropologistes sans Frontières

How might such an NGO of anthropologists be constituted? In a presentation I made on this topic early in 2008, Professor Margaret Walker, an eminent philosopher at Arizona State University, suggested that anthropologists might well consider founding a group similar to Médecins Sans Frontières (Doctors without Borders), the France-based, Nobel Prize–winning international organization of physicians who provide medical care in desolate and desperate areas of the world without presuming to pass judgment on the political and military conflicts that precipitate truly dire human need. As with that organization of member-physicians around the world, anthropologists from the international community would volunteer (accepting only subsistence wages and living expenses) to provide anthropological expertise to United Nations peacekeeping forces and to other intervening military forces deployed on peacekeeping missions that can demonstrate that they are eager to promote stability, keep or restore peace, and minimize the risk of doing harm to the very clients they were sent to protect.

Professor Walker suggested calling that approach "Anthropologists without Borders." That is a constructive suggestion, and I think, finally, that anthropologists may need to make their expertise available without being beholden to, or sitting in judgment of, any of the parties to the conflicts that generate the human suffering that only they can help alleviate.[30] The AAA Executive Committee could authorize a subsidiary nonprofit organization of this title, and assist in attracting private donations and foundation funds to support its operation. If the concern over this matter is truly as great as the present controversy would suggest, that subsidiary organization ought in turn to have little difficulty in attracting a stable of qualified volunteers. This strikes me as a far better way to supply such expertise than relying on an international PMC that has a somewhat shadowy reputation and is currently under investigation in two nations for criminal fraud and corruption. It also strikes me as more readily appealing to skeptical scholars who would assuredly feel morally compromised if classified merely as civilian employees of the Department of Defense.

As to the matter that initially prompted the writing of this book—namely, the controversy among learned colleagues in anthropology and the social sciences about the professional propriety of working with the U.S. military or other national security forces—the AAA CEAUSSIC Commission Report itself concludes:

> We have found no single model of "engagement," so issuing a blanket condemnation or affirmation of anthropologists working in national security makes little sense. [We conclude] there is nothing inherently unethical in the decision to apply one's skills in a security context. Instead, the challenge for all anthropologists is finding ways to work in or with these institutions, seeking ways to study, document, and write openly and honestly to an anthropological audience about them, in a way that honors the discipline's ethical commitments.

The report itself, and especially its concluding observations, advice, and illustrations for individual members, suggest the complexity of these choices. My efforts in this book have been geared toward engaging those complexities and bringing the methodology of applied philosophy itself to bear upon some of these vexed questions, in order to aid esteemed colleagues, engaged in vital research and public service, to have greater confidence in their own good-faith efforts to evaluate and ultimately justify the moral worthiness of these activities.

Notes

1. These comments reflect the immediate aftermath of the AAA's 107th annual meeting in San Francisco in November 2008. See Vergano and Weise (2008).

2. This myopia is confronted forcefully, in detailed historical context, in Fluehr-Lobban (1994). This analysis is largely responsible for the first explicit recognition by the AAA of these responsibilities, enshrined in the Code of Ethics of 1998, wholly retained in the 2009 revisions. That concept, notably absent from discussions in the 1960s and 1970s, now pervades contemporary discourse about professional ethics in anthropology.

3. This is an apparent reference to the two members of HTS teams, IZ3 Nicole Suveges and AF1 Michael Bhatia, referenced in John Stanton's *Pravda* article in the preceding chapter, as well as to the recent serious injury to Paula Loyd, who has since died. I have seen no accounts in the press, or on Mil_Ant_Net or critical blogs, of other reported deaths or injuries beyond these three. If those facts are correct, they serve as further indication of the inevitable tendency toward sensationalism and hyperinflation of rumor surrounding these activities, especially in the absence of concrete evidence.

4. I would beg to differ from this considered judgment only on one very significant point. Moral philosophers, and far more important, exasperated victims of such harm, would likely object that it is not that "harm" itself is "not an absolute concept" or that it is somehow culturally contextualized. Being savagely beaten merely for having been the tragic victim of the criminal actions of others constitutes "harm" in any cultural context! Rather, the correct conclusion to draw is that ignorant cultural outsiders (in this case, high-minded social scientists committed to the principle of transparency) are likely to make seriously erroneous judgments about the sorts of behavior that finally cause harm to occur.

5. I owe this observation to Professor J. W. Schneewind of Johns Hopkins University, who first noted that the announcements of lectures at the University of Königsberg contained descriptions of lectures by Kant on this topic at least as early as 1772–1773. For a more detailed account, I am pleased to cite the work of a former student, Felicitas Munzel, *Kritischer Kommentar zu Kants Anthropologie in pragmatischer Hinsicht (1798)*. "Kant-Forschungen, Band 10." (Hamburg: Felix Meiner Verlag, 1999). The first full-length English treatment of this subject is by Holly Wilson, *Kant's Pragmatic Anthropology*, published in my Philosophy Series by the State University of New York Press in 2006. In chapter 1 of that work, she notes that Kant began to teach a distinct course in anthropology in his 18th year at Königsberg, during the winter semester of the academic year 1772–1773. He began lecturing on and advocating for a distinct "discipline" or study of anthropology in his lectures on metaphysics as early as 1762, at which time this was not a distinct subject in any university curriculum elsewhere in Europe. Thus, every bit as much and perhaps more than even Montaigne, Montesquieu, or Rousseau, by all accounts Kant deserves to be recognized as the modern "father" of this subject as a distinct academic discipline in the university (Wilson 2006: 7f.), particularly inasmuch as more recent scholars, such as Herder and Dilthey, who bequeathed to anthropology the vexing concept of "Kultur," were themselves Kant's students and intellectual heirs.

6. What places the admonition to *do no harm* at the top of any subsequent list of prima facie duties (see the discussion of these in chapter 2, note 6) that might be generated from this principle is that, first and foremost, it is the sort of strategy or practice to which those affected by it or subject to it could be expected to give their consent. The precise interpretation of this point is disputed by contemporary Kantians with respect to policies like suicide and voluntary euthanasia, to which autonomous moral agents also might conceivably consent. But Kant himself roundly condemned such practices on the basis of his fundamental principle, and no one disputes that admonitions against the doing of harm to self and others are, for the most part, the most clear and compelling examples of strict or "perfect" duties of justice: that is, forms of behavior that are strictly forbidden as constituting strategies to which no autonomous moral agent could willingly and knowingly give their rational consent.

7. I suspect Horowitz had in mind Kant's specific injunction, the so-called second form of his "categorical imperative," not to use persons merely as means—in this case, merely as the means of scientific discovery and advancement of human knowledge (and presumably also the researcher's scholarly career).

8. Fluehr-Lobban argues incorrectly that this principle, as we know it, emerged only in the wake of a 1972 Supreme Court decision, *Canterbury v. Spence*, pertaining to biomedical research. As we noted in chapter 1, however, the grounds for this decision rest explicitly on the first fundamental finding of the Nuremburg Doctor's Trials and the resulting code, which held that, above all, a patient's knowledge and consent were required as justification for medical experimentation (see chapter 1, notes 5 and 6). Thus, the longstanding philosophical recognition of this principle considerably antedates this case. Indeed, as I am arguing here, it is quite possible to interpret the most salient features of Kant's moral philosophy along these lines. The precise nomenclature is recent, though quite a bit older than Fluehr-Lobban acknowledges. The underlying philosophical principle, however, has been acknowledged for centuries. Thus, "informed consent" is not merely a recent and limited development in "professional ethics," but rather the application and interpretation within a contemporary professional context of a longstanding, widely recognized, and culturally invariant moral principle.

9. A more comprehensive account (or thumbnail sketch) of Kantian ethics in the context of his larger philosophical enterprise, including his academic focus on the importance of anthropology, still intended for comprehension by the nonspecialist, can be found in my introduction to "Kantian Ethics and the Basis of Duty" (Lucas and Rubel, 2007: 165–69). My own thinking on this subject is deeply indebted to the earliest work of Onora O'Neill, in her pathbreaking study, *Acting on Principle: An Essay on Kantian Ethics* (1975; see "Onora Nell"). See her own reflections from that perspective on the topic of "informed consent" in the context of bioethics in *Rethinking Informed Consent in Bioethics* (Cambridge University Press, 2007).

10. These comments summarize the results of Mill's careful analysis of unfettered public discourse and the importance of freedoms of speech and the press, found especially in the third chapter of his seminal essay *On Liberty* (1859).

11. Sissela Bok's pathbreaking study *Lying: Moral Choice in Public and Private Life* (New York: Random House, 1978), raises a number of these concerns. Her account of the burden of proof and procedures for moral justification in instances of lying, secrecy, or deception, particularly what she terms the "Principles of Veracity and Publicity," address the concerns I have raised here, with sustained reference to the philosophies of Mill, Kant, and Aristotle. That early work is thought by many of my colleagues in moral philosophy, however, to contain serious conceptual inconsistencies, to prove frustratingly inconclusive regarding the principles I have attempted to set forth more clearly in this essay, and to equivocate generally between utilitarian and deontological accounts of justification in a manner that is no longer necessary or appropriate in the light of the kind of Kantian reasoning I invoke here, as exemplified in the work of philosophers like Habermas, John Rawls, Christine Korsgaard, Barbara Herman, and most especially (in my opinion) Onora O'Neill. Nevertheless, the book remains a refreshing historical and practical study of a topic that had been routinely neglected.

12. It was often necessary to clarify boundaries of good practice and rein in tendencies to abuse power when presiding over panels of scholars convened to evaluate fellowships and research grant proposals at the National Endowment for the Humanities during my tenure there. Naturally, the tendency of rejected applicants was to suppose that treachery, injustice, or incompetence had been practiced by their colleagues behind the "veil of secrecy" imposed on such deliberations. Generally, however, this was not permitted to occur.

Likewise, scholars have their own horror stories of "rank and tenure committee" abuses under the cloak of secrecy, many (but, sadly, not all) of which are largely unfounded. Some years ago I was asked to provide a confidential external review of an application for tenure that had been denied and appealed. The unsuccessful candidate had published a book in a philosophy series that I edited, which book, and series, had been impugned in a "secret" letter submitted to the university provost by one of the candidate's disgruntled departmental colleagues outside the normal review process. Apart from the libel I had sustained, I found it interesting that, in the all-male department of this eminent Southern, quite "WASPish" university, the candidate in question was female, Jewish, and had written a highly original study of Maimonides. Fortunately, I was able to document my editorial procedure and produce copies of numerous qualified, anonymous (secret?) referees' reports on her work, justifying its publication according to conventional practice. The provost and the tenure committee finally concurred with my judgment that the original decision was a product of malevolent "clandestinity" rather than a valid confidential judgment of the candidate's merits. The decision was reversed, and the deserving tenure candidate reinstated. Scholars in this country have far more to fear in this respect from one another than from the agents of their government, Professor Price's researches notwithstanding.

13. As with all things "Foucauldian," this charge is an exaggeration, though perhaps not nearly so great a one as the entire controversy surrounding military anthropology. In his case, moreover, all such exaggerations unmask something genuine and uncomfortable lying beneath the normal range of self-conscious practice. Here, I think, the deliberate exaggeration goes right to the heart of the matter.

14. To be fair, Robert Rubinstein reminds me, Chagnon's work (but certainly not Lewis's) did receive some government, if not MIS, support from the Atomic Energy Commission.

15. The limitations to which I am referring are neatly reflected in the AAA members' various blog comments for or against the current revisions, to the effect that this sort of legislative project is finally inappropriate and doomed to failure. They can be found appended to Jaschik's report at http://www.insidehighered.com/news/2009/02/19/anthro.

16. See David Price's comments on the importance of sustaining this professional dialogue in an interview conducted after the annual AAA meeting with Josh Keller of the *Chronicle of Higher Education*, "The Ethics of a Code for Anthropologists," (December 5, 2008). http://chronicle.com/weekly/v55/i15/15a00601.htm.

17. Resolution A/44/34 was voted on favorably at the 72nd Plenary Meeting of the U.N. General Assembly on December 4, 1989, although it did not go fully into force until 2001. The text can be found at http://www.un.org/documents/ga/res/44/a44r034.htm.

18. Most recently, while engaged in presenting a paper designed to distinguish the kinds of military anthropology he does, and the value-orientation he brings to this task, from exclusive focus on the HTS program and the specific complaints of its critics, Brian Selmeski unintentionally revealed that this wider antipathy toward the military and toward any forms of engagement with it was still widely prevalent among members of the AAA, including those whose views on the military he quoted (and responded to) from the preceding day's business meeting (Selmeski 2008). His paper eloquently stated the case I have summarized above.

19. A more recent British editorial condemnation of HTS (*Nature* 2008) demonstrates greater nuance in describing just what aspects of HTS it finds objectionable. In contrast to the AAA Executive Committee's earlier resolution, for example, it finds the idea of anthropologists working with military forces in the manner described above to be "[i]n theory . . . a good idea," and its authors go on to argue in principle that "the insights of science have much to offer strategies in a war zone—not least through training combat troops to understand the local cultures within which they operate." Their editorial questions (as I have as well) the propriety of having a private military contractor supervise the arrangement, and focuses entirely on much-publicized failures (such as the deaths of the three HTS team members noted earlier) without acknowledging competing claims of achievement or success. That strikes me

as perhaps a rush to judgment. What I advocate instead is a thorough program review prior to issuing such a finding.

20. While this fact was widely known in military and international law circles, it is only now coming to full public attention and recognition through current congressional investigations. In 2002 and 2003, long before any public concerns over the Guantánamo Bay detention facility had been raised, the top lawyers for each of the four branches of military service had objected to the use of illegal interrogation techniques: "Major General Jack Rives, Deputy Judge Advocate General of the Army, wrote that approving what he called exceptional interrogation techniques could be interpreted as giving official approval to methods that members of the armed forces had always been taught were unlawful. He wrote that some of the proposed techniques amounted to violations of civilian and military law." See, for example, "Newly Released Documents Show Military Lawyers Strongly Objected to US Interrogation Policy," by Gary Thomas, in *Voice of America News* (July 29, 2005). http://voanews.com/english/archive/2005-07/2005-07-29-voa49.cfm?CFID=73354837&CFTOKEN =82035700.

21. Col. Steve Kleinman, a career intelligence officer, first witnessed and ordered a halt to illegal methods of interrogation in Iraq in 2003, and informed his superiors that these practices were abusive and illegal. See the report of his congressional testimony in "Air Force Instructor Details Harsh Interrogations," by Joby Warrick, in the *Washington Post* (September 26, 2008), p. A17. Army Specialist Joseph Darby (now a sergeant in the Army Reserve) first notified investigators of the abuses at Abu Ghraib. See "Abu Ghraib" in Rubel and Lucas, *Case Studies in Ethics for Military Leaders*, 2nd ed. (New York: Pearson, 2006), pp. 39–44. The details of these abuses reported in the *New Yorker* (Hersh 2004) were entirely dependent upon information derived from these military sources. Finally, Maj. Gen. Antonio Taguba, U.S. Army, investigated the abuses, issued a full report to Congress, and was disciplined and forced to resign by Secretary of Defense Donald Rumsfeld. See Taguba's account in "Ethical Leadership: Your Challenge, Your Responsibility," 11th Annual Stutt Lecture, U.S. Naval Academy (March 22, 2005): http://www.usna.edu/ethics/Publications/TagubaPg1-24_Final-1.pdf.

22. Gen. Anthony C. Zinni, USMC, Maj. Gen. Paul E. Eaton, U.S. Army, and Lt. Gen. Mark Newbold, USMC, all retired, were among the top generals to denounce the handling of the war in Iraq. Many, like Zinni, had opposed it from the outset, and were ostracized. See his initial exposé in 2003, "The Obligation to Speak the Truth," 7th Annual Stutt Lecture, U.S. Naval Academy (March 27, 2003): http://www.usna.edu/ethics/Publications/TagubaPg1-24_Final-1.pdf. For an analysis of this case, see Martin L. Cook, "The Revolt of the Generals: A Case Study in Professional Ethics," *Parameters*, vol. 38 (Spring 2008): 4–15, http://www.carlisle.army.mil/usawc/Parameters/08spring/cook.htm, and Col. Don L. Snider, "Dissent and Strategic Leadership," Carlisle, PA: Strategic Studies Institute (February 19, 2008), http://www.strategicstudiesinstitute.army.mil/pubs/display.cfm?pubID=849.

23. Further evidence of the impact those past misdeeds had on present military judgment is evident in *Washington Post* reporter Karen J. Greenberg's account (Greenberg 2009) of the exemplary handling of detainees at Guantánamo Bay in the first months after 9/11, when, as she suggests, "military officers on the ground tried to do the right thing with the recently captured detainees but were ultimately defeated by civilian officials back in Washington," in the days before (as she says) "Gitmo became Gitmo."

24. Here I think it best to begin, as I suggested in an earlier chapter, by confining professional jurisdiction to those with terminal degrees in the field, and perhaps also membership in the professional or disciplinary organization. This would help, at least, in avoiding having to take responsibility for the behavior of individuals who are, at best, only marginally qualified as "anthropologists."

25. I am, of course, quite well aware of the historical and resulting habitual administrative association of anthropology with sociology, since both these social sciences emerged from my own discipline. That historical association, however, is no more meaningful than the equally frequent historical and administrative association of philosophy with "religious studies," the latter in fact a multidisciplinary endeavor that encompasses historians, linguists, archaeologists, and anthropologists alongside more traditional theologians and ethicists. Anthropology is administratively at home within a number of other disciplines, and has about as little to do methodologically or substantively with sociology as it does with history, political science, or, for that matter, psychology or biology. If the historical association with sociology in particular, or even the dubious classification of "social science" generally, are leading anthropologists to shoulder the lion's share of the blame for the behavior of colleagues in these other disciplines, then perhaps it is simply time for the traditional partners to petition for divorce, rather than to continue tearing their own profession apart for the sins of others.

26. The AAA has since acted on this proposal, and established this new consultative body in January 2009. It is described (http://www.aaanet.org/issues/policyadvocacy/Friends-CoE.cfm) as "an *ad hoc* consultative body of anthropologists who have agreed to serve the membership in an advisory capacity on questions about the ethical implications of research and practice decisions/choices/issues. The benefit of such a body to the membership is the availability of a dynamic and diverse network of practitioners who can provide multiple viewpoints on both broad and specific issues that concern the membership regarding ethical considerations in anthropological research and practice. They complement the Committee on Ethics by providing continuity and institutional memory, as well as bringing to bear their own experience, professional expertise and contacts with practitioners representing a tremendous breadth of theoretical orientation, methodological approach, field sites, disciplinary focus and research experience." As Committee on Ethics chair Dena Plemmons remarks, "The mere fact of a code isn't what makes us ethical practitioners. We can learn to be ethical professionals, through negotiation, through practice,

through doing but not, I suspect, through words on paper." The conversations and reflections this new body will elicit should go a long way toward actualizing that mature, more collegial vision of ethical practice.

27. Pulitzer Prize–winning reporter Steven Fainaru of the *Washington Post* offers a graphic description of this "moral murkiness" (Fainaru 2008a, 2008b). His accounts of these tragedies could equally well apply to HTS members Bhatia, Suveges, and Loyd.

28. These are among the findings of the Montreux Document on Pertinent International Legal Obligations and Good Practices for States Related to Operations of Private Military and Security Companies during Armed Conflict, issued in Montreux, Switzerland, in cooperation with the International Committee of the Red Cross (September 17, 2008). This is an extremely complex matter, but the deliberation of this body of international lawyers and representatives of signatory states (including the U.S.) did seem to conclude that individuals employed in PMCs who, for example, wear uniforms, carry weapons, and are otherwise embedded with combat troops are, at least, not immune from deliberate attack by opposing forces. See Part One, Section A (4–8), and especially Section E (25, 26 (b)), pp. 5, 9. The complete document is available at http://www.icrc.org/web/eng/siteeng0.nsf/htmlall/montreux-document-170908/$FILE/Montreux-Document.pdf. Last accessed November 27, 2008.

29. Prior to 2007, the UCMJ pertained to U.S. civilians only when "serving with or accompanying an armed force in the field" at a "time of war." The Defense Reauthorization Act of 2007 amended this language to include "contingency operations" ordered by the Executive Branch, as well as wars declared by Congress, specifically to extend legal jurisdiction over U.S. civilians serving with or accompanying an armed force in the field. The constitutional status of this extension, however, is yet to be tested in court. In addition, these jurisdictional arrangements address only DOD-retained contractors. Those like Blackwater, Inc., employed to provide security to State Department and embassy personnel, do not fall under these provisions, while the role of companies headquartered in other countries (like Britain, Australia, and South Africa), and employing "third-party nationals" (TCNs) is wholly anomalous. At this writing, for example, the five employees of the former Blackwater Worldwide (which has since changed its company name to "Xe") are currently under indictment in Utah for manslaughter in the deaths of 17 Iraqi civilians killed in Monsour Square in Baghdad in September 2007. They are being tried under MEJA, the "Military Extraterritorial Jurisdiction Act," which subjects U.S. citizens to trial in the United States for committing criminal acts abroad. There is widespread belief among lawyers, however, that this attempt at redefining or broadening the jurisdictional boundaries of this act will not survive a court test.

30. A recent work, Robert Rubinstein's *Peacekeeping under Fire* (Rubinstein 2008), offers a detailed historical analysis of peacekeeping operations along with a cogent analysis of the manner in which cultural anthropology has contributed and can meaningfully continue to contribute to such morally worthy efforts to lessen violence, resolve conflict, and restore stability and the rule of law in the aftermath of armed conflict.

Appendix

Code of Ethics of the American Anthropological Association
Approved February 2009

I. Preamble

Anthropological researchers, teachers and practitioners are members of many different communities, each with its own moral rules or codes of ethics. Anthropologists have moral obligations as members of other groups, such as the family, religion, and community, as well as the profession. They also have obligations to the scholarly discipline, to the wider society and culture, and to the human species, other species, and the environment. Furthermore, fieldworkers may develop close relationships with persons or animals with whom they work, generating an additional level of ethical considerations.

In a field of such complex involvements and obligations, it is inevitable that misunderstandings, conflicts, and the need to make choices among apparently incompatible values will arise. Anthropologists are responsible for grappling with such difficulties and struggling to resolve them in ways compatible with the principles stated here. The purpose of this Code is to foster discussion and education. The American Anthropological Association (AAA) does not adjudicate claims for unethical behavior.

The principles and guidelines in this Code provide the anthropologist with tools to engage in developing and maintaining an ethical framework for all anthropological work.

II. Introduction

Anthropology is a multidisciplinary field of science and scholarship, which includes the study of all aspects of humankind—archaeological, biological, linguistic and sociocultural. Anthropology has roots in the natural and social sciences and in the humanities, ranging in approach from basic to applied research and to scholarly interpretation.

As the principal organization representing the breadth of anthropology, the American Anthropological Association (AAA) starts from the position that generating and appropriately utilizing knowledge (i.e., publishing, teaching, developing programs, and informing policy) of the peoples of the world, past and present, is a worthy goal; that the generation of anthropological knowledge is a dynamic process using many different and ever-evolving approaches; and that for moral and practical reasons, the generation and utilization of knowledge should be achieved in an ethical manner.

The mission of American Anthropological Association is to advance all aspects of anthropological research and to foster dissemination of anthropological knowledge through publications, teaching, public education, and application. An important part of that mission is to help educate AAA members about ethical obligations and challenges involved in the generation, dissemination, and utilization of anthropological knowledge.

The purpose of this Code is to provide AAA members and other interested persons with guidelines for making ethical choices in the conduct of their anthropological work. Because anthropologists can find themselves in complex situations and subject to more than one code of ethics, the AAA Code of Ethics provides a framework, not an ironclad formula, for making decisions. Persons using the Code as a guideline for making ethical choices or for teaching are encouraged to seek out illustrative examples and appropriate case studies to enrich their knowledge base.

Anthropologists have a duty to be informed about ethical codes relating to their work, and ought periodically to receive training on current research activities and ethical issues. In addition, departments offering anthropology degrees should include and require ethical training in their curriculums.

No code or set of guidelines can anticipate unique circumstances or direct actions in specific situations. The individual anthropologist must be willing to make carefully considered ethical choices and be prepared to make clear the assumptions, facts and issues on which those choices are based. These guidelines therefore address *general* contexts, priorities and relationships which should be considered in ethical decision making in anthropological work.

III. Research

In both proposing and carrying out research, anthropological researchers must be open about the purpose(s), potential impacts, and source(s) of support for research projects with funders, colleagues, persons studied or providing information, and with relevant parties affected by the research. Researchers must expect to utilize the results of their work in an appropriate fashion and disseminate the results through appropriate and timely activities. Research fulfilling these expectations is ethical, regardless of the source of funding (public or private) or purpose (i.e., "applied," "basic," "pure," or "proprietary").

Anthropological researchers should be alert to the danger of compromising anthropological ethics as a condition to engage in research, yet also be alert to proper demands of good citizenship or host-guest relations. Active contribution and leadership in seeking to shape public or private sector actions and policies may be as ethically justifiable as inaction, detachment, or noncooperation, depending on circumstances. Similar principles hold for anthropological researchers employed or otherwise affiliated with nonanthropological institutions, public institutions, or private enterprises.

A. Responsibility to people and animals with whom anthropological researchers work and whose lives and cultures they study.

1. Anthropological researchers have primary ethical obligations to the people, species, and materials they study and to the people with whom they work. These obligations can supersede the goal of seeking new knowledge, and can lead to decisions not to undertake or to discontinue a research project when the primary obligation conflicts with other responsibilities, such as those owed to sponsors or clients. These ethical obligations include:

- To avoid harm or wrong, understanding that the development of knowledge can lead to change which may be positive or negative for the people or animals worked with or studied
- To respect the well-being of humans and nonhuman primates
- To work for the long-term conservation of the archaeological, fossil, and historical records
- To consult actively with the affected individuals or group(s), with the goal of establishing a working relationship that can be beneficial to all parties involved

2. In conducting and publishing their research, or otherwise disseminating their research results, anthropological researchers must ensure that they

do not harm the safety, dignity, or privacy of the people with whom they work, conduct research, or perform other professional activities, or who might reasonably be thought to be affected by their research. Anthropological researchers working with animals must do everything in their power to ensure that the research does not harm the safety, psychological well-being or survival of the animals or species with which they work.

3. Anthropological researchers must determine in advance whether their hosts/providers of information wish to remain anonymous or receive recognition, and make every effort to comply with those wishes. Researchers must present to their research participants the possible impacts of the choices, and make clear that despite their best efforts, anonymity may be compromised or recognition fail to materialize.

4. Anthropological researchers should obtain in advance the informed consent of persons being studied, providing information, owning or controlling access to material being studied, or otherwise identified as having interests which might be impacted by the research. It is understood that the degree and breadth of informed consent required will depend on the nature of the project and may be affected by requirements of other codes, laws, and ethics of the country or community in which the research is pursued. Further, it is understood that the informed consent process is dynamic and continuous; the process should be initiated in the project design and continue through implementation by way of dialogue and negotiation with those studied. Researchers are responsible for identifying and complying with the various informed consent codes, laws and regulations affecting their projects. Informed consent, for the purposes of this code, does not necessarily imply or require a particular written or signed form. It is the quality of the consent, not the format, that is relevant.

5. Anthropological researchers who have developed close and enduring relationships (i.e., covenantal relationships) with either individual persons providing information or with hosts must adhere to the obligations of openness and informed consent, while carefully and respectfully negotiating the limits of the relationship.

6. While anthropologists may gain personally from their work, they must not exploit individuals, groups, animals, or cultural or biological materials. They should recognize their debt to the societies in which they work and their obligation to reciprocate with people studied in appropriate ways.

B. Responsibility to scholarship and science

1. Anthropological researchers must expect to encounter ethical dilemmas at every stage of theirwork, and must make good-faith efforts to

identify potential ethical claims and conflicts in advance when preparing proposals and as projects proceed. A section raising and responding to potential ethical issues should be part of every research proposal.

2. Anthropological researchers bear responsibility for the integrity and reputation of their discipline, of scholarship, and of science. Thus, anthropological researchers are subject to the general moral rules of scientific and scholarly conduct: they should not deceive or knowingly misrepresent (i.e., fabricate evidence, falsify, and plagiarize), or attempt to prevent reporting of misconduct, or obstruct the scientific/scholarly research of others.

3. Anthropological researchers should do all they can to preserve opportunities for future fieldworkers to follow them to the field.

4. Anthropologists have a responsibility to be both honest and transparent with all stakeholders about the nature and intent of their research. They must not misrepresent their research goals, funding sources, activities, or findings. Anthropologists should never deceive the people they are studying regarding the sponsorship, goals, methods, products, or expected impacts of their work. Deliberately misrepresenting one's research goals and impact to research subjects is a clear violation of research ethics, as is conducting clandestine research.

5. Anthropological researchers should utilize the results of their work in an appropriate fashion, and whenever possible disseminate their findings to the scientific and scholarly community.

6. Anthropological researchers should seriously consider all reasonable requests for access to their data and other research materials for purposes of research. They should also make every effort to insure preservation of their fieldwork data for use by posterity.

C. Responsibility to the public

1. Anthropological researchers should make the results of their research appropriately available to sponsors, students, decision makers, and other nonanthropologists. In so doing, they must be truthful; they are not only responsible for the factual content of their statements but also must consider carefully the social and political implications of the information they disseminate. They must do everything in their power to insure that such information is well understood, properly contextualized, and responsibly utilized. They should make clear the empirical bases upon which their reports stand, be candid about their qualifications and philosophical or political biases, and recognize and make clear the limits of anthropological expertise. At the same time,

they must be alert to possible harm their information may cause people with whom they work or colleagues.

2. In relation with his or her own government, host governments, or sponsors of research, an anthropologist should be honest and candid. Anthropologists must not compromise their professional responsibilities and ethics and should not agree to conditions which inappropriately change the purpose, focus or intended outcomes of their research.

3. Anthropologists may choose to move beyond disseminating research results to a position of advocacy. This is an individual decision, but not an ethical responsibility.

IV. Teaching

Responsibility to Students and Trainees

While adhering to ethical and legal codes governing relations between teachers/mentors and students/trainees at their educational institutions or as members of wider organizations, anthropological teachers should be particularly sensitive to the ways such codes apply in their discipline (for example, when teaching involves close contact with students/trainees in field situations). Among the widely recognized precepts which anthropological teachers, like other teachers/mentors, should follow are:

1. Teachers/mentors should conduct their programs in ways that preclude discrimination on the basis of sex, marital status, "race," social class, political convictions, disability, religion, ethnic background, national origin, sexual orientation, age, or other criteria irrelevant to academic performance.

2. Teachers'/mentors' duties include continually striving to improve their teaching/training techniques; being available and responsive to student/trainee interests; counseling students/ trainees realistically regarding career opportunities; conscientiously supervising, encouraging, and supporting students'/trainees' studies; being fair, prompt, and reliable in communicating evaluations; assisting students/trainees in securing research support; and helping students/trainees when they seek professional placement.

3. Teachers/mentors should impress upon students/trainees the ethical challenges involved in every phase of anthropological work; encourage them to reflect upon this and other codes; encourage dialogue with colleagues on ethical issues; and discourage participation in ethically questionable projects.

4. Teachers/mentors should publicly acknowledge student/trainee assistance in research and preparation of their work; give appropriate credit for coauthorship to students/trainees; encourage publication of worthy student/trainee papers; and compensate students/trainees justly for their participation in all professional activities.

5. Teachers/mentors should beware of the exploitation and serious conflicts of interest which may result if they engage in sexual relations with students/trainees. They must avoid sexual liaisons with students/trainees for whose education and professional training they are in any way responsible.

V. Application

1. The same ethical guidelines apply to all anthropological work. That is, in both proposing and carrying out research, anthropologists must be open with funders, colleagues, persons studied or providing information, and relevant parties affected by the work about the purpose(s), potential impacts, and source(s) of support for the work. Applied anthropologists must intend and expect to utilize the results of their work appropriately (i.e., publication, teaching, program and policy development) within a reasonable time. In situations in which anthropological knowledge is applied, anthropologists bear the same responsibility to be open and candid about their skills and intentions, and monitor the effects of their work on all persons affected. Anthropologists may be involved in many types of work, frequently affecting individuals and groups with diverse and sometimes conflicting interests. The individual anthropologist must make carefully considered ethical choices and be prepared to make clear the assumptions, facts and issues on which those choices are based.

2. In all dealings with employers, persons hired to pursue anthropological research or apply anthropological knowledge should be honest about their qualifications, capabilities, and aims. Prior to making any professional commitments, they must review the purposes of prospective employers, taking into consideration the employer's past activities and future goals. In working for governmental agencies or private businesses, they should be especially careful not to promise or imply acceptance of conditions contrary to professional ethics or competing commitments.

3. Applied anthropologists, as any anthropologist, should be alert to the danger of compromising anthropological ethics as a condition for engaging in research or practice. They should also be alert to proper demands of hospitality, good citizenship and guest status. Proactive

contribution and leadership in shaping public or private sector actions and policies may be as ethically justifiable as inaction, detachment, or noncooperation, depending on circumstances.

VI. Dissemination of Results

1. The results of anthropological research are complex, subject to multiple interpretations and susceptible to differing and unintended uses. Anthropologists have an ethical obligation to consider the potential impact of both their research and the communication or dissemination of the results of their research on all directly or indirectly involved.
2. Anthropologists should not withhold research results from research participants when those results are shared with others. There are specific and limited circumstances however, where disclosure restrictions are appropriate and ethical, particularly where those restrictions serve to protect the safety, dignity or privacy of participants, protect cultural heritage or tangible or intangible cultural or intellectual property.
3. Anthropologists must weigh the intended and potential uses of their work and the impact of its distribution in determining whether limited availability of results is warranted and ethical in any given instance.

VII. Epilogue

Anthropological research, teaching, and application, like any human actions, pose choices for which anthropologists individually and collectively bear ethical responsibility. Since anthropologists are members of a variety of groups and subject to a variety of ethical codes, choices must sometimes be made not only between the varied obligations presented in this code but also between those of this code and those incurred in other statuses or roles. This statement does not dictate choice or propose sanctions. Rather, it is designed to promote discussion and provide general guidelines for ethically responsible decisions.

VIII. Acknowledgments

This Code was drafted by the Commission to Review the AAA Statements on Ethics during the period January 1995–March 1997. The Commission members were James Peacock (Chair), Carolyn Fluehr-Lobban, Barbara Frankel, Kathleen Gibson, Janet Levy, and Murray Wax. In addition, the following individuals participated in the Commission meetings: philosopher

Bernard Gert, anthropologists Cathleen Crain, Shirley Fiske, David Freyer, Felix Moos, Yolanda Moses, and Niel Tashima; and members of the American Sociological Association Committee on Ethics. Open hearings on the Code were held at the 1995 and 1996 annual meetings of the American Anthropological Association. The Commission solicited comments from all AAA Sections. The first draft of the AAA Code of Ethics was discussed at the May 1995 AAA Section Assembly meeting; the second draft was briefly discussed at the November 1996 meeting of the AAA Section Assembly.

The Final Report of the Commission was published in the September 1995 edition of the *Anthropology Newsletter* and on the AAA web site (http://www.aaanet.org). Drafts of the Code were published in the April 1996 and 1996 annual meeting edition of the *Anthropology Newsletter* and the AAA web site, and comments were solicited from the membership. The Commission considered all comments from the membership in formulating the final draft in February 1997. The Commission gratefully acknowledges the use of some language from the codes of ethics of the National Association for the Practice of Anthropology and the Society for American Archaeology. Subsequent revisions to this Code were initiated by the passing of a resolution, offered by Terry Turner at the AAA Business Meeting held in November of 2007, directing the AAA Executive Board to restore certain sections of the 1971 version of the Code of Ethics. A related motion, introduced by John Kelly, directed the Executive Board to report to the membership a justification of its reasoning if a decision was made to not restore, in total, the language proposed in the Turner motion.

On January 20, 2008, the Executive Board tasked the Committee on Ethics, whose membership included Dena Plemmons (acting chair), Alec Barker, Katherine MacKinnon, Dhooleka Raj, K. Sivaramakrishnan and Steve Striffler, with drafting a revised ethics code that "incorporates the principles of the Turner motion while stipulating principles that identify when the ethical conduct of anthropology does and does not require specific forms of the circulation of knowledge." Six individuals (Jeffrey Altshul, Agustin Fuentes, Merrill Singer, David Price, Inga Treitler and Niel Tashima) were invited to advise the Committee in its deliberations.

On June 16, 2008, the Committee on Ethics issued its report to a newly formed subcommittee of the Executive Board created to deal with potential code revisions. The subcommittee (consisting of TJ Ferguson, Monica Heller, Tom Leatherman, Setha Low, Deborah Nichols, Gwen Mikell and Ed Liebow) examined the Committee on Ethics report and solicited the input of the Committee on Ethics; the Commission of the Engagement of Anthropology with the US Security and Intelligence Communities; the Committee on Practicing,

Applied and Public Interest Anthropology; and the Network of Concerned Anthropologists, asking these groups to advise before making its own recommendations to the larger Executive Board. After examining the input of these groups, the EB subcommittee forwarded its recommendations to the entire Executive Board August 8. Subsequent to these activities, AAA President Setha Low reached out to a number of stakeholders to solicit their input. On September 19, 2008, the Executive Board approved a final version of the Code of the Ethics.

IX. Other Relevant Codes of Ethics

The following list of other Codes of Ethics may be useful to anthropological researchers, teachers and practitioners:

Animal Behavior Society
1991 Guidelines for the Use of Animals in Research. *Animal Behavior* 41:183–86.

American Board of Forensic Examiners
n.d. *Code of Ethical Conduct.* (American Board of Forensic Examiners, 300 South Jefferson Avenue, Suite 411, Springfield, MO 65806).

American Folklore Society
1988 Statement on Ethics: Principles of Professional Responsibility. *AFS-News* 17(1).

Archaeological Institute of America
1991 Code of Ethics. *American Journal of Archaeology* 95: 285.
   1994 *Code of Professional Standards.* (Archaeological Institute of America, 675 Commonwealth Ave., Boston, MA 02215-1401. Supplements and expands but does not replace the earlier Code of Ethics).

National Academy of Sciences
1995 *On Being a Scientist: Responsible Conduct in Research.* 2nd edition. Washington, DC: National Academy Press (2121 Constitution Avenue, NW, Washington, DC 20418).

National Association for the Practice of Anthropology
1988 *Ethical Guidelines for Practitioners.*

Sigma Xi
1992 Sigma Xi Statement on the Use of Animals in Research. *American Scientist* 80: 73–76.

Society for American Archaeology
1996 *Principles of Archaeological Ethics*. (Society for American Archaeology, 900 Second Street, NE, Suite 12, Washington, D.C. 20002-3557).

Society for Applied Anthropology
1983 *Professional and Ethical Responsibilities*. (Revised 1983).

Society of Professional Archaeologists
1976 *Code of Ethics, Standards of Research Performance and Institutional Standards*. (Society of Professional Archaeologists, PO Box 60911, Oklahoma City, OK 73146-0911).

United Nations
1948 *Universal Declaration of Human Rights*.
   1983 *United Nations Convention on the Elimination of All Forms of Discrimination Against Women*.
   1987 *United Nations Convention on the Rights of the Child*.
   2007 *United Nations Declaration on Rights of Indigenous Peoples*.

References

AAA, 1998. "Code of Ethics of the American Anthropological Association." Approved June 1998. http://www.aaanet.org/issues/policy-advocacy/Code-of-Ethics.cfm. Accessed November 27, 2008.

AAA, 2007. "American Anthropological Association Executive Board Statement on the Human Terrain System Project." October 31, 2007. http://dev.aaanet.org/issues/policy-advocacy/Statement-on-HTS.cfm. Accessed November 27, 2008.

Abedi, 1990. "Oral life worlds: Shi'ite socialization in Pahlavi Iran." *Debating Muslims: Cultural Dialogues in Postmodernity and Tradition*. Eds. Michael J. J. Fischer and Mehdi Abedi. Madison: University of Wisconsin Press: 3–94.

Abu-Lughod, 1991. "Writing against culture." *Recapturing Anthropology: Working in the Present*. Ed. Richard Fox. Santa Fe, NM: School of American Research Press: 137–62.

Arend, 1999. *Legal Rules and International Society*. Oxford: Oxford University Press.

Avant, 2002. "Privatizing military training: A challenge to U.S. Army professionalism." *The Future of the Army Profession*. Eds. Don M. Snider and Gayle L.Watkins. New York: McGraw-Hill: 179–96.

Bender, 2007. "Efforts to aid US roil anthropology." *Boston Globe*, October 8, 2007.

Benedict, 1946. *The Chrysthymum and the Sword*. Boston: Houghton Mifflin Company.

Berreman, 1971. "Ethics, responsibility, and the funding of Asian research." *Journal of Asian Studies* 30, no. 2.

Berreman, 2003. "Ethics versus realism in anthropology: Redux." *Ethics and the Profession of Anthropology*, 2nd ed. Ed. Carolyn Fluehr-Lobban. Walnut Creek, CA: AltaMira Press: 51–83.

Caplan, 2003. *The Ethics of Anthropology: Debates and Dilemmas*. Ed. Pat Caplan. London: Routledge.

Carafano, 2008. *Private Sectors, Public Wars: Contractors in Combat*. Westport, CT: Praeger Publishers.

CEAUSSIC, 2007. "Final Report of the AAA Ad Hoc Commission on the Engagement of Anthropology with U. S. Security and Intelligence Communities." November 4, 2007. http://www.aaanet.org/pdf/Final_Report.pdf. Accessed November 27, 2008.

Chagnon, 1997. *Yąnomamö: The Fierce People*, 5th ed. New York: Holt, Rinehart and Winston.

Clarke, 2008. "Going the distance in Iraq," *Washington Post*, November 27, 2008, A29.

Clifford and Marcus, 1986. *Writing Culture: The Poetics and Politics of Ethnography*. Eds. James Clifford and George E. Marcus. Berkeley: University of California Press.

Condominas, 1994. *We Have Eaten the Forest: The Story of a Montagnard Village in the Central Highlands of Vietnam*. New York: Kodansha.

Constable, 2009. "A terrain's tragic shift: Researcher's death intensifies scrutiny of U.S. cultural program in Afghanistan." *Washington Post*, February 18, 2009, C1, C8.

Fainaru, 2008a. *Big Boy Rules: America's Mercenaries Fighting in Iraq*. Philadelphia: Da Capo Press.

Fainaru, 2008b. "Soldier of misfortune." *Washington Post*, December 1, 2008, C1–C2.

Ferguson and Whitehead, 1992. *War in the Tribal Zone: Expanding States and Indigenous Warfare*. Santa Fe, NM: School of American Research Press.

Fluehr-Lobban, 1994. "Informed consent in anthropological research: We are not exempt." *Human Organization* 52, no. 1: 1–10. Reprinted in Fluehr-Lobban 2003: 159–77.

Fluehr-Lobban, 2003. *Ethics and the Profession of Anthropology*, 2nd ed. Ed. Carolyn Fluehr-Lobban. Walnut Creek, CA: AltaMira Press.

Fluehr-Lobban, 2003a. "Ethics and anthropology: 1890–2000." Pp. 1–28 in Carolyn Fluehr-Lobban, ed., *Ethics and the Profession of Anthropology*, 2nd ed. Walnut Creek, CA: AltaMira Press.

Fluehr-Lobban, 2003b. "Darkness in El Dorado: Research ethics, then and now." Pp. 85–106 in Carolyn Fluehr-Lobban, ed., *Ethics and the Profession of Anthropology*, 2nd ed. Walnut Creek, CA: AltaMira Press.

Fluehr-Lobban, 2008. "New ethical challenges for anthropologists: The terms 'secret research' and 'do no harm' need to be clarified." *The Chronicle of Higher Education Review* 55, no. 12 (November 2008): B11.

Frese and Harrell, 2003. *Anthropology and the United States Military: Coming of Age in the Twenty-First Century*. Eds. Pamela R. Frese and Margaret C. Harrell. New York: Palgrave Macmillan.

Fosher, 2008. "Yes, both, absolutely: A personal and professional commentary on anthropological engagement with military and intelligence organizations." Invited chapter in the edited volume *Anthropology and Global Counterinsurgency*. University of Chicago Press, forthcoming.

Fosher, 2009. *Under Construction: Making Homeland Security at the Local Level*. Chicago: University of Chicago Press.

Fujimura, 2003. "Integrating diversity and understanding the other at the U.S. Naval Academy." Pp. 147–51 in P. Rese and M. C. Harrell, eds., *Anthropology and the United*

States Military: Coming of Age in the Twenty-first Century. New York: Palgrave Macmillan.

Geertz, 1973. *The Interpretation of Cultures.* New York: Basic Books, 1973.

Glenn, 2009. "Anthropologists adopt new language against secret research." *Chronicle of Higher Education* (February 19, 2009).

Gonzalez, 2007. "We must fight the militarization of anthropology." *Chronicle of Higher Education* (February 2, 2007): B20.

Greenburg, 2009. "When Gitmo was (relatively) good." *Washington Post,* January 25, 2009, B1, B4.

Gusterson, 2007. "Anthropology and militarism." *Annual Review of Anthropology* 36: 155–75.

Habermas, 1984/1987. *The Theory of Communicative Action,* Vols. I/II, trans. Thomas McCarthy. Boston, MA: Beacon Press.

Habermas, 2000. "Bestiality and humanity: A war on the border between law and morality." Pp. 306–16 in William Joseph Buckley, ed., *Kosovo: Contending Voices on Balkan Interventions.* Grand Rapids, MI: William B. Eerdmans.

Habermas, 2001. *The Postnational Constellation.* Cambridge, MA: MIT Press.

Habermas, 2004. *The Divided West.* Trans. Jeffrey Craig Miller. Cambridge: Polity Press, 2006.

Hegel, 1807. *Hegel's Phenomenology of Spirit.* Trans. A. V. Miller. Oxford: Oxford University Press, 1977.

Hersh, 2004. "The Grey Zone." *The New Yorker* (May 24, 2004).

Horowitz, 1967. *The Rise and Fall of Project Camelot: Studies in the Relationship between Social Science and Practical Politics.* Cambridge, MA: MIT Press.

Jaschik, 2009. "Anthropologists toughen ethics code." *Inside Higher Ed* (February 19, 2009). http://www.insidehighered.com/news/2009/02/19/anthro.

Jonson, 2000. *A Short History of Medical Ethics.* Oxford: Oxford University Press.

Kuhn, 1962/1970. *The Structure of Scientific Revolutions,* 2nd ed. Chicago: University of Chicago Press, 1970.

Latour and Woolgar, 1979. *Laboratory Life: The Construction of Scientific Facts.* Princeton, NJ: Princeton University Press.

Lesser, 1981. "Franz Boas." Pp. 1–25 in Sydel Silberman, ed., *Totems and Teachers: Key Figures in the History of Anthropology,* 2nd ed. Walnut Creek, CA: AltaMira Press, 2004.

Lucas, 2001. *Perspectives on Humanitarian Military Intervention.* Response by General Anthony C. Zinni, U.S. Marine Corps (retired). The Fleet Admiral Chester W. Nimitz Memorial Lecture Series on National Security Affairs, University of California, Berkeley. Berkeley: University of California Institute of Governmental Studies.

Lucas, 2003. "The role of the international community in the just war tradition: Confronting the challenges of humanitarian intervention and preemptive war," *Journal of Military Ethics* 2, no. 2: 128–43.

Lucas, 2004. "From *jus ad bellum* to *jus ad pacem:* Rethinking just war criteria for the use of military force for humanitarian ends." Pp. 72–96 in Donald Scheid and Deen K. Chatterjee, eds., *Ethics and Foreign Intervention.* New York: Cambridge University Press.

Lucas, 2005. "Defense or offense: Two streams of just war tradition." In Peter A. French and Jason A. Short, eds., *War and Border Crossings: Ethics when Cultures Clash*. Lanham, MD: Rowman & Littlefield.

Lucas, 2007. "Methodological anarchy: Arguing about war, and getting it right." *Journal of Military Ethics* 6, no. 3: 246–52.

Lucas, 2008. "The morality of military anthropology." *Journal of Military Ethics* 7, no. 3: 165–85.

Lucas and Rubel, 2007. *Ethics and the Military Profession: The Moral Foundations of Leadership*, rev. ed. New York: Longman/Pearson.

Lucas and Tripodi, 2006. "Case Studies in Humanitarian Intervention." In W. R. Rubel and G. R. Lucas, eds., *Case Studies in Military Ethics*. New York: Longman/Pearson.

Mason, 2006. *Oppenheimer's Choice*. SUNY Series in Philosophy. Ed. G. R. Lucas Jr. Albany: State University of New York Press.

McFate, 2005a. "Anthropology and counterinsurgency: The strange story of their curious relationship." *Military Review* (March–April 2005).

McFate, 2005b. "The military utility of understanding adversary culture." *Joint Forces Quarterly* 38 (3rd Quarter, 2005): 42–47.

Mead, 1942. *And Keep your Powder Dry: An Anthropologist Looks at America*. New York: Berghahn Books, 2000. Introduction by Hervé Vareene.

Mintz, 1981. "Ruth Benedict." Pp. 103–24 in Sydel Silverman, ed., *Totems and Teachers: Key Figures in the History of Anthropology*, 2nd ed. New York: AltaMira Press, 2004.

Montreaux, 2008. "Montreux document on pertinent international legal obligations and good practices for states related to operations of private military and security companies during armed conflict." Montreux, Switzerland: International Committee of the Red Cross (September 17, 2008). http://www.icrc.org/web/eng/siteeng0.nsf/htmlall/montreux-document-170908/$FILE/Montreux-Document.pdf. Accessed November 27, 2008.

Munzel, 1999. *Kritischer Kommentar zu Kants Anthropologie in pragmatischer Hinsicht (1798)*. "Kant-Forschungen, Band 10." Hamburg: Felix Meiner Verlag.

Nature, 2008. "Failure in the field: The U.S. military's human terrain programme needs to be brought to a swift close." *Nature* 456 (December 11, 2008): 676.

NCA, 2007. "Pledge of non-participation in counterinsurgency." Network of Concerned Anthropologists. http://concerned.anthropologists.googlepages.com. Accessed November 27, 2008.

Nuti, 2006. "Smart card: Don't leave military base without it," *Anthropology News* (October 6, 2006): 15–16.

Nuti and Fosher, 2007. "Reflecting back on a year of debate with the Ad Hoc Commission." *Anthropology News* 48, no. 7: 3–4.

Orend, 2006. *The Morality of War*. Peterborough, Ont.: Broadview Press.

Packer, 2006. "Knowing the enemy." *The New Yorker* (December 16, 2006): 60–69.

Pels, 1999. "Professions of duplexity." *Current Anthropology* 40, no. 2 (April 1999).

Pels and Salemink, 2000. *Colonial Subjects: Essays on the Practical History of Anthropology*. Ann Arbor: University of Michigan Press.

Petraeus, 2007. *Counterinsurgency*. Eds. D. H. Petraeus and J. F. Amos. Army Field Manual 324. Washington, DC: U.S. Government Printing Office.

Price, 1997. "Anthropological research and the Freedom of Information Act." *Cultural Anthropology Methods* 9, no. 1: 12–15.

Price, 1998a. "Gregory Bateson and the OSS: World War II and Bateson's assessment of applied anthropology." *Human Organization* 75, no. 4: 379–84.

Price, 1998b. "Cold War anthropology: Collaborators and victims of the national security state." *Identities* 4, no. 3–4: 389–430.

Price, 2003. "Anthropology sub rosa: The CIA, the AAA, and the ethical problems inherent in secret research." Pp. 29–49 in Carolyn Fluehr-Lobban, ed., *Ethics and the Profession of Anthropology*, 2nd ed. Walnut Creek, CA: AltaMira Press.

Price, 2004. *Threatening Anthropology: McCarthyism and the FBI's Surveillance of Activist Anthropologists*. Durham, NC: Duke University Press.

Price, 2008. *Anthropological Intelligence: The Development and Neglect of American Anthropology in the Second World War*. Durham, NC: Duke University Press.

Price and Gonzalez, 2007. "When anthropologists become counterinsurgents," *Counterpunch*. Eds. Alex Cockburn and Jeffrey St. Clair. September 27, 2007. http://www.counterpunch.org/gonzalez09272007.html. Accessed November 27, 2008.

Rehm, 2007. "Anthropologists and war." Guest host Susan Page, *USA Today*. *The Diane Rehm Show*. WAMU Public Radio, Washington DC. Wednesday, 10 October 2007 at 10–11 A.M. EDT. http://wamu.org/programs/dr/07/10/10.php. Accessed November 27, 2008.

Rodin, 2002. *War and Self-Defense*. Oxford: Oxford University Press.

Rohde, 2007. "Army enlists anthropology in war zones," *The New York Times*, October 5, 2007. http://www.nytimes.com/2007/10/05/world/asia/05afghan.html?pagewanted=1&_r=1&sq=David%20Rohde&st=cse&scp=2. Accessed November 27, 2008.

Rubinstein, 1988. "Anthropology and international security." Pp. 17–34 in Robert A. Rubinstein and Mary LeCron Foster, eds., *The Social Dynamics of Peace and Conflict*. Dubuque, IA: Kendall/Hunt Publishing Co., 1997.

Rubinstein, 2001. *Doing Fieldwork: The Correspondence of Robert Redfield and Sol Tax*. New Brunswick, NJ: Transaction Books.

Rubinstein, 2003. "Politics and peace-keepers: Experience and political representation among United States military officers." Pp. 15–27 in P. R. Frese and M. C. Harrell, eds., *Anthropology and the United States Military: Coming of Age in the Twenty-first Century*. New York: Palgrave Macmillan.

Rubinstein, 2006. "Anthropology, Peace, Conflict, and International Security." San Jose, CA: 106th Annual Meeting of the American Anthropological Association.

Rubinstein, 2008. *Peacekeeping under Fire: Culture and Intervention*. Boulder, CO: Paradigm Publishers.

Rubinstein, 2008a. "Ethics, Engagement, and Experience: Anthropological Excursions in Culture and the Military." Seminar on "Scholars, Security and Citizenship." Santa Fe, NM: School of Advanced Research on the Human Experience. July 24–25, 2008.

Sahlins, 1965. "The established order: Do not fold, spindle, or mutilate." Pp. 71–79 in Irving Louis Horowitz, ed., *The Rise and Fall of Project Camelot: Studies in the Relation-*

ship between Social Science and Practical Politics. Cambridge, MA: MIT Press. Speech delivered at the November 1965 annual meeting of the American Anthropological Association.

Sahlins, 2000. *Culture in Practice*. New York: Zone Books.

Said, 1978. *Orientalism*. New York: Pantheon Books, 1978.

Salmoni and Holmes-Eber, 2008. *Operational Culture for the Warfighter: Principles and Applications*. Quantico, VA: Marine Corps University Press.

Schachtman, 2008. "Montgomery McFate: Use anthropology in military planning." *Wired Magazine* 16, no. 10 (September 22, 2008). Available online at http://www.wired.com/politics/law/magazine/16-10/sl_mcfate. Accessed November 27, 2008.

Schachtman, 2008a. "Army social scientist set afire in Afghanistan." *Wired Magazine/ Danger Room* (November 6, 2008). http://blog.wired.com/defense/2008/11/army-socialsci.html. Accessed November 27, 2008.

Schachtman, 2009. "'Human Terrain' contractor guilty of manslaughter." *Wired Magazine/Danger Room* (February 3, 2009). http://blog.wired.com/defense/2009/02/human-terrain-c.html. Accessed February 9, 2009.

Schachtman, 2009a. "Human Terrain contractors' pay suddenly slashed." *Wired Magazine/Danger Room* (February 13, 2009). http://blog.wired.com/defense/2009/02/more-hts-mania.html.

Selmeski, 2007a. "Who are the security anthropologists?" *Anthropology News* 48, no. 5 (May 2007): 11–12.

Selmeski, 2007b. "Military cross-cultural competence: Core concepts and individual development." Centre for Security, Armed Forces & Society Occasional Paper Series No. 1. Kingston, Ont.: Royal Military College of Canada, May 16, 2007.

Selmeski, 2008. "Anthropology for the (military) masses: A moral-practical argument for educational engagement." San Francisco: 107th Annual Meeting of the American Anthropological Association (November 22).

Sides, 2006. *Blood and Thunder*. New York: Random House.

Silverman, 2004. *Totems and Teachers: Key Figures in the History of Anthropology*, 2nd ed. Ed. Sydel Silverman. New York: AltaMira Press.

Silverman and Metraux, 1981. "Margaret Mead." Pp. 198–221 in Sydel Silverman, ed., *Totems and Teachers: Key Figures in the History of Anthropology*, 2nd ed. New York: AltaMira Press, 2004.

Silvert, 1965. "American academic ethics and social research abroad: The lesson of Project Camelot." American Universities Field Staff Reports (West Coast South American Series), vol. 12, no. 3 (July 1965). Reprinted pp. 80–106 in Irving Louis Horowitz, ed., *The Rise and Fall of Project Camelot: Studies in the Relationship between Social Science and Practical Politics*. Cambridge, MA: MIT Press.

Simons, 1997. *The Company They Keep: Life Inside the U.S. Army Special Forces*. New York: The Free Press.

Singer, 2008. *Corporate Warriors: The Rise of the Privatized Military Industry*, updated edition. Ithaca, NY: Cornell University Press.

Sobel, 1999. *Galileo's Daughter*. New York: Walker & Co.

Stanton, 2008. "U.S. Army Human Terrain System in disarray: Millions of dollars wasted, two lives sacrificed." *Pravda*, July 23, 2008. English language version available online at http://english.pravda.ru/topic/Human_Terrain_System-607. Accessed November 27, 2008.

Stanton, 2009. "U.S. government takeover of Human Terrain System." *Pravda* (February 11, 2009). http://cryptome.info/0001/hts-bailout.htm.

Stockman, 2009. "Anthropologist's war death reverberates." *Boston Globe* (February 12, 2009). http://www.boston.com/news/world/middleeast/articles/2009/02/12/anthropologists_war_death_reverberates/?page=1. Accessed March 9, 2009.

Sullivan, 2009. "Partnering with social scientists." *Marine Corps Gazette* 93, no. 1: 53–57.

Thucydides, 1998. *The Landmark Thucydides*. Trans. Richard Crawley. Ed. Robert P. Strassler. New York: Touchstone Books.

Tierney, 2000. *Darkness in El Dorado: How Scientists and Journalists Devastated the Amazon*. New York: W.W. Norton.

Tiron, 2009. "Panel says Pentagon relies too heavily on contractors." *The Hill* (February 12, 2009). http://thehill.com/the-executive/panel-says-pentagon-relies-too-heavily-on-contractors-2009-02-12.html. Accessed February 21, 2009.

Vergano and Weise, 2008. "Should anthropologists work alongside soldiers?" *USA Today*, December 9, 2008, 5D.

Vitoria, 1539/1557. "De juri belli/De Indis." Pp. 233–92 in Anthony Pagden and Jeremy Lawrance, eds., *Francisco de Vitoria: Political Writings*. Cambridge: Cambridge University Press, 1991.

Wakin, 1992. *Anthropology Goes to War: Professional Ethics and Counterinsurgency in Thailand* Monograph #7, University of Wisconsin Center for Southeast Asian Studies. Madison: University of Wisconsin Press, 2007.

Walzer, 1977. *Just and Unjust Wars*. New York: Basic Books.

Watson, 1968. *The Double Helix*. Kingsport, TN: Kingsport Press.

Whitehead, 1919. *An Enquiry Concerning the Principles of Natural Knowledge*. Cambridge: Cambridge University Press.

Whitehead, 1920. *The Concept of Nature*. Cambridge: Cambridge University Press.

Whitehead, 1925. *Science and the Modern World*. New York: Macmillan, 1925.

Wilson, 2006. *Kant's Pragmatic Anthropology: Its Origin, Meaning, and Critical Significance*. SUNY Series in Philosophy. Ed. G. R. Lucas Jr. Albany: State University of New York Press, 2006.

Winnick, 2008. "Anthropology and the military: A summary of related 2007 annual meeting events." *Anthropology News*, no. 1 (January 2008): 18–19.

Wolf and Jorgensen, 1970. "Anthropology on the war path in Thailand." *New York Review of Books* 15: 26–35.

Wrage, 2007. "By invitation: Anti-corruption efforts—the price of the UK's capitulation on corruption." *Ethical Corporation* (February 6, 2007). Available online at http://www.ethicalcorp.com/content.asp?ContentID=4877. Accessed November 27, 2008.

Index

AAA. *See* American Anthropological Association

Abu Ghraib prison, 7, 62, 82, 146, 188

Advanced Research Projects Agency, anthropologists and, 65–66. *See also* Defense Advanced Research Projects Agency)

Afghanistan: anthropologists in, 5, 7, 81, 109, 123, 131, 133, 148, 150, 155, 156; controversy over, 125–26, 109, 125; Human Terrain System in, vii, 19n2, 81, 109, 122, 125–26, 133, 145, 147, 150, 155; war in, 35, 39, 55, 71, 81, 123

Agency for International Development. *See* United States Agency for International Development (USAID)

AIR. *See* American Institutes for Research

Al Qaeda, 122; use of narrative by, 3

Algeria: French army in, 3

Allende, Salvador; assassination of, 61

American Anthropological Association Code of Ethics: censure of Boas by, 51, 53–54, 69, 75n1, 75n2, 76n5; and cooperation with the military, 65, 85, 86, 88, 89, 111, 114, 133, 183; and essentializing culture, 16; and the Human Terrain System, 84, 123, 125; professional ethics in, 70. *See also* Code of Ethics of the American Anthropological Association

American Institutes for Research (AIR), 70, 83, 114, 126

American University (Washington, D.C.): and Project Camelot, 58

Amos, James F.: as coauthor of FM 3-24, 4

Anthropologists: and clandestine or secret research, 7–8, 25, 26, 51–52, 62, 63, 66–67, 69, 82, 84, 113, 118, 125, 133–34, 140–41; as citizens, viii, 31–37, 51–52, 53; collaboration of, with governments, viii, 7, 26, 32, 34, 36, 37, 70, 81–82, 84–85; definition of, 189; ethical guidelines for, 16, 41, 134, 143, 167, 181–83, 190; in Human Terrain System,

About the Author

George R. Lucas, Jr., is professor of philosophy and Class of 1984 Distinguished Chair of Ethics in the Vice Admiral James B. Stockdale Center for Ethical Leadership at the United States Naval Academy (Annapolis, Maryland), and visiting professor of ethics at the Naval Postgraduate School (Monterey, California). From 1990 through 1995, he was assistant director of the Division of Research Programs at the National Endowment for the Humanities in Washington, D.C.

Professor Lucas has taught at Georgetown University, Emory University, Randolph-Macon College, the Catholic University of Louvain, Belgium, and served as Philosophy Department chairman at the University of Santa Clara in California. He has received research fellowships from the Fulbright Commission and the American Council of Learned Societies and a number of grants in education and research from the National Endowment for the Humanities. He has served three times (in 1986, 1990, and 2004) as director of National Endowment for the Humanities Summer Institutes for College and University Faculty, and also served a three-year term (1998–2001) on the national Board of Officers of the American Philosophical Association (APA), for which he was chairman of the APA Committee on Career Opportunities.

Professor Lucas received his Ph.D. in philosophy from Northwestern University in 1978. He is the author of four previous books, more than fifty journal articles, translations, and book reviews, and has also edited several book-length collections of articles in philosophy and ethics. Among these titles are *Perspectives on Humanitarian Military Intervention* (2001), *Lifeboat Ethics: The Moral Dilemmas of World Hunger* (1976), *Poverty, Justice, and the Law: Essays on Needs, Rights, and Obligations* (1986), *The Rehabilitation of Whitehead: An Analytic and Historical Assessment of Process Philosophy* (1989), and *The Genesis of Modern Process Thought*, which was named an "Outstanding Academic Selection" in 1983 by *Choice*. He was invited to contribute essays to three volumes in the prestigious Library of Living Philosophers series, on Charles Hartshorne, Paul Weiss, and Hans-Georg Gadamer, respectively, the last of which was awarded the 1993–1994 Pergamon Prize from the Elsevier Science Foundation in Oxford, England (awarded biennially to the author of the most outstanding essay on the history of European ideas). Dr. Lucas is also coeditor (with Captain Rick Rubel, U.S. Navy, retired) of the textbook *Ethics and the Military Profession: The Moral Foundations of Leadership* and a companion volume, *Case Studies in Military Ethics* (2007). These texts are used in core courses devoted to ethical leadership at the United States Naval Academy, the United States Air Force Academy, and at Naval ROTC units at more than fifty-seven colleges and universities throughout the United States.

A summa cum laude graduate in physics from the College of William and Mary, Professor Lucas is a member of Phi Beta Kappa and Omicron Delta Kappa, and received the Sigma Xi Research Award in 1971 for his work in intermediate energy particle physics, published in *The Physical Review* (1973).

No under items - human & rts or Universal Decl g—
UN -

.175 deception?

56 - Both Boas + Cancelot are ref. to in ways that done
accord w/ their substance